CAD/CAM SYSTEMS

MECHANICAL ENGINEERING

A Series of Textbooks and Reference Books

EDITORS

L. L. FAULKNER

Department of Mechanical Engineering
The Ohio State University
Columbus, Ohio

S. B. MENKES

Department of Mechanical Engineering
The City College of the
City University of New York
New York, New York

1. Spring Designer's Handbook, *by Harold Carlson*
2. Computer-Aided Graphics and Design, *by Daniel L. Ryan*
3. Lubrication Fundamentals, *by J. George Wills*
4. Solar Engineering for Domestic Buildings, *by William A. Himmelman*
5. Applied Engineering Mechanics: Statics and Dynamics, *by G. Boothroyd and C. Poli*
6. Centrifugal Pump Clinic, *by Igor J. Karassik*
7. Computer-Aided Kinetics for Machine Design, *by Daniel L. Ryan*
8. Plastics Products Design Handbook, Part A: Materials and Components; Part B: Processes and Design for Processes, *edited by Edward Miller*
9. Turbomachinery: Basic Theory and Applications, *by Earl Logan, Jr.*
10. Vibrations of Shells and Plates, *by Werner Soedel*
11. Flat and Corrugated Diaphragm Design Handbook, *by Mario Di Giovanni*
12. Practical Stress Analysis in Engineering Design, *by Alexander Blake*
13. An Introduction to the Design and Behavior of Bolted Joints, *by John H. Bickford*
14. Optimal Engineering Design: Principles and Applications, *by James N. Siddall*
15. Spring Manufacturing Handbook, *by Harold Carlson*

16. Industrial Noise Control: Fundamentals and Applications, *edited by Lewis H. Bell*
17. Gears and Their Vibration: A Basic Approach to Understanding Gear Noise, *by J. Derek Smith*
18. Chains for Power Transmission and Material Handling: Design and Applications Handbook, *by the American Chain Association*
19. Corrosion and Corrosion Protection Handbook, *edited by Philip A. Schweitzer*
20. Gear Drive Systems: Design and Application, *by Peter Lynwander*
21. Controlling In-Plant Airborne Contaminants: Systems Design and Calculations, *by John D. Constance*
22. CAD/CAM Systems Planning and Implementation, *by Charles S. Knox*
23. Probabilistic Engineering Design: Principles and Applications, *by James N. Siddall*
24. Traction Drives: Selection and Application, *by Frederick W. Heilich III and Eugene E. Shube*
25. Finite Element Methods: An Introduction, *by Ronald L. Huston and Chris E. Passerello*
26. Mechanical Fastening of Plastics: An Engineering Handbook, *by Brayton Lincoln, Kenneth J. Gomes, and James F. Braden*
27. Lubrication in Practice, Second Edition, *edited by W. S. Robertson*
28. Principles of Automated Drafting, *by Daniel L. Ryan*
29. Practical Seal Design, *edited by Leonard J. Martini*
30. Engineering Documentation for CAD/CAM Applications, *by Charles S. Knox*
31. Design Dimensioning with Computer Graphics Applications, *by Jerome C. Lange*
32. Mechanism Analysis: Simplified Graphical and Analytical Techniques, *by Lyndon O. Barton*
33. CAD/CAM Systems: Justification, Implementation, Productivity Measurement, *by Edward J. Preston, George W. Crawford, and Mark E. Coticchia*
34. Steam Plant Calculations Manual, *by V. Ganapathy*
35. Design Assurance for Engineers and Managers, *by John A. Burgess*

OTHER VOLUMES IN PREPARATION

CAD/CAM SYSTEMS

Justification, Implementation, Productivity Measurement

Edward J. Preston
Computervision Corporation
Edison, New Jersey

George W. Crawford
Mark E. Coticchia
Westinghouse Electric Corporation
Pittsburgh, Pennsylvania

MARCEL DEKKER, INC New York and Basel

Library of Congress Cataloging in Publication Data

Preston, Edward J., [date]
CAD/CAM systems. Justification, implementation, productivity measurement

(Mechanical engineering ; 33)
Includes index.
1. CAD/CAM systems. I. Crawford, George W. II. Coticchia, Mark E. III. Title. IV. CAD/CAM systems. V. Series
TS155.6.P74 1984 670.42'7 84-17049
ISBN 0-8247-7257-1

MARCEL DEKKER, INC.
270 Madison Avenue, New York, New York 10016

Current printing (last digit)
10 9 8 7 6 5 4 3 2 1

PRINTED IN THE UNITED STATES OF AMERICA

The authors wish to thank their families and their companies for the support they gave throughout this project

Preface

In this age of technological explosion, we hear the term *breakthrough* so often that it has almost become meaningless. Yet, now and then, there is a development that one can truly label a breakthrough, for example, computer-aided design/computer-aided manufacturing (CAD/CAM). The Center for Productivity of the National Science Foundation said of this fast-emerging technology: "CAD/CAM has more potential to radically increase productivity than any development since electricity."

CAD/CAM allows one to perform many highly technical tasks essential to science and industry—and perform them far faster, more easily, more accurately, and more economically than by traditional methods. A computer-aided design and manufacturing system is one capital expenditure that could allow your business or organization to fully recover initial costs in less than a year—out of savings alone.

CAD/CAM systems speed many tedious steps in the normal concept-to-production cycle. For example, in engineering, construction, and manufacturing, up to 80% of all drawings are spin-offs from earlier designs. Imagine the potential time-savings with a system that provides almost instant access to original design and quick accurate editing or manipulation of that old design to produce a new one.

If there is one word that sums up the significance of CAD/CAM, it is *productivity*, a prime concern of both industries and nations. They all want to make use of their resources to offset the spiraling cost of materials and skilled personnel. With experienced designers and draftsmen at a premium, CAD/CAM offers a unique way to increase the productivity of this scarce and valuable resource.

Companies in every field of industry, from electronics to automobiles, from mapping to plant design, are using CAD/CAM to increase design and drafting throughput and trim product development time and costs. As you will see, the impact on the bottom line can be quite dramatic.

Yet, amazingly, a start-to-finish evaluation and selection of a CAD/CAM system can take up to 9 months to complete, even though the associated costs for companies in this mode can be staggering. This seemingly lengthy process can be attributed to two major issues. The first is the very competitiveness of the industry itself. New CAD/CAM companies, each with their own set of buzz words and acronyms to dazzle the prospect with, announce start-up almost monthly. It is often said that buying a system is a lot more difficult than selling one. The second can be identified as the customer "waiting for the better mousetrap to be built." (A very dangerous attitude, more on this in Chapters 1–6.)

No less than 15 areas of major concern must be satisfied before a suitable and palatable decision can be reached regarding vendor selection.

Price of system
Performance (software capability)
"Report cards" from surrounding users
Annual research and development expenditures
Regular new product announcements
A justifiable expenditure
Market share of vendor (sliding/gaining/static)
Proximity of postsale support
Evidence of system obsolesence
Turnkey versus third-party issues
Two- versus three-dimensional considerations
Benchmarking (Do I need to do this?)
Vendor's commitment to CAD/CAM only
System integration with other existing computers (communications)
Ease of implementation for engineering and manufacturing

This volume will address three of the most important above-mentioned areas.

This book is unique in that all efforts to date have focused on a single discipline and the ways in which a given software package would impact it (e.g., how the hardware and software of a given vendor have affected the overall printed circuit board design and drafting process). The handicap that besets the authors with this applications approach is that one must take a snapshot of current software capabilities while relating productivity gains that may be derived. Given that the CAD/CAM industry is truly software-driven and can change literally on a day-to-day basis, the information from an applications approach would be dated before a book could be published. So, specific feature/function/benefit studies will not be dealt with in any detail, but rather only in a cursory sense to make a statement clearer. We feel it is more useful to relate thoughts on broader-based topic areas, and in so doing, this book should attract three separate readership levels:

The *justification* process will be aimed at the company president who is concerned with return on investment and related subjects.

The *implementation* section will assist the CAD/CAM selection committee members with ideas on successful start-up procedures.

The *productivity measurement* portion will be targeted for potential users as well as existing CAD/CAM users and will be on ways to evaluate system productivity from a design/drafting standpoint.

Edward J. Preston

George W. Crawford

Mark E. Coticchia

Contents

Preface v

JUSTIFICATION

1. Getting Started 3
2. Qualitative Rationales for CAD/CAM: A Case Study 11
3. Service Bureau Considerations 69
4. Cost Justifying a CAD/CAM System 81
5. Request for Proposal 99
6. Benchmarking 133

IMPLEMENTATION

7. Introduction 139
8. Facility Planning 141

9. Facility Organization and Administration 155

10. Personnel Planning 163

11. Personnel Development and Organization 171

12. Training 189

13. System Planning and Organization 199

14. Systems Administration 205

15. Preventive Maintenance 235

PRODUCTIVITY MEASUREMENT

16. Evaluation 249

GLOSSARY

Glossary of Common CAD/CAM Terms and Concepts 315

Index 355

CAD/CAM SYSTEMS

JUSTIFICATION

1

Getting Started

Once it has been determined that an effort should take place to examine the computer-aided design/computer-aided manufacturing (CAD/CAM) industry for eventual system selection, the first logical step is the formation of the CAD/CAM select committee. It is essential that *all* interests of the company be kept in mind when committee members are chosen. To do this correctly, your present *and* future product cycle should be as well-defined as possible. If you do not have a well thought out cycle, ask yourself two questions: (1) What is it you do? (2) How are you currently doing it? Be cognizant of your business plan one year out, three years out, and so on. This can be vital in helping in eliminating from consideration the CAD/CAM vendors who do not have the total capability necessary to do the job you need to have done. Some examples are discussed below.

If you have decided among other things, to eliminate outside service bureaus currently doing your engineering analysis finite-element modelling (FEM),finite-element analysis (FEA) you would not want to consider a low-end system with only two-dimensional (2-D) capabilities. This would narrow the choice of suppliers substantially. If your product is made up of both mechanical and electrical components, it would be in your best interest to examine only those systems that are multiapplicational *and* associative. This would also whittle down the list of potential vendors, in that some are purely limited to only one engineering discipline. Getting back to the product cycle, an example of a true engineering and manufacturing organization which will benefit from both sides of the CAD/CAM acronym appears in Chapter 4 (Fig. 7). Steps A-F of the illustration encompass the CAD capability, G-K refer to the CAM capability. The committee, therefore, should have representation from all iteration areas. This is not to suggest that a representative from each and every area be on the committee. Rather, the committee should include a person who has all the engineering information and interests, someone who has all the manufacturing interests, and so on who can represent collective groups within departments. In summary, each member should be a person who is sensitive to the inner workings and problems of all the major work areas. Typically, CAD/CAM committees have these recurring positions involved:

1. Engineering representative
   Design
   Drafting
   Analysis (FEM, etc.)
   Checking
2. Manufacturing representative
   Tool and fixture design and drafting
   Numerically controlled (NC) tape preparation
   Robotics
   Prototypes
   NC operations
3. Management of information services
   Communications to existing mainframe systems
   Communications to other CAD/CAM systems
   Analysis considerations
   Data storage
   Bill of material (BOM) considerations
4. Technical publications/illustrations
   Creation of nondimensioned drawings that refer directly to engineering drawings (very often a duplication of effort)
5. Facilities planning
   Group chartered with graphically illustrating growth/contraction within the company itself
6. Head of CAD/CAM committee
   Person chartered to disseminate all collected materials

A method often used to assist the committee for decision making is the vendor factor comparison chart. Because there are so many systems of comparable price with similarities in capability, prospects often benefit from a scheme that assesses these areas of importance and ultimately provides an overall numerical rating for each vendor. Let us take the list that was discussed in the preface, add upon it, and go through the exercise.

Vendor Factor Comparison

Category	Importance[a]	Vendor A Rating	Vendor A Point extension[b]	Vendor B Rating	Vendor B Point extension[b]
Delivery schedule	3	7	(21)	10	(30)
Vendor concern for us	9	6	(54)	4	(36)
Vendor support	9	10	(90)	4	(36)
Proximity of support	8	9	(72)	7	(56)
Future offering (R&D)	8	9	(72)	7	(56)
Lease commitment	6	10	(60)	6	(36)
Operating system	8	4	(32)	4	(32)
Data comm. to other devices	7	7	(49)	9	(63)
Data base associativity	10	6	(60)	4	(40)
Applications packages	7	10	(70)	5	(35)
Upward compatibility	10	7	(70)	6	(60)
Conversion risk	10	6	(60)	3	(30)
Dollars ($)	1	5	(5)	5	(5)
Data base admin. capability	6	10	(60)	4	(24)
System reliability	7	7	(49)	4	(28)
Environment requirements	2	6	(12)	3	(6)
Virtual machine	—	—	—	—	—
Obsolescence	5	7	(35)	4	(20)
Report cards from users	8	8	(64)	7	(56)
Justification assistance	6	10	(60)	2	(12)
Market share of vendor	8	5	(40)	3	(24)
Ease of use	7	9	(63)	8	(56)
Totals			(1039)		(727)

[a]Importance and rating factors were measured on a scale (1-10) low-1, high-10.
[b]Point extension = importance factor × rating factor. The evaluation team simply has to fill in the blanks and add the scores.

While this exercise has proven to be very useful for the committee, overall support from your local sales representative, his support team, the regional sales manager, and so on can be vital to you in the selection process. After all, this is a lengthy complicated process with heavy vendor contact. When done, you want to come away feeling good about the organization that has supported and will continue to support you *after* the purchase order has been signed. The ultimate selection is usually based primarily on emotional issues.

In that this is both a physically as well as psychologically demanding process at times requiring extensive travel, long days, and possible in-fighting as a result of differing opinions, it would be wise to keep in mind the employee who would most likely hold up under these rigors. And also, of course, make the *best* decision for your company.

Simply put, you want to be sure you have a healthy cross section on the committee. You want to avoid the risk of a decision being made by members because of overzealousness or no decision being made because of a "why change now" philosophy. Of course, a good way to check on this or any other aspect discussed in this book, is to talk to your local CAD/CAM user community. They are willing to share their experiences on these matters. What follows is a guide that many CAD/CAM vendors use to determine "what it is you do" and "how are you presently doing it." From the information learned, a vendor will:

1. Better understand your product cycle
2. Be able to prepare a solid cost justification analysis
3. Be in a position to recommend the optimum system configuration (hardware and software)

CAD/CAM Vendor Survey

Company name and address:

Survey conducted by:

Survey Date:

Key contacts:

Decision maker and title:

Nature of business:

Do you have a committee investigating CAD/CAM?

If yes, list chairman and committee members:

Fiscal year ends:

Over how many years do you amortize equipment?

Do you capital lease equipment?

What requirements do you have for payback justification? For return on investment?

Do you currently have funds budgeted for the acquisition of a CAD/CAM system? How much

What vendors are you currently examining?

Are there any other corporate divisions using CAD/CAM equipment? If yes, list division, CAD/CAM vendor, and application area.

Does your competition use CAD/CAM technology? If so, list competitor and CAD/CAM vendor.

Has a system configuration been prepared? If so, please describe (hardware and software).

Do you expect any additional costs resulting from: (1) room preparation(s), (2) dedicated CAD/CAM system manager, (3) training, (4) other? If so, how much?

Outline your product cycle flow from concept to shipping. Refer to Figure 7, Chapter 4, payback return on investment (ROI) computation.

What is your procedure for generating:

Bid proposals/quotations?

Technical illustrations/publications?

Is there a space planning (facilities) group within your organization? If so, how much effort is expended by this group in updating existing or generating new drawings for your facility?

Work Analysis

Average monthy hours—drafting (multiapplication—MD, PC/ES/WD etc.)

Discipline(s)	Design engineers	Drafters
Mechanical example:		
Layout		
Assembly		
Subassembly		
Detail		
Bill of material (BOM)		
Other		

Discipline(s)	Design engineers	Drafters
Electrical example:		
Layout		
Artwork		
Drill drawing		
Assembly drawing		
Parts list		
Schematic		
Other		

What is the "mix" of prep time and actual board time for each of the above-mentioned activities (state in %)?

Do you use numerically controlled (NC) equipment in your company? (Include planned purchases.) If yes, please list name and model number for each.

Explain the system currently used for NC tape generation.

How many NC programmers are dedicated to this activity?

Number of design engineers Burdened rate/hour

Number of drafters/detailers Burdened rate/hour

Number of NC programmers? Burdened rate/hour

Number of shifts worked in the drafting department:

Are you currently working overtime in the design/drafting area? If so, how much?

Are service bureaus relied on for any of your design/drafting efforts; If so, state amount in dollars per annum.

How much backlog do you currently have?

Number of new personnel hired in the past 12 months
- Design engineers
- Drafters
- NC programmers
- Other technical personnel

Number to be hired in the next 12 months
- Design engineers
- Drafters
- NC programmers
- Other technical personnel

Turnover rate for design engineers
Turnover rate for drafters
Turnover rate for NC programmers
Turnover rate for other technical personnel

What percentage of time is spent on
  Generating new drawings?
  Revising existing drawings?

How many new drawings do you create each month?

Do you use repetitive symbols? If yes, explain.

Explain the procedure used to generate the required bills of material.

Explain checking procedure.

Please relate your thoughts regarding the perceived overall impact to your organization from our designer system.
  For example:

  What current "bottlenecks" will be removed by implementing a CAD/CAM system in your operation?

  Do you feel any new problems will result from introducing this technology to your organization?

  How will CAD/CAM assist you in marketing your product before your competition does?

---

*Vendors note

Please feel free to add any additional thoughts not covered in this survey that might better describe your current operation. The more they know about your situation, the more they can help.

2

Qualitative Rationales for CAD/CAM: A Case Study

PROLOGUE

In early 1981, Simmonds Precision Products of Vergennes, Vermont broke with long-established tradition regarding their capital equipment acquisition practices. They did this for two reasons (1) to gain immediate entry into the world of computer graphics, and (2) to position themselves for a longer range strategy leading to computer-integrated engineering and manufacturing operations.

The following case study discusses the justification process, management role, and measurement factors for two critical periods in the Simmonds experience, March 1980 through February 1981, the period leading to the "buy" decision, and May 1981 through December 1982, the period of installation, training, and performance evaluation.*

THE COMPANY

A discussion of the company and its operating environment will be of interest to the discerning computer-aided design/computer-aided manufacturing (CAD/CAM) observer, serving to calibrate similarities between the Simmonds situation and their own, as well as indexing the relative credibility of Simmonds' findings.

---

*This case study was reprinted courtesy of Mr. Ron Van Nostrand of Simmonds Precision Products of Vergennes, Vermont, and Auerbach Publishing of Pennsauken, New Jersey.

As have many American corporations, Simmonds has struggled over the years (and continues to struggle) with the short-term earnings versus long-range strategy dilemma. Examination of past experience would show that financial decisions were invariably biased towards quarter-to-quarter growth in earnings, a Simmonds hallmark in the financial community. This financial orientation, while tempered by current long-range strategies, is still reflected in Simmonds day-to-day operations, toughminded, pragmatic, conservative, placing emphasis on tight management control of fiscal operations.

Simmonds capital equipment justification process mirrors this conservatism:

Related statements of savings are developed using raw labor dollars plus *variable* burden only.

Resultant savings are *halved* for payback calculation purposes (i.e., after-tax savings).

Payback period, return on investment (ROI), and net present value calculations are required.

Two year or better payback is required for approval at the division level.

These requirements are augmented by quarterly capital ''want list'' scrubs which progressively cull out the ''nice to have's'' leaving ''hard'' requirements to compete for available dollars.

This is not to suggest a paucity of capital purchases (49% of Simmonds total plant and equipment base has been purchased in the past three years, 67% in the last five), rather, it reflects a determination to assure the best possible application of these funds and a thorough testing of their supporting rationale.

THE JUSTIFICATION PROCESS—PAYBACK STARTS HERE

Simmonds ''first pass'' CAD/CAM analyses were based on then available source data, being primarily published or presented by turn-key computergraphic manufacturers, major airframers, or other large corporations with sizable investments and substantially mature CAD/CAM operations. Virtually all of these users endorsed their CAD/CAM operation in glowing terms for the most part, reporting enormous productivity gains, often on the order of 10, 20, or even 40 to 1.

Looking through this window into the CAD/CAM world, it took little imagination to project a two-year or better payback for Simmonds and several such scenarios were readily developed. However, under progressively detailed examination, it became evident that these lacked the substance of a credible proposal (major corporations were not necessarily suitable role models for small- to medium-sized companies), nor were CAD/CAM systems manufacturers a reliable source of impartial user references. Further probing into these claims, we found a rather disturbing absence of consistency or associated back-up data. It also seemed that much of the information highlighted was out of context in terms of incurred total costs as well as incidence of occurrence. For example, while there may be instances of 20:1 payback, if these represent but 1% of the total cycle activity, then a "20:1 productivity gain" statement is somewhat misleading. In the same vein, omission of sizable service contract costs, training, programming, and administrative costs further contributes to a skew toward overstated "savings."

Considerably sobered, we round-filed these early pro formas and returned to square one with a revised set of actions, prominent among them to:

Develop cost/utility/applications profiles for candidate systems.

Develop an independent index of small- to medium-size users, applications, and system productivity assessments.

Investigate various approaches to capital procurement rationale, methodology, and "selling" technique.

By either attending or collecting proceedings from different system user group symposiums, a roster of companies were developed whose applications and/or financial situations were similar to those at Simmonds, . . . some 15 companies in all. Extensive follow-on discussions with their CAD/CAM people yielded a considerably revised and enlightened insight to realistically achievable payback expectations for a company such as ours.

We viewed achievability as a fundamental aspect. Why? Aside from the substantial funds involved, we had come to appreciate that a CAD/CAM proposal is a benchmark document with an attendant responsibility of providing a firm and credible foundation for the associated CAD/CAM proposals we knew would inevitably follow.

With this in mind, we set out to identify those systems which could consistently demonstrate mature capabilities for known Simmonds applications as well as deliver performance consistent with Simmonds requirement of itself "excellence, rather than efficient mediocrity" and "to earn a high return on invested capital."

Contending with a persistent inclination to favorably color our findings, we discovered that hard, near-term (i.e., two-year) savings opportunities were far fewer than originally envisioned, but nonetheless, proceeded to evaluate these in the traditional manner operationally and financially.

Simmonds' initial CAD/CAM applications were identified in three areas, the engineering, manufacturing, and graphics departments.

ENGINEERING

As might be expected, engineering, the data base developer and "table setter" for downstream CAM applications was the primary source. We had confirmed early on that, due to the nature of our business and other organizational factors, our printed circuit (PC) design area presented the greatest opportunity for high productivity gains, with mechanical design having potential (initially) for some lesser, unquantified applications and savings.

Fortunately, our design group had excellent historical PC design data for both manual designs and those partially designed on our automated drafting system (acquired in 1975). Four-year records (1977–1980) of labor hours, categorized by discipline and design element and designs per annum, provided a solid baseline for developing detailed comparative analyses.

While vendor benchmarking played a confirming role in the final system selection process, *it was not considered as a factor in our PC design savings analysis. There were several reasons for this*: the atypical expertise of the benchmark conductor, the small size (one or two designs) and the inability to factor in operator variables, schedule pressure, in-process design changes or the issue of relative design complexity, constraints, and density. Further, these benchmarks had been, as is typical, thoroughly prepared and debugged, with inputs required well in advance of the actual demonstration. We instead went back to our user data, and, discarding highs and lows, keyed on five companies whose experience was deemed most representative in terms of their product lines and design complexity factors (Fig. 1).

Figure 2 depicts PC savings projections as a function of Simmonds' anticipated volume, while Figure 3 provides a more detailed comparison of the relative differences between then present and proposed design methods. It is important to note here that the quantities shown in Figure 2 reflect new designs as well as all complete redesigns, such as the number of complete design iterations. We will come back to this point during the evaluation discussion.

	Manual hours (actual)	Computer-aided drafting hours (actual)	CAD/CAM (estimated)*
Schematics	22	22	16
Feasibility analysis	5	5	1
Design and layout	40	40	20
Fabrication drawing	6	6	2
Assembly drawing	32	6	2
Artwork	40	10	0
Checking	30	30	11
Total	175	119	52

Figure 1 Printed circuit design elements: Labor hours requirements. Note: *CAD/CAM estimations for each category are based on the averaged labor-hour requirements of five companies with similar applications.

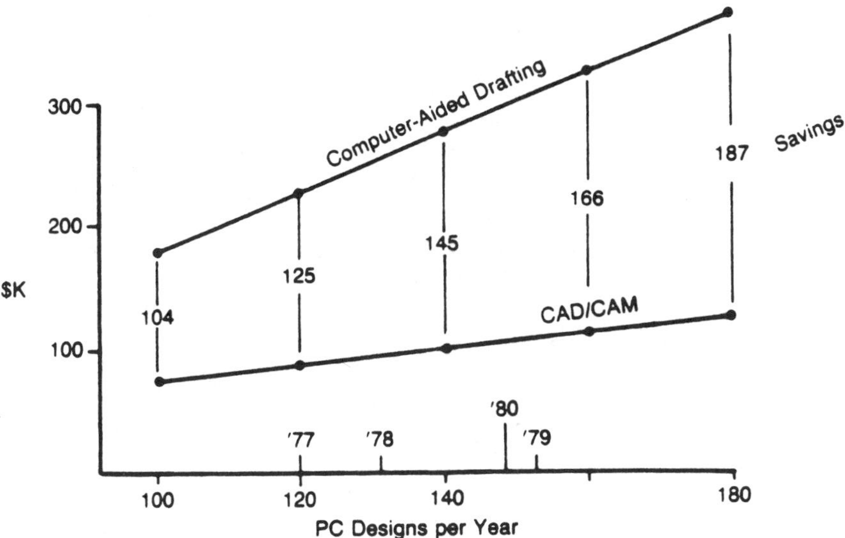

Figure 2 Computer-aided design-printed circuit design. Savings and volume.

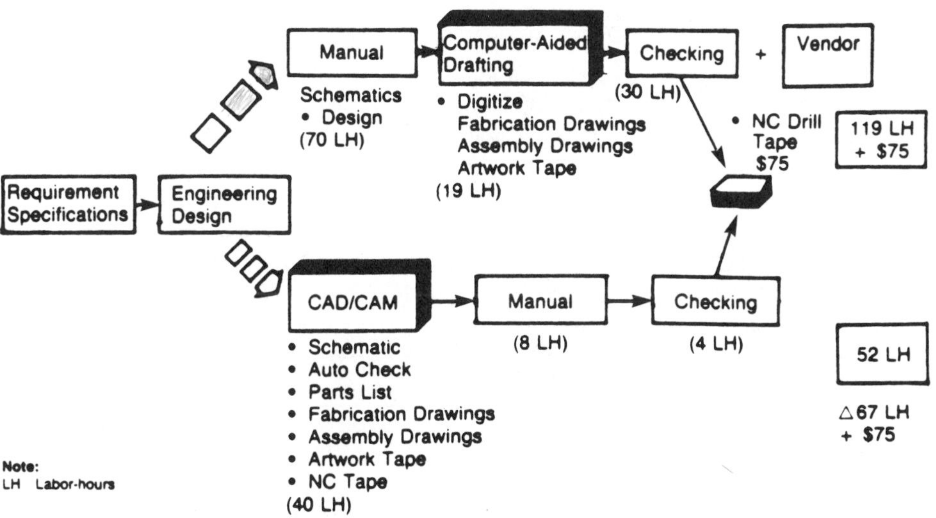

Figure 3 CAD/PC design engineering.

This, then, was our base-line position regarding PC design savings, $145,000 per annum, a figure we felt could be consistently realized, and one which comprised the cornerstone of our proposal.

There were, by the way, some interesting anecdotes associated with this comparative process, one of which serves to highlight a basic CAD/CAM truth.

We noticed during our survey, that there was a wide variation between reported performance by two companies with similar printed circuit applications and identical turnkey systems, one begrudging a 1.2:1 payback at best, the other judging 4:1 or better. We were puzzled by this disparity in that both were specialty houses with competitive base-line positions. We spoke at length with the design managers of each operation, and while it was evident that both were operational experts, the similarity ended there. The major difference lay in their *respective attitudes about their CAD system*. The former was disappointed with the relative "unfriendliness" of the system and the investment and duration of training required to attain reasonable proficiency. He and his design people had apparently made some major compromises as a result and were utilizing only a small part of the system's total PC design capability.*

The latter manager, who heads a major East Coast PC design house, boasted of being "probably the best PC design house in the country," before acquiring their CAD system and yet he was still estimating a 4:1 increase in output. Why so much better than his counterpart? His answer has since formed the basis of our daily operating perspective. He said, "I'll tell you something. There are a lot of people out there who think that you buy a CAD/CAM system, plug it in, and that's all there is to it. Well, I've got news for them . . . getting a system is just the beginning . . . you've got to put your shoulder to the wheel, keep it there, and push like heck." Two years later, with systems much improved and substantially "friendlier," we still value this good advice.

Unfortunately, we had little historical detail available for our mechanical design operations, nor could content equivalency be so readily ascertained. We did, however, have a good idea of where the major advantages would lie (Fig. 4). Although we referenced these projected benefits in our proposal, augmenting them with other companies' reported savings, we opted not to "create" a Simmonds savings statement. Reason? We felt there was insufficient data to develop a predictable model, and were uncertain about the extent of measurable savings available to early mechanical design operations, particularly in view of the up-front training, custom programming, and data base development required. There is a substantial amount of work to be done here before the savings start to accrue. (For example, we were surprised to find that even basic piece-part hardware libraries were unavailable.)

---

*We witnessed identical situations at the CAD/CAM facilities of two other major corporations we visited, one of whom had finally relegated their CAD system almost exclusively to the design of tools and fixtures.

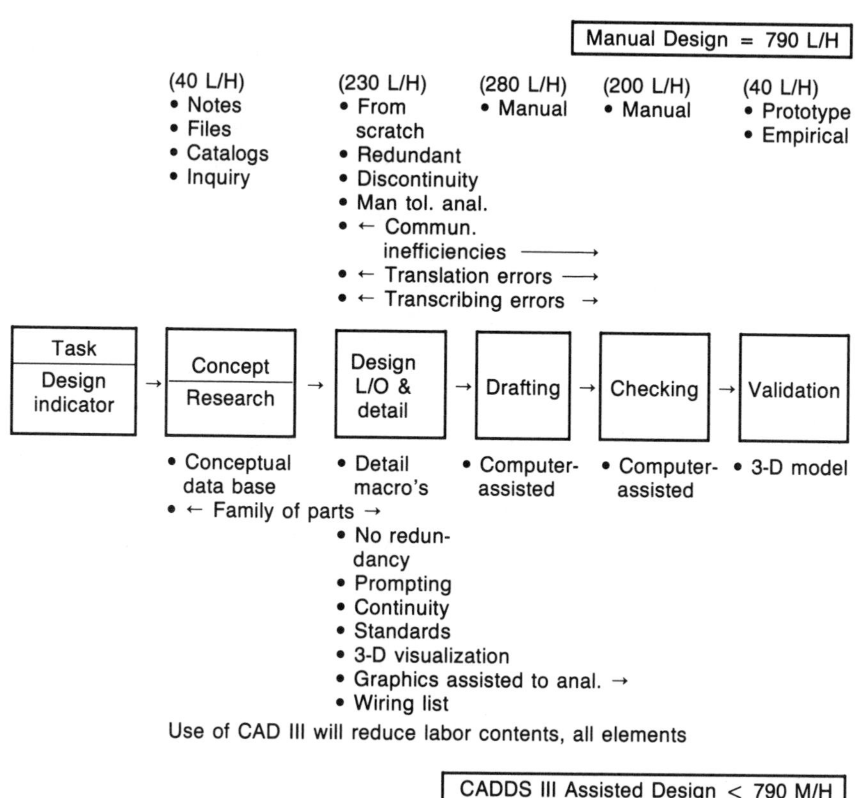

Figure 4 Major mechanical design activity.

In a related, highly specialized area of proprietary design practice, we confidently projected $42K/annum of savings, but as we will see in our critique, they occurred in a manner quite different than that planned.

MANUFACTURING

Our manufacturing people also took a cautious approach in their savings projections, limiting their commitment to $18.6K/annum, all related to NC programming efficiencies for our NC lathes and machining centers. As we will see further on, it was well that we were not overly aggressive here.

GRAPHICS

Projected graphics savings, which we felt were realistic and well thought out, are depicted in Figure 5, which bottom-lined at $35K/annum. We would also be in for some surprises here. As the reader can see, these were tied to projected productivity improvements in the generation of illustrations for proposals, technical publications, and manuals.

That was it, the tangible savings as we could best assess them, some $240K per year. Not bad but not nearly enough as it turned out.

Subsequent financial analyses provided a relative dimension to our problem; as indicated 40-month payback versus the 24 months or better we were looking for.

While discouraged at the time by the magnitude of our short-fall, we realized that this was to be a significant turning point in our capital proposal justification process.

It had been evident from the outset that there were two additional factors, powerful factors, which any CAD/CAM proposal should consider, intangibles and the long-range strategic role of CAD/CAM.

Available evidence suggested that a strong case could be made for quantifying intangibles. For example, we were tempted to apply a Lockheed study's findings that:

> Use of interactive graphics produces more ideas and better designs resulting in 15% fewer design changes.

We also looked at the ability of a CAD/CAM system to catalyze a high degree of standardization, as presented in Figures 6–9.

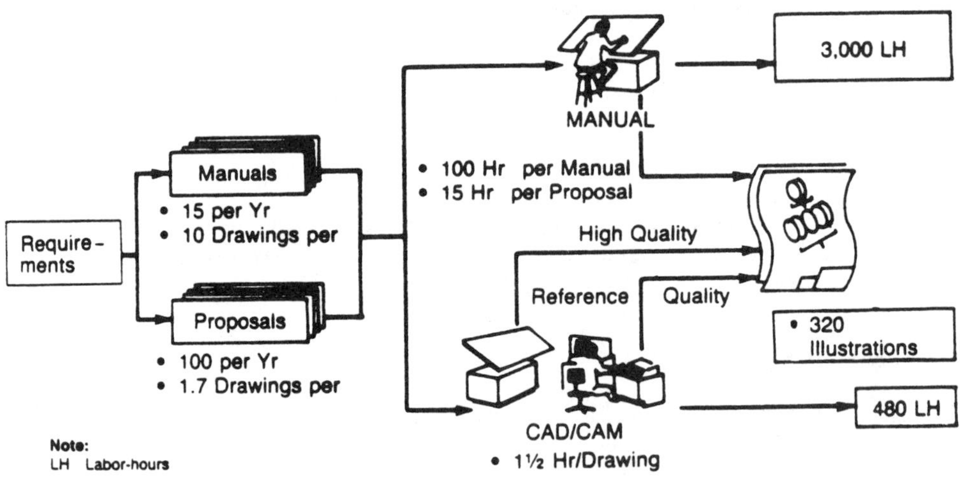

Figure 5 Proposals/publications.

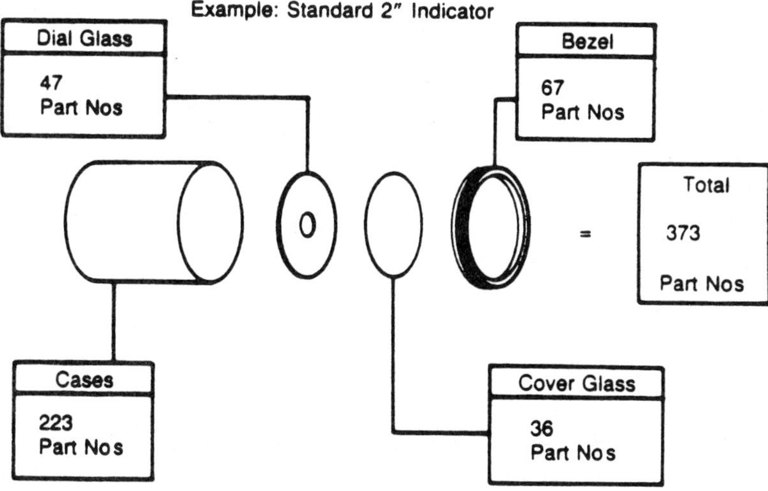

Figure 6 Part number proliferation in the absence of standards.

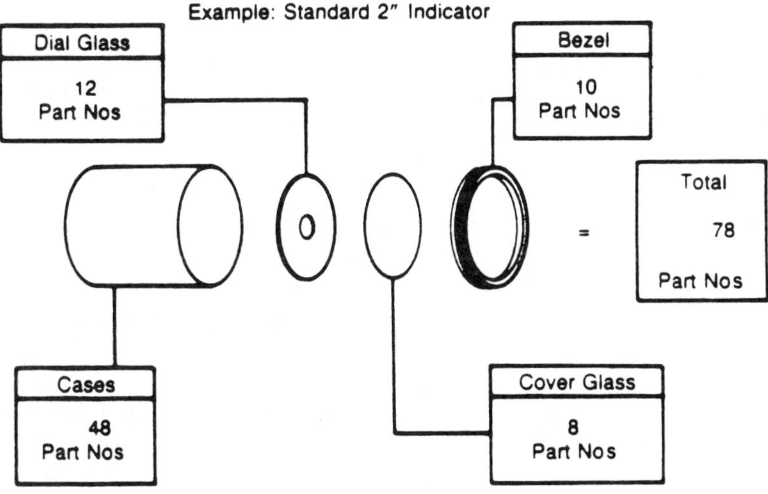

Figure 7 Part number control with CADDS III standards.

- Load Item Master
- Generate Product Structure
- Make/Buy Decision
- Process by Analyst
- Cut Requisition
- Cut Order
- Place Order
- Expedite Order
- Write Q.C. Insp. Analysis
- Set Up Bin in Stockroom
- Set Up Location Card
- Receive & Notify Planner
- Inspect
- For Make Items:
  - Write Operation Sheet
  - Write Planning Card
  - Set Up Machine(s)
  - Inspect
- Kit Additional Part
- Handle Add'l. Part in Assy.
- Add One More Part to Inventory

Figure 8 Standardization.

Creativity and its enhancement were also thematic to much of our source data. Of the various testimonies to CAD's impact on creativity, we found Carl Sagan's views on this subject more persuasive:

> Computer graphics have now reached a state of sophistication that permits important and novel kinds of learning experiences in arts and sciences, and in both cerebral hemispheres. There are individuals, many of them analytically extremely gifted, who are impoverished in their abilities to perceive and imagine spatial relations, particularly three-dimensional geometry. . . . Computer graphics is an extraordinary tool for improving our ability to visualize three-dimensional forms—a skill extremely useful in graphic arts, in science, and in technology.

Other reasonably supportable intangibles were directly related to resource acquisition and utilization, such as the ability to use lesser skilled people for higher order design activities, and, as a consequence, derive a reduction in the costs associated with hiring experienced designers and illustrators.

While presenting the preceding factors for consideration, we elected not to quantify or include them in our projected savings. There was a good reason for this. We had been exposed as well to the obverse side of intangibles; caveats which seldom find their way into mainstream CAD/CAM euphorics. The organizational, psychological, and physiological factors which may impede, or, in some instances, prevent a successful CAD/CAM installation.

These uncertainties were weighed, and in our judgment, comprised a degree of offsetting risk sufficient to engender a ''wait and see'' position relative to intangibles.

From a strategic viewpoint, we saw CAD/CAM as being both compelling and inevitable, a focal point for divisional synergy and productivity improvement. We specifically proposed that CAD/CAM:

Is the primary building block for developing systems and methodologies which would strengthen Simmonds' leadership position in the marketplace.
Is a highly visible commitment to designing and producing higher quality products at lower cost and with fewer errors.
Is an effective new business tool. Automated graphics would enable faster turnaround or better quality proposals.
Would generate a higher level of customer confidence.
Would drive the integration of engineering and manufacturing.

While thoroughly convinced that CAD/CAM was a necessary component of our division's future vitality and competitive posture, we were, at least for the moment, stymied by the seemingly irreconcilable short-term financial tests.

It was at this point (late 1980) that top management stepped in. Robert I. August, then Divisional President, encouraged a continuation of the study and consulted with Chairman of the Board, Geoffrey R. Simmonds. While these discussions are not a matter of record, two related 1980 strategy statements are.

1. Apply Simmonds' resources to produce extraordinary results, recognizing that establishing priorities for critical new investments are essential management disciplines.
2. Make strategic investments to insure long-term competitiveness.

The issue at hand, then, was to judge whether this proposal, this system, was consistent with the intent of these strategies. The baton had been passed and Geoffrey Simmonds moved decisively. Within weeks, Bob Langford, a CAD/CAM consultant, was auditing our proposal and examining its assumptions. It soon became evident that there was a strong coincidence in our respective approaches, with both emphasizing conservatism and built-in compensation for variables and unknowns. In retrospect, Bob's contributions went far beyond this auditory role and the justification process. He stressed three points which put our anxieties into proper perspective:

1. That we might, in fact, not realize *any* net savings in the first year-and-a-half, or so.
2. That savings could occur in ways or areas not recognized at that time; that by the end of the first two years, we may find that the majority of our savings would be in these, as yet unidentified, applications.
3. That there would be a significant reduction in the number of design and documentation errors (whether this improvement would be measurable was another matter).

The details were not as important as the underlying message of support. The final critical link was in place; an intermediary to tie up loose ends at the detail level and provide the necessary assurance at the board room level.

The Board of Directors approved our CAD/CAM capital request in March 1981 and with that approval, a highly visible component of Simmonds' long-range strategy was moved into place.

IMPLEMENTATION

While the implementation details of Simmonds' CAD/CAM system go beyond the scope of this discussion, the subject of payback invites a brief highlighting of the factors and tactics which were influential in achieving this payback:

A balanced approach to training and work assignment, getting several applications under way in parallel, rather than serially. This early hands-on familiarization started the thought germination processes for several unforeseen applications.

A well-managed, full-time, centralized, and highly compatible design group.

Doing what we knew best and resisting the temptation to immediately be all things to all people. And resisting, as well, any notion that the system would make us expert in areas in which we were not already competent.

Avoiding, at least at the outset, high-pressure, short-fused jobs which would jeopardize the building of confidence and credibility. We operated under the premise that an unbroken string of successful tasks was necessary to integrate the system into the operational mainstream.

Gaining early acceptance was a key factor. We judged project engineering confidence and support to be essential during the early training stages. Recognizing that there was justifiable concern with the risk of their tightly managed projects becoming CAD/CAM "guinea pigs," we budgeted a "kitty" to provide incentives in the form of guaranteed rebates to cover any overruns. As it turned out, we rebated some 110 hours, while saving thousands of hours in the aggregate.

Virtual 100% system reliability, due, in some measure, to a well-designed facility with a dependable environmental control system and mainframe located in a separate, contaminant-free area.

In terms of payback measurement strategy, we followed another Bob Langford recommendation, "Don't try to track or quantify every savings you come across. 'Collecting' savings can easily become an all-consuming and self-serving end unto itself, thereby obscuring or even roadblocking the more significant, strategic aspects of the system."

Consistent with this counsel, we reported only those savings for which either sufficiently comparable historical data existed, or where pre-CAD/CAM estimates formed the basis for analysis.

CLOSING THE LOOP: REALITY VERSUS EXPECTATIONS

Recalling our expectations, we recognized three distinct elements of CAD/CAM:

1. The foundation applications upon which our base-line payback depended.
2. The intangible or strategic benefits.
3. The catalytic, synergistic aspects, which, while not fully understood at the time, were seen as having conceptually sound bases.

These factors are discussed below by application, rather than in turn, so as to maintain continuity of thought. While many of the results are perhaps unique to Simmonds' particular situation, they are presented with the belief that every company possesses similar, tailored opportunities for productivity gains.

Foundation Applications

By way of review, these were in the area of: (1) printed circuit design, (2) a proprietary analytical application, (3) NC programming, and (4) proposal/publications graphics.

Printed circuit design savings were seen as comprising the primary vehicle for early system payback. Our objectives were ambitious and near term: "Save 67 hours per standard design, plus $75 in vendor fees."

There were, in effect, two distinct periods in our first 20 months experience; the first twelve months, and the ensuing eight months. During the first year, PC operations proceeded to plan, with normal mix complexity and schedule pressures. Training, initially projected at six months to bring operators to an intermediate degree of system fluency, turned out to be reasonably accurate. (Some systems manufacturers claim a three-month period.) This training was on company time, in answer to an often asked question.

All PC design objectives were met, with a few bonuses thrown in. Design time was, in fact, reduced from 119 to 45-55 hours. Tracking of this data, by the way, is fairly straightforward at Simmonds, using a computerized engineering project information and control system, which tracks tasks weekly, by project elements and departmental skill codes.

Our CAD/CAM systems' auto-route feature exceeded expectations by consistently producing a 90-95% completion after component placement had been accomplished by our designers. Another point of interest, we believe that autoplace, a software program for locating circuit components within the board's "keep in" areas is an excellent tool for logic device placement, but it cannot compete with a seasoned designer on analog circuit layout. Simmonds is fortunate in having several excellent PC designers, which has undoubtedly enhanced the system's auto-route performance.

During the first year, several measurable peripheral benefits attended Simmonds PC design activity.

We found ourselves doing four and sometimes five feasibility layouts in the time it previously took to do one, thus enabling a higher degree of design and cost predictability early in the proposal stages.

We were able to determine, with certainty, the absolute minimum number of layers required for a given design. This led to considerable recurring savings over the life of a program. By setting up execute files, "number of layers" design rule variants were serially exercised during an unattended third shift, with the results available for us first thing in the morning.

Our system, in addition to saving $75/board in NC drill tape costs, proved to be compatible with a far broader, and therefore, more competitive printed circuit board vendor base. Our purchasing people exploited this opportunity to drive an additional $150/board (average) cost reduction.

This also resulted in a three-week reduction in turnaround time.

In a situation which is definitely unique to Simmonds but, nonetheless of interest, we saved another $750-1000 per design. Here's how. With our earlier digitizing system, we had a single source for artmasters in Toronto, Canada with an eight day turnaround. Whenever we were in a schedule bind (most of the time) our designer would drive to Toronto, stay over to coordinate and expedite, then return with the artwork. This necessarily involved customs coordination, carnets, value-added duty, lost man-days (with overtime adding further insult), vendor premium payments, meals, motel and transportation expense, all added to our cost-of-sales.

During May 1982, having barely assessed our first year of PC operations, total pandemonium broke loose: 14 new programs descended on us, a combination of commercial, military, and space systems, all scheduled for completion during the period ending in December. While this volume of design work (107 printed circuit designs) far exceeded that of any prior such period (220% of preceding eight months) the figures alone provide little perception of the schedule intensity or explosion of new technical requirements which characterized this period. These were substantive and state-of-the-art, necessary for improved system performance and reliability and included individually heat-sinked components, heat-dissipating thermal "ladders," specified layers, specified component locations, specified pin inputs/outputs, and specified test point locations. These contraints, taken singly, add considerable complexity to the design problem. Digital Equipment Company's (DEC) automated design manual, for instance, states that "pre-assigned component placement (alone) may increase design time by 100%." Taken in the aggregate, the effect is exponential. Compound these factors with a series of "what if" analyses to determine the minimum number of total layers required, add scores of in-process change, pull the schedule in a month, and still meet original cost objective. That was the task.

We therefore believe that the essence here was rather one of capabilities and system growth, a dynamic transition from "standard" printed circuit skills to a consistently demonstrated mastery of designs described by our board producers as among the most technically advanced they had seen.

All were delivered on time and at or below bid.

We recognized a number of other intangibles during this period: Being in the business of hardware, not paper, we continued to search for ways to reduce the PC boards production cycle. By combining our mutual requirements, we were able to influence a local design house to buy a photoplotter. (This plotter translates digitized data to printed circuit artmasters.) This enabled us to drop our work off at night and pick it up in the morning. A virtual 100% reduction in cycle time. When you add to this a negotiated reduction of $8000/annum versus (then) present costs, and a further savings of $10,000/annum in express delivery charges (we had been dealing with an artmaster house in Arizona, and by express delivering both ways, we achieved a four-day cycle, at a Δ cost of $60) you start to gain an appreciation of the less obvious ways in which a CAD/CAM system can influence cost and operations. Another subtle benefit we found was that, with the flexibility and editing ability of CAD, we were producing a great number of drawings on a C size format (22 × 17 in.), which formerly required either D (34 × 22 in.) or F size (33 × 34 in.) formats, or in the case of most schematics, two or three sheets. There are efficiencies here which transcend the paper savings, for instance, user convenience, reduced reproduction time for the engineering and manufacturing printrooms, savings in storage space, reduction in user errors, particularly with schematics, elimination of the photo reduction process for SCDs, to name a few.

There was an interesting sidelight to this aspect which threw quite a curve into our productivity measurement program.

Simmonds measures its design groups' productivity by using the number of 8½ × 11 in. drawing units (DU) produced during a period as the numerator for a number of quantitative and qualitative calculations (i.e., hours per DU, errors per DU, etc.).

We were puzzled for a while, in that the perceived level of activity was somehow not being reflected by the drawing unit count. It finally dawned on us that this drawing "compression" was the reason. We then constructed, from prior years historical data, a "standard" Simmonds drawing of 4.43 DUs for use in future calculations.

In the course of analyzing our PC operations, we also realized that "complexity indexing" would be necessary if we were to be able to accurately measure our productivity gains (Fig. 9). Using this approach, we developed a board-by-board composite profile for this period:

No. of designs	Complexity factor	≅ Standard designs
3	3.5	10.5
4	3.0	12.0
13	2.5	32.5
15	1.5	22.5
72	1.0	72.0
107	1.38	149.0

The B-1B program required more detailed modulation per its Figure 10 profile.

Having developed a consistent methodology for quantifying these factors, we were now able to measure comparative PC design costs and savings for the first 12 months in a relatively straightforward fashion. These amounted to $154,000, excluding any of the aforementioned intangibles.

Measuring the next eight months was a little more complicated. We were at a saturation point, facility and staffwise, which necessitated constructing a "would have cost" model, incorporating contract help, overtime, and other variables attendant to the extreme work crunch experienced during this period.

These variables notwithstanding, the "would have cost" model, which was given the benefit of every conceivable doubt, reflected a requirement of 17,572 hours. With our CAD/CAM system, the task was accomplished in exactly 5171 hours, for a productivity gain of 3.4:1.

A point of clarification. This comparison was vis-a-vis our computer-assisted drafting system. Had it been compared to a manual design effort, the "would have cost" scenario would reflect an increase to 25,841 hours versus the 5171, for a 5:1 gain.

However, using the former data set, raw cost savings still amounted to some $344,000 for these eight months, for a total of $498,000 for the first 20 months of PC operations, again, excluding any intangibles.

There is one more area for comment before wrapping up this PC design commentary. Over the past 20 months, we have come to believe that achieving targeted cost and schedule reductions may be only part of the story.

Using our four-year trend data, we also observed that after adjusting for relative level of program requirements, atypical "spikes," reduced requirements from a sister division, and effects of inflation, that PC design iterations (new, plus redesign) are running some 25% fewer than in past years. While this conclusion is relatively untested at this point, we are leaning towards a belief that this may well be the case, due to the more thorough, upfront feasibility analyses, plus

DESCRIPTION	BASELINE
Board Size	3 × 5
Working area	12 in.^{2}
Number of layers	2
1. Component density	80%
2. Number of holes	200
3. Predetermined I/O's	None
4. Predetermined comp. location	None
5. Design restraints	Minor
6. Type of circuitry	Analog
7. Changes while design in process (level of risk)	Low

1. If < than 80% deduct 10%
   If > than 80% < 90% add 10%
   If > than 90% = 100% add 25%

2. If < 200 deduct 10%
   If > 200 < 400 add 25%
   If > 400 < 600 add 50%
   If > 600 < 800 add 75%
   If > 800 = 1000 add 100%

3. If no add 0%
   If yes see table for factor;
   < 10 add 10%
   > 10 < 25 add 25%
   > 25 < 50 add 30%
   > 50 < 75 add 40%
   > 75 < 100 add 50%

Baseline = 100%
Complexity = Baseline ± Factor

4. If no add 0%
   If yes see table for factor;
   < 10% add 10%
   > 10% < 25% add 25%
   > 25% < 50% add 50%
   > 50% < 75% add 75%
   > 75% = 100% add 100%

5. If design restraints;
   None deduct 10%
   Minor add 0%
   Major add 10%

6. If circuitry is;
   > 50% Analog add 0%
   > 50% Digital add 10%

7. If level of risk is;
   High add 20%
   Medium add 15%
   Low add 0%
   None deduct 10%

Figure 9 PCB complexity index.

the additional 2–3 weeks now available for design maturation prior to "drop dead" release dates.

The second area of projected savings, $42,000/annum, involved a proprietary mechanical design process which ideally lends itself to significant computer graphics enhancement.

This task evolved along somewhat different lines than originally envisioned. Whereas we initially considered automation of the existing process, we subsequently decided to re-examine the process itself. (This is a very important and

Description	Standard (1, 0) PC board	B-1B PC board
Board size	3 × 5 in.	4.5 × 6 in.
Component to board density	80%	85–100%
Number of layers	2	6–12
Type of circuitry	Analog	Digital
Thermal considerations	None	All boards required (individual) heatsinking of components to chassis.
Heatsink laminated to PC boards	None	Due to thermal considerations heat "ladder" required for each card for heat transfer (new technology).
Predetermined component location	None	Due to thermal considerations and circuit sensitivity all boards had at least 50% of components preplaced.
Predetermined input/output locations	None	All four boards had at least 90% of I/O pins on I/O connector predetermined.
Special layerings	None	Predetermined layering schemes on all boards (i.e., signal layers, ground layers, and voltage).
Circuit changes while PC design in process	< 3	I.D. > 20 per board Ind. < 5 per board
Design complexity	Baseline	Using the average PC design as baseline and reviewing the complexity of B-1B designs it becomes evident that the B-1B designs are 3-5 times more complex than non-B-1B designs.
Specified test point locations (added after board design underway)	None	30–50

Figure 10 PCB standards.

beneficial aspect of the CAD/CAM conversion process, that is, the rethinking and functional brainstorming of tasks rather than merely automating existing techniques.) This departure from plan provides a good example of other expectations confirmed. Looking back at a key statement from our justification package, "CAD/CAM might be likened to a catalyst, whereby its presence will cause a host of peripheral activities to initiate . . . activities, which until now, have had no supportive vehicle for their implementation."

At the time, we had no idea just how far-reaching this aspect would be. By focusing our attention on the various supportive building blocks for the initial task, we have developed many new approaches to solving not only the basic problem, but several subtier problems, some of which have generated major productivity improvements in their own right:

A 20:1 reduction in one analysis turnaround time
A 5:1 improvement in another
A 9:1 reduction in chargeable mainframe time
The ability to solve extremely complex aircraft attitude versus system accuracy problems with higher accuracy and less hardware
A virtual elimination of errors during one data conversion process
The automation of extensively detailed matrix worksheets
An improvement to the manufacturing fabrication process

Therefore, while not ascribable to our CAD/CAM system per se, we nonetheless see a strong correlation. Recalling an earlier comment, the foregoing typify micro rather than macro task productivity gains.

Ironically, the prime task, which involves the use of customer design data as a direct tape input to our system, is on a back burner pending development of policy for releasing these data sets to Simmonds.

Strategically, the idea has been well received, with several major customers complimenting Simmonds progressive and imaginative approach to solving this (their) problem.

Finally, the overall study has led to a much earlier-than-planned introduction of finite-element modeling and analysis as a resident design tool. Our CAD/CAM system creates the mesh model and nodal data from already existing design geometry, which is then transferred via tape to a PDP-11 for analysis. A powerful new design capability, in place long before its intended time.

The third area of projected savings, \$18.6K, was in numerical controlled (NC) programming, an element we approached with caution, at least in terms of early payback. As it turned out, we accomplished some basic training and coordination, but the enormous printed circuit and graphics workloads, being worked three shifts, effectively preempted our manufacturing engineers from spending any appreciable period on the system during the first 20 months of operations. Savings were nil, in fact, there was a net loss here, as reconciled further on.

The fourth area of projected near-term benefits was in the production of exploded view and assembly graphics for proposal, publications, and program support. At the outset, we had taken a rather simplistic view of savings opportunities here, and we have since been most pleasantly surprised by the breadth of applications being developed by our various graphics operators. Some examples are given below.

On the B-1 program, where all Program Evaluation and Review Techniques (PERT) charts and work breakdown structures were done on our CAD/CAM system, the project engineer estimated direct labor-hour savings of eight labor-months. In that our drafting department was fully committed to other workload at the time, we would have had to use our graphics staff, plus several job shoppes, at a Δ cost of $30,000 or so. Even at that, schedule compliance would have been doubtful at best, considering the number of changes flowing in at the eleventh hour. As it was, we met schedule with two junior CAD operators, enabling the graphics department to, instead, concentrate on a critical and simultaneously due customer presentation.

Our graphics people developed a way to reformat our "layered" approach to design, (there are 255 available "layers"), and modify existing printed circuit assembly drawings for publications purposes. This reduces a 24-32 hour illustrating job to 4-6 hours, for a 6:1 productivity improvement.

Schematics, which in all too many past instances involved four iterations from conception to tech manual (brown paper bag stage → final sketch → drafting version → tech pubs-suitable version) are now being done once, with the primary purpose being the required input statement for PC board autorouting.

All software flow diagrams, program charts, drawing trees, etc. (approximately 350/annum) are being done on the system by a CAD clerk. Production time varies from 15 minutes to an hour versus manual times of 2-6 hours. Ease of change further enhances this figure, as does the lower hourly rate of a CAD clerk, compared to an illustrator.

On a recent proposal for a major system retrofit, existing design geometry was accessed on the system to produce the supporting illustrations. The graphics specialist accomplished this estimated 1000-hour task in just over 200 hours.

Here's a classic, with a moderate productivity increase but leveraging a significant response from our customer, the Air Force, and other participating companies and customer divisions. One of our program managers designed an extensive test equipment utilization and applications chart for his program, one which would have typically involved dozens of individual charts, all tied together with from-to notes. Our graphics people instead designed a single global chart on our CAD system, 23 feet long, which is substantially easier to interpret and follow. We have received as many plaudits for this effort as for any of our far more complex accomplishments, it being described as a "stimulus and breakthrough in terms of better understanding total program requirements."

Another instance, involving a major aircraft engine manufacturer, where a CAD layout of customer envelope geometry resolved a very complex "whose problem *is* it?'' question, evoked the following written statement from the project engineer, ''Had the (CAD/CAM) system been available for use at the inception of this project, I believe this entire job would have been successfully completed months ago.''

The various foregoing ''incremental'' examples are intended to be representative and they are not, by any means, direct bottomline indicators. Now let us see what these incremental improvements have produced at the bottomline, in terms of quality and staffing impact.

Quality

There are two ways to look at Simmonds' error-reduction experience:

First, *logically* we have observed, day in and day out, that despite the increased complexity of current designs, the CAD/CAM methodology, with its built-in design aids and readily available, high clarity check prints, typically leads to error-free results, error-free that is, in terms of faithfully translating a given input to a desired output.

Secondly, *statistically* we can look at some historical trend data related to the cost of errors. Since 1981, Simmonds has systematically tracked eleven categories of ECR causal and cost factors, including those due to (1) design errors and (2) drafting errors, on both design verification test (DVT) and production releases, occurring within the prior 12-month period.

Using our prototype shop's pilot production records, we observed a reduction from .26 errors per drawing unit in 1981, to about .20 in 1982. A 24% reduction. Next, looking at monthly financial reports and our document control center records, we plotted our trend insofar as production released drawings are concerned. In 1981, our cost to correct design and drafting errors was $78,000 for 5500 released drawing units or about $14 per drawing unit. In 1982, the cost was $85,000 for over 9000 releases, for a cost of $9.50 per drawing unit, a 32% reduction.

Staffing Impact

Looking at Simmonds engineering direct labor staff for 1976, 1980, and 1982, and normalizing it for non-drawing-related effects of staff growth in the projects, software, and applications groups, we see the following:

	1976	1980	1982
D/L Staff	102	96	164[a]
Less: P.E., S/W, Applic.	18	10	37
Net Staff	84	86	127
Des/Drft/Ch'k & CADDS Staff	23	24	24
% of Organization	27%	28%	19%

[a]Plus 32 job shoppers, of which 6 (also 19%) are designers and draftspeople.

We can see here that, in terms of relative organizational content, the design and drafting staff has been reduced by 32% when compared to the 1979–1980 period. This reflects a high degree of correlation with the improvement in drawing output, which reflected a 35% improvement, as shown below:

Standard Drawings/Person/Year

	Drawing ÷	Net staff	=	Standard Drawings/Person
1980	1345	24.06	=	55.9
1981	1410	22.8	=	61.8 ↑ 10%
1982	2160	28.6	=	75.5 ↑ 35% (vs. 1980)

Any bottomline discussion would be incomplete without a final reconciliation of estimated savings. Simmonds 20-month financial position reflects the following:

Gross savings		$546K
Less		
Service contract	39	
Training	41	
Library and procedure development	12	
Net savings	=	454K
After tax savings	=	227K
Basic system amortization	=	70%
Planned system amortization	=	50%

CONCLUSIONS

While we wince at equating savings with value received, Simmonds' measurable savings for this period, excluding consideration for schedule, quality, or other intangibles, were immense.

This does not, however, alter a basic recommendation that potential users conduct their own thorough examination of CAD/CAM not as a mystical design and manufacturing cure-all, but in the light of its own intended operating environment.

Of equal import is total organizational involvement and commitment for the bad times as well as good.

Timing is a key element, both in terms of the selected system's maturity for its primary applications as well as the timing of its acquisition. For instance, if Simmonds' management had not acted quickly and system delivery had not been pulled in four months, we would have missed or possibly ruined our greatest period of payback opportunity.

As might be expected, there were surprises, both positive and negative:

The system has proved to be friendlier than expected in some areas and far more difficult in others.

Reliability has far exceeded expectations.

We have experienced none of the psychological or physiological problems frequently cited by other users. In fact, it would appear that quite the opposite has occurred, that the dedicated CAD team is a particularly cheerful group with a lower than average number of problems or absenteeism.

We discovered that many problems which are literally unsolvable by conventional means are routinely solved on our CAD/CAM system.

We found that a full-time applications programmer and instructor, although not planned for, is almost a necessity. This type of person has also proven to be scarce and expensive.

The tremendous flexibility, utility, and payback of graphics applications has far exceeded our original expectations.

Productive operator time on the system, originally estimated at six hours per day, based on various published studies, has proved to be an understatement. Through necessity and staff limitations, Simmonds' CAD/CAM group has worked extended 10-hour shifts, maintaining a consistently high output of quality work. Of course, this doesn't "just happen." There is some attention to detail required here . . . comfortable, properly supportive chairs, good lighting (without glare), storage rather than raster cathode ray tubes (CRTs), correct eyeglass focal length (not set up for 18-in. reading distance, but rather, 26–30-in. CRT screen distance), a quiet environment, out of mainstream traffic and commotion and, finally, properly maintained temperature and humidity controls.

The speed and quality of drawings and graphics from our electrostatic plotter continue to amaze us. The value of timely check prints and in-process working drawings cannot, in our opinion, be overestimated.

If there was a major disappointment, it was our inability to spread the system user base. We, in effect, cash-cowed our shooting star, due primarily to hardware limitations (five terminals), the overwhelming printed circuit workload, and a shortage of qualified instructors (one). Looking back, we appreciate that this was an extremely austere beginning, much more so than we realized at the time.

These, then, are some of the Simmonds' observations, all leading to an inescapable conclusion, that while a CAD/CAM system promotes higher productivity in many ways, operationally and strategically, this role is soon eclipsed by the realization that in the final analysis CAD/CAM is an indispensable and fundamental tool.

As our current divisional president, Arlen VanKoevering, recently reported to Geoffrey Simmonds, "we could not have made it through this past year . . . without CAD/CAM."

What follows are additional stand-alone rationales that support the previous case study. They are intentionally kept generic so as to be of assistance to the widest possible readership.

DESIGN

Starting from a rough sketch or possibly just an idea, the designer uses the graphic display as if it were a drafting board to construct the geometry of a design. Several parts can be displayed simultaneously so the designer can ensure that they fit together properly and that there will be no interference upon assembly.

After completion of geometric definition, design analysis functions are invoked to determine various properties. The results of the analysis often require changes in the design geometry, and a fresh analysis of the new design. This iterative process is performed at the CAD workstation, without the traditional shuttling of the part design between the analysis and design groups.

Computer-assisted design is at its best in designing families of parts (parametric parts). The part can be designed so that the variable parameters are input data. The part can then be called up as a library function specifying the values of the required parameters. In this way the design of the entire family of parts can be completed in little more time than is required to produce the design for one part.

Most CAD systems provide some form of layering. A layer is simply one way of describing the part. This can be a particular geometric view (e.g., rough cast shape, or finished shape), or a nonpictorial way of describing the part (e.g., bill of material or automatically programmed tools (APT) part program). The layering is used heavily throughout the design process, in drafting, checking, and NC part programming to name only a few uses.

Some typical design application areas are: the design of configurations, space allocation, structures, buildings, ducting, forgings, castings, machine parts, sheet metal parts, electrical systems, printed circuits, and mechanical linkages.

ANALYSIS

Some of the design analysis functions commonly available will now be explained. In this technique, the part is subdivided into a number of small rectangles or triangles which are analyzed separately. The total effect on the part is the sum total of all of the subdivisions.

The analysis is performed by a large computer. Until graphics was used, the geometric input into the analysis program was manual and tedious. To obtain the input it was necessary to make a large-scale accurate drawing of the part shape. An engineer then drew in the elements, with smaller and more numerous elements near suspected problem areas. Each element was then numbered and the coordinates of the nodal points were measured manually. All this information was then converted into a punched card deck which was input to the mainframe computer for analysis. If the analysis indicated a problem area, the part geometry in that area was changed and the entire process repeated.

The availability of a universal graphics data base changes all that. Now the data bases of the parts to be analyzed are called up. The finite-element grid is generated automatically through software developed for finite elements. The engineer has the ability to change any portion of this grid pattern if he or she so desires. The elements are numbered and the precise coordinates of the nodal points are obtained automatically by the graphics system. This information is output from the system in a format that requires no human intervention before being input to a computer for analysis. Should the analysis indicate that the part geometry required modification, this is done rapidly at the CRT terminal and the entire process repeated.

It should be noted that the finite-element analysis is usually performed on a larger computer than that which supports the CAD system. The CAD system essentially performs housekeeping details, preparing input for the larger mainframe. This is no small aid. The CAD system eliminates a very time-consuming task by handling the bulk of input preparation for finite-element analysis programs.

Additional design analysis functions typically include dynamic and static clearances; tolerance between mating parts, structural section properties, hydraulic circuit properties, stress analysis, and deflection analysis.

Mass Properties

The feature of a CAD system that has perhaps the widest application is that of "mass properties." This feature automatically gives the perimeter, area, center of gravity, and moments of inertia of any cross-section. The properties of the cross-section when rotated about any axis to form a solid are also given: exposed surface area, volume, weight, center of gravity, and moments of inertia. Applications range from weight calculation to contour roll die design.

Stackups

The ability to display an assembly of various components is used to good advantage in axial stack-up calculations. In this application the engineer has all the components of interest displayed on the screen. In the time it would normally take to describe the requirements to a drafter, the engineer is able to identify the areas where a nominal clearance is wanted and obtain its value.

Finite-Element Analysis

Many parts are subject to severe heat transfer and stress conditions. One mathematical tool used to calculate the effects of these on a given part is "finite-element model analysis."

DESIGN REVIEW

Checking the accuracy of drawings can be accomplished using either a graphics terminal or a hardcopy output. It is often found that a large plot of a part is a very useful tool for design reviews. The engineer essentially has a very precise drawing of the components, and can visually spot errors in stacking, blends, undersize fillets, and so on, in much the same way that these errors are spotted after the part is made. A CAD system also allows the user to zoom in and magnify any local area of the screen to any magnification. This enables the drafter to check for dimensional errors, providing a verification capability that does not exist without CAD.

Layering is useful in design review. Placing a geometric representation of the minimum-sized rough shape over a view of the maximum-sized succeeding shape (through to the finished part) provides a fast way to determine whether it is possible to perform the operation.

DATA BASE CREATION

Once the designer is satisfied that the part design has been sufficiently optimized, the drawing is entered into the data base. The data base will contain all the information pertaining to the part. The part can be retrieved by other designers for incorporation into their design or for checking compatability. The central data base allows full use to be made of the information entered into the CAD system.

DRAFTING

A draftsman accesses the data base and retrieves the part design. The detail work is now performed. Lines and fillets are trimmed. Layout lines are removed. Areas are crosshatched. Drilled holes are identified. Dimensions are added (generally available in English, metric, or both types of units). Tolerances are noted. All necessary text is placed on the drawing.

Company standards for drawings can be easily enforced by programming the standard into the system. Aids to the draftsman include transformations to assist in developing oblique, isometric, and perspective views, and the capability to replicate details which appear at various places on the design.

Additional views can be quickly generated. Although the drafter works with the design as if it were just a drawing, it is important to realize that this is not just an image on the CRT. It is precise geometric data stored in the data base which can be manipulated to suit various needs; the CRT merely makes the data visible.

Common applications include surface contour and styling drawings, layouts for preliminary design, exploded views, floor plans, perspective drawings, dimensioned drawings, isometric drawings, nondimensioned master drawings for production design, logic diagrams, charts, graphs, symbolic diagrams, assembly layouts, fixture layouts, interference problem layouts, subassembly drawings, assembly drawings, module drawings, clearance drawings, and stack-up drawings.

TOOL DESIGN

A tooling engineer retrieves the part program from the bata base and designs tooling for the part. The fully defined geometry is particularly useful in designing holding devices for machining complicated parts. The CAD system generally enables the designer to rotate the part on any axis and measure from any datum. This makes it simple to measure dimensions which are necessary to design tooling and extremely difficult to obtain by ordinary methods.

Typical applications are the design of holding fixtures, dies, glass layouts, and templates of many kinds.

NUMERICAL CONTROLLED (NC) PART PROGRAMMING

In producing a numerical control (NC) part program, the accurate geometric definition of the part that is present in the data base is employed by the part programmer. The presence of this eliminates the step of defining the part geometry from drawings, which is the first step in traditional (APT-like) NC programming. Auxiliary statements concerning cutting speed, feed rate, coolants, tool changes, and so on must be entered. The definition of the cutter path is then normally specified interactively, rather than by the traditional APT process of mentally envisioning the cutter path. The part program can often be done through a graphic presentation of the machining operation (if the CAD system is of the refresh type, this is often accomplished through antimation). The resulting NC part program is usually in APT/CL file format.

Typically NC programming can be done for 2, 2½, 3, 4, and 5 axis machining and machines including milling machines, lathes, punch presses, drilling machines, and most other digitally controlled machines.

INSPECTION

Inspection of parts with complex shapes can be aided through the use of CAD. The use of various cut planes allows the part to be measured by an inspector, after which the CAD system generates a view of the part design cut on the same plan as the measurement was taken. This allows simple determination of the intended design nominal dimension; and, consequently, rapid decisions are possible as to whether the part is within specifications.

BENEFITS

There are many benefits of CAD, only some of which can be easily measured. Some of the benefits are intangible, reflected in improved work quality, more pertinent and usable information and improved control, all of which are difficult to quantify. Other benefits are tangible, but the savings from them show up far downstream in the production process, so that it is difficult to assign a dollar figure to them in the design phase. On the other hand, there are some benefits which are directly measurable.

Here we have a checklist of potential benefits which may be derived from a CAD system.

Increased Productivity

Increased productivity translates into a more competitive position for the firm because it will reduce staff requirements on a given project. This leads to lower costs, in addition to speeding response on tight timetable projects.

Productivity improvement depends on: degree of detail (more detail, greater productivity), degree of repetitiveness or symmetry (more repetition, greater productivity), extensiveness of library of commonly used entities, drawing complexity (greater complexity, greater productivity). Because productivity improvement varies so much with different applications, it is impossible to give a firm figure for it. Productivity improvement ratios of up to 100:1 can truly be found, but it would be untrue to suggest that figure is typical.

Shorter Production Lead Time

Interactive CAD is inherently fast and also speeds up the tedious process of making and compiling material takeoff information by hand. Thus, such systems can produce a finished drawing and associated reports in a relatively short time.

In the development of a product, certain parts of the critical path are dependent on engineering flow time. The tremendous productivity of engineers working with CAD tends to greatly reduce the prominence of design, drafting, and analysis as a time critical item.

The flow time will not experience a reduction of the same magnitude as the productivity improvement since other tasks will become critical, but a significant shortening of the critical path to manufacturing can be expected.

Design Analysis

The design analysis routines available in a CAD system help to consolidate the design process into a more logical work pattern. Rather than having a back and forth exchange between design and analysis groups, the same person can perform the analysis, while remaining at a CAD workstation. This helps to improve the concentration of designers, since they are interacting with their designs in a real-time sense. Generally, the designers retain their train of thought more easily. Because of the fast analysis possible, designs can be produced which are closer to an optimum design. There is a time saving to be derived from analysis routines, both in designer time, and also in absolute time. This saving results both from the rapid performance of the design analysis and from the time no longer lost while the design finds its ways from the designer's drawing board to the top of the design analyst's queue and back again.

An example of the success of this is drawn from the General Electric experience with the T700 engine. In designing an engine, weight is a primary parameter. During the design of an engine, weights of each part in each design alternative must be calculated. In the past this had been done manually by breaking each part into simple geometrical shapes, the volumes of which could be calculated. Through the use of CAD and its mass properties design analysis function, the mass properties were obtained in 25% of the time formerly taken.

Better Designs

Since design changes are usually easier to make and analyze with a CAD graphics system, more alternate solutions can be tried in the available development time. Consequently, an improvement in design quality can be expected.

Reduction in Processing Errors

Interactive CAD systems provide an intrinsic capability for avoiding design, drafting, and documentation errors. Data entry, transposition, and extension errors that crop up quite naturally during material take-off calculations in the preparation of a bill of material are virtually eliminated. One key reason for such accuracy is simply that no manual handling of information is required once the initial drawing has been developed. Errors are further avoided because interactive CAD systems perform time-consuming repetitive duties such as multiple symbol placement, sort by area and by like item at high speeds with consistent and accurate results.

Still more errors can be avoided because a CAD system, with its interactive capabilities can be programmed to question input which may be erroneous (e.g., a tolerance of .00002 in., perhaps there was one too many 0's). The success of this checking would depend on the ability of the system designers to determine what input is likely to be incorrect, and hence, what to question.

Improved Accuracy

There is also a high level of dimensional control, far beyond the levels of accuracy attainable manually. Mathematical accuracy is often to 14 significant decimal places. The accuracy delivered by interactive CAD systems in three-dimensional (3-D) curved space designs is so far beyond that offered by manual methods that there is no real comparison.

Computer-based accuracy pays off in many ways. Parts are labeled by the same recognizable nomenclature and number throughout all drawings. In some CAD systems, a change entered on a single item can appear throughout the entire documentation package effecting the change on all drawings that utilize the part.

Such accuracy also shows up in the form of fewer ECOs, more accurate material and cost estimates, and tighter procurement scheduling. These last two points are especially important in such cases as long lead time material purchases.

Numerical Control (NC) Part Programming

One typical NC programming language is automatically programmed tools (APT). This is a powerful and versatile language, but has three potential disadvantages. The first is that the user must learn a language with its own syntax and grammar. Unless the user already has computer programming experience, he or she is exposed to some entirely alien concepts. A second disadvantage is that the part programmer must interpret the engineering drawings (with the possibility of error) and define the geometry of the part for APT. The third disadvantage is that the programmer has to mentally visualize the tool path while programming. Experience has shown that these disadvantages either prevented capable machine shop personnel from becoming part programmers or else made the learning time unacceptably long. Computer-aided design, on the other hand, uses language easily understood by machine shop personnel. This eases the problem of ''computer shock'' and eliminates the need to learn an alien language. Since the geometry of the part is defined in the CAD data base, there is no need to go through the process of extracting the part geometry from the drawings. The geometry is already given, precisely as the designer specified it. The graphic display and interactive nature of the system eliminates the need to envision the cutter path, since the user is provided with a visual verification of every step in the process.

These advantages have a significant impact on the time necessary to produce an NC tape, and to train an NC part programmer. General Electric's experience with the design and manufacute of the T700 engine indicated that NC tapes were produced in one-half the time taken by conventional APT programming, and that the time required to train methods personnel to make NC tapes was reduced by a factor of 6.

Tool Design

The ability to obtain a view of a part from any desired angle (provided by CAD) is a great aid in designing tooling. For example, in the design of holding fixtures for machining compound angles, information which, using traditional methods, takes days to calculate, can be simply obtained by automatic measurement from the CAD system.

Drawing once more on the GE T700 engine experience, it was found that using CAD, tool design time was reduced to 12–25% of the time taken by traditional methods and the cost of making glass layouts was reduced 60%.

Improved Engineering Change Order Procedures Control

Control of engineering changes is significantly improved. Original drawings and reports are stored in the data base of the CAD system. This makes them much more accessible than documents kept in a drawing vault. They can be quickly checked against new information. Since data storage is extremely compact, historical information from previous drawings can be easily retained in the system's data base for easy comparison with current design/drafting needs.

Standardized Design/Drafting/Documentation Procedures

The single data base and operating system is common to all workstations in a CAD system. Consequently, the system provides a natural standard for design/drafting procedures. All work is handled in a standardized, well-structured manner. Interactive CAD can also integrate office procedural rules into its basic system framework. Using interactive CAD, drawings are "standardized" as they are drawn; there is no confusion as to proper procedures because the entire format is "built into" the system program.

Understandable Drawings

Interactive CAD is equally adept at creating and maintaining isometrics and oblique drawings, as the simpler orthographics. All drawings can be generated and updated with equal ease. Thus, an up-to-date version of any drawing type is always available.

In general, understanding a drawing relates directly to the projection used. Orthographic views are less comprehensive than isometrics. Both are less understandable than a perspective view. Most actual construction drawings are "line drawings." The addition of shading increases comprehension. Different colors further enhance understanding.

Comprehension of the scale, or size of engineered features, also directly relates to the project used (see Fig. 1).

End of measuring (scaling) drawings changes with projection.

Shorter and Easier Training of New Personnel

Interactive CAD systems are highly effective in helping new personnel become acquainted with standardized, routine operations. The reason is that CAD programs "prompt" the user at the screen, in a step-by-step manner.

This ability of an interactive CAD system to support training of new personnel not only accelerates their learning, but also frees senior members of the organization so that they can concentrate on more responsible tasks. Because they are built into each task, the trainee is automatically presented with the company standards and specifications.

Documentation Preparation

Computer-aided design systems often can produce a bill of material in the required format as an addition to the design/drafting process. With purchase specifications stored in the CAD data base, coded data can serve to meet scheduling and production control needs. The time which engineers previously spent doing tedious documentation can now be put to more productive use.

Project Management Enhancements

The appeal of interactive CAD as a drawing and documentation tool should by now be clear. There are, however, some management advantages that may be less evident, although very relevant.

Computer-aided design provides a high-level video communication capability, much like a television network. An interactive CAD display at design review conferences enables project managers to implement almost instantly changes to the data base. Interactive CAD can be the equivalent of bringing all the original tracings to a conference room for progress inspection and review. In essence, each project manager can run a tighter ship by being better informed on the status of a project.

Accounting Information

The use of a CAD system provides accounting information greatly superior to that available from a traditional system. Typically, a system keeps records of the time it was used by user, by project number, and by specific part or drawing. The time is automatically determined from log-on and log-off time. This allows easy, accurate costing of individual projects.

Since the information is cumulative, it can be used for the inevitable system audits. These are extremely important in determining system utilization and productivity figures. These figures are useful in determining what type of capital expenditures to make to upgrade system capacity (for instance, whether to extend the system or buy another one), to determine whether the system is cost-effective, and to determine how well it meets expectations.

Almost all CAD systems contain the following hardware: a computer with disc and magnetic tape for secondary storage, one or more plotters, graphics terminals, alphanumeric terminals, and some form of printer.

There are normally two types of workstations, design and input. Input workstations, normally not found in 3-D mechanical design systems, generally include a large digitizer and an alphanumeric terminal. Design stations usually include a graphics terminal, a form of cursor control, and an alphanumeric terminal (either a CRT or hardcopy terminal).

The Central Processing Unit

Functioning as the "brain" of a CAD system, the central processing unit (CPU) is usually a minicomputer. The CPU does all the mathematical calculations necessary and directs all activity within the system. It acts as the master controller and manager of all workstation input and editing, storage activities, and plotting.

The CPU directs plotters in precisely what to draw, copies disc data onto magnetic tapes for semiactive storage, reads magnetic tapes of drawings and/or documentation for revision or other reuse, and transmits data to and from much larger computers.

In terms of accuracy, most minicomputers conform to similar standards. A typical CPU has a 16-bit word. Almost all systems have a hardware floating point number processor, which greatly speeds calculations involving floating point numbers. The accuracy of a system normally depends on the number of words used to store numbers. Using multiple precision, giving a total of 64 bits per number, a typical system provides accuracy to 14 decimal places. This, however, is not always the case. There may be systems which do not provide sufficient accuracy for your business' purposes. Characteristically, memory capacity ranges from 32,000 to 256,000 words, providing space for the multitasking which the CAD system is designed to handle. The range of execution speed of an instruction is typically 300–1000 nsec.

Finally, the CAD computer often can be connected to other computer systems to expand the storage capacity, processing capacity, or to benefit from more elaborate analysis programs and large data files.

Graphics Terminal

The most visible part of a CAD system from the user's point of view, is the graphics terminal. Using state-of-the-art technology virtually all CAD systems are provided with some form of cathode ray tube (CRT) similar to those used in televisions, oscilloscopes, and radars. Cathode ray tubes are available in many sizes and configurations, and with various capabilities. The majority of CAD systems provide either a "storage" CRT or a "refresh"CRT.

In storage CRTs an electron beam "paints" the image on the screen by "stroking" vectors on the screen's phosphor surface and a wire grid directly behind the screen. Resolution, the number of addressable points on the screen, is very good, typically providing an addressable matrix of 4096 × 4096 points on a 19-in. diagonal screen. After being drawn, the lines remain clear and bright because there are several electron "flood guns" which provide enough voltage to keep the phosphor "on" once activated by the main beam. Therefore, it is possible to maintain the image for an indefinite period. The major disadvantage to a storage screen is that when the user removes a line from a part (in the data base), the change is not seen until the system "repaints" the entire image. This is because it is impossible to selectively erase a storage screen, the entire screen must be cleared to remove any line. Depending on the complexity of the image, and the speed of data transmission to the terminal, repaint time can vary from one second to several minutes. This type of terminal is the less expensive of the two types, with prices typically in the $5000–$12,000 range.

Raster refresh CRTs operate by sending an electron beam across the screen, left to right and top to bottom at a continuous sweep rate. The screen is coated with phosphor. An image is created by a system of activating a light or dark dot at any given spot on the screen by turning the beam on or off as the beam passes it. This process is termed "rasterization." Resolution is usually not as good with a refresh terminal as it is with a storage tube, typically with an addressable matrix of 1024 × 1024 points on a 21-in. diagonal screen. On CAD systems with refresh screens, any change made to the part in the data base is seen instantly since the image on the screen is always being refreshed as the beam passes a particular point on the screen. Therefore, selective erasure and antimation are possible. Since images on a refresh screen last only a few hundredths of a second, the screen must be refreshed quickly. "Flickering" of the image is observed if the refresh rate is too slow. The minimum refresh speed to avoid "flicker" is generally stated as 30 refreshes per second, with a recommended speed of 40–50 refreshes per second.

A variation on this is a vector refresh CRT. An electron beam draws each line on the screen in a series of strokes. This is very similar to the method employed by the storage tube except that there is not the continuous energizing which keeps a line bright. This type of screen shares the fine resolution of the storage tube, but must be refreshed since it is not a storage tube. Therefore, selective erasure is possible. A refresh screen is the more expensive of the two types, with prices in the $10,000–75,000 range.

A brief discussion of essential computer productivity might be helpful at this point.

COMPONENTS

Digitizers

Some CAD systems include a digitizer. This is not normally a part of a 3-D mechanical design system. A manual digitizer has a cursor which can be moved about a large smooth table. It is oriented via a standard x-y coordinate system, through which the computer can detect its location. The cursor generally has a cross-hair target.

Drafters find the digitizer not unlike their drafting boards. It tilts, raises, and lowers. Some digitizers are available with backlighting for easy tracing or with free-floating cursors. Automatic raster scanners can be used to digitize continuous tone photographs and line drawings. Automatic line followers reduce a drawing to a series of lines rather than stream of points. By recording only the information needed to reproduce the lines, the output is condensed. However, a line-follower operator must intervene in the entry process to determine the direction to follow at line intersections.

The digitizer can be used to input from a rough schematic or large layout drawing, input and edit from check-plots, or perform freehand edits of previously stored drawings. High resolution digitizers, typically 42 × 60 in. typically provide resolution and accuracy of .001 in.

Alphanumeric Terminal

Nearly all CAD systems employ an alphanumeric terminal along with the graphics terminal. This is used to enter supplemental information, commands (if there is no cursor-type menu), alphanumeric input, and system commands via a keyboard. The terminal receives messages from the system, design analysis output, program listings and error messages. The advantage of a separate terminal is that these messages can be displayed and entered without erasing or overwriting the image on the graphics screen.

The terminal is either a CRT or a hardcopy terminal. Each type has its advantages. The CRT provides much faster output and does not produce masses of scrap paper. The hardcopy terminal provides a permanent listing, often desirable in debugging or for permanent records.

Cursor Control

The cursor is generally a bright spot on the screen which indicates where lettering or drawing will be placed. There is normally a method by which the position of the cursor can be read by the computer. Therefore, controlling the cursor position enables one to enter locational information into the computer. This can be used in a geometric sense, such as defining a point. A more sophisticated utilization interprets the cursor position as the selection of an item from a menu (the screen is divided into sections, one of which corresponds to each menu section). There are three basic divisions in cursor control devices.

The first type are those which control the cursor without a direct physical relationship to the screen (from the viewpoint of a user). One of these is thumbwheels. There are two thumbwheels used to control the cursor, one of which controls the horizontal position of the cursor, the other the vertical. The thumbwheels are turned to change the position of the cursor. A joystick is a single stick which normally stands straight up. It can be pushed in any direction, causing the cursor to move in the direction. A rock ball is similar to a joystick except there is no stick. The cursor is controlled by rotating the ball in the direction which the user desires the cursor to move in.

Another type of device is the light pen. Contrary to popular belief, the light pen does not project light, but rather detects light from the screen. The cursor follows the light pen, with the computer seeking the position of the light pen by trying to place the bright cursor under the pen. With the pen, the user actually points to the position on the screen which he wishes to input. The light pen, coupled with a refresh screen, provides a very natural method of selecting from a menu. The menu can be placed on the screen, and after pointing to the desired item on it, replaced with the drawing.

The third type of device is a digitizing tablet and pen. This type of tablet detects the position of the pen, and moves the cursor to a corresponding position on the screen. Since the tablet and screen are separate, this provides a means for natural menu selection in a system using a storage tube screen. The menu can be permanently placed on the tablet. Then to select a menu item, the pen is merely touched to the correct block on the tablet. Therefore, the user can see the menu items without busying the screen with the menu (which could not be selectively erased on a storage tube).

Hardcopy Unit

There is normally a hardcopy unit provided to quickly make copies of the screen. The screen can be copied in a few seconds. These copies can be used as permanent records of intermediate steps or on occasions when a rough hardcopy of the screen is desired. These units are not suitable for final drawings since they are not as accurate as plotters.

Output Plotters

There are many types of plotters available for use on CAD systems including high speed drum plotters, flatbed plotters, and computer-output microfilm plotters.

A typical drum-type plotter operates under computer control by rolling paper on a drum (generally mounted horizontally) past axially moving pens. These units are fast and can make drawings of essentially unlimited length, but are limited in width to the width of the drawing drum.

As the name suggests, a flatbed plotter has a flat horizontal drawing surface with the paper lying flat. It is suitable for highly accurate, finished quality drawings. On most flatbed plotters the pens move and the paper remains stationary. Free-floating or carriage-driven drafting heads can plot at speeds of up to 40 in./sec with accuracy of up to .001 in., repeatability of up to .004 in., and resolution of up to .0001 in.

These pen plotters use a holder for an ink pen or scribing tool. Most plotters work with several pens of different colors to achieve multicolor plots.

Electrostatic plotters do not use pens and are the fastest type of plotter. They print dots at densities up to 200 dots per inch. The dots overlap to achieve continuity. Although their accuracy and resolution are not equal to those of good flatbed plotters, these units can produce fairly high-quality, low-cost drawings quickly and quietly. Their major disadvantage is that the original drawing must be rasterized or converted to a series of consecutive printed lines made up of discrete points. Because of this, however, they will plot at the same speed regardless of the drawing density. These speeds can reach close to 1/2 ft^2/sec. On a drawing with many lines this is tremendously faster than a pen plotter. An advantage that these plotters share with drum plotters is that the plot can be virtually any length; typically the limit on length is in excess of 400 ft.

Computer output microfilm (COM) plotters produce drawings on 35-mm film to be used in aperture cards or in roll form. It is much faster than pen, nearly 50 times faster than a pen plotter or electrostatic plotting. It is, therefore, less expensive. Typically a COM plot can be produced and photographically enlarged to original size at less than one-tenth of the cost incurred in producing the same drawing on a pen plotter. Another advantage of COM is that drawings can be conveniently stored. On microfilm, even the largest company's file of drawings can probably be fit in a few cabinets. (With a CAD system, however, this advantage is minimized, since the aim is to store drawings in the data base, not as physical drawings.)

Disadvantages of COM plotting are: the user cannot write on the film; graphic enlargements of microfilm result in drawings which are inferior in accuracy and overall quality to those produced on a pen plotter, and color is difficult to obtain.

Secondary Storage

The CAD data base is normally maintained on magnetic disks, along with much of CAD system software. Disks provide rapid access to the information stored on them due to their random access configuration. The average access time for disk units provided with most CAD systems is 25–40 msec. Computer-aided design systems generally have the capability of handling multiple disk drives, totaling at least 150 megabytes of storage. Some systems provide the capability of supporting configurations of up to 1500 megabytes.

Magnetic tape drives are normally available. They are used as disk backup and for permanent archival file storage. Information access is not nearly as rapid from a magnetic tape as it is from a disk, since the tape is a sequential storage device. Therefore, to access any piece of information, all the information preceding it must first be read. For archival files and backup, however, the infrequent usage makes the slow access time perfectly acceptable. Information transfer rates from magnetic tape are typically one-half as fast as for disks. However, this is still extremely rapid, often in excess of 50,000 bytes per second. Magnetic tape is an extremely compact and inexpensive method of storing large amounts of data. A single tape can store up to 125 megabytes, at a media cost of about 1/100,000 cents per byte.

This might be an ideal opportunity to pause and examine some of the hardware devices referred to in this chapter.

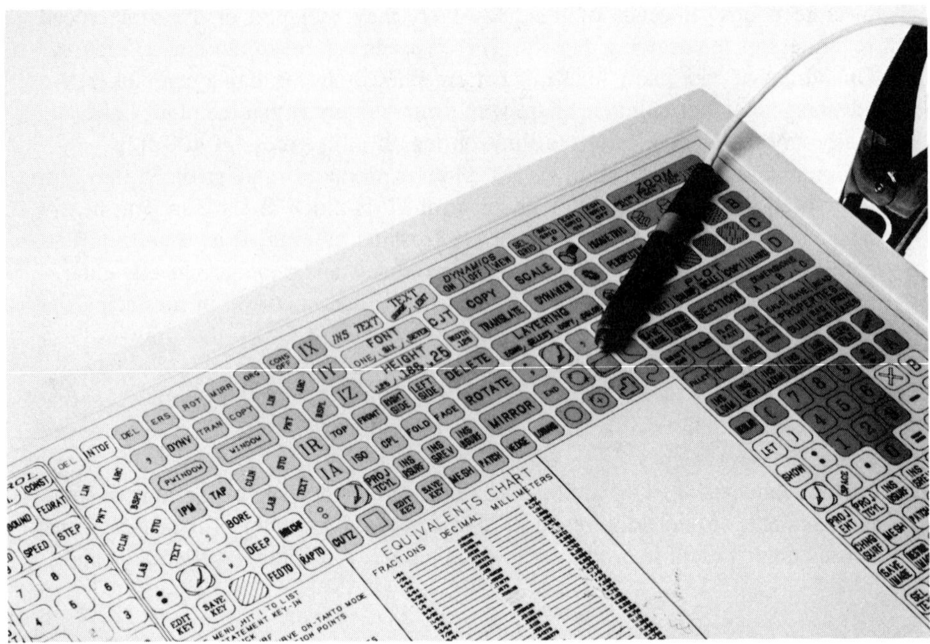

Figure 11 Designer menu tablet and pen. (Reprinted with permission from Computervision Corporation, Bedford, MA.)

Figure 12 A workstation keyboard. (Reprinted with permission from Computervision Corporation, Bedford, MA.)

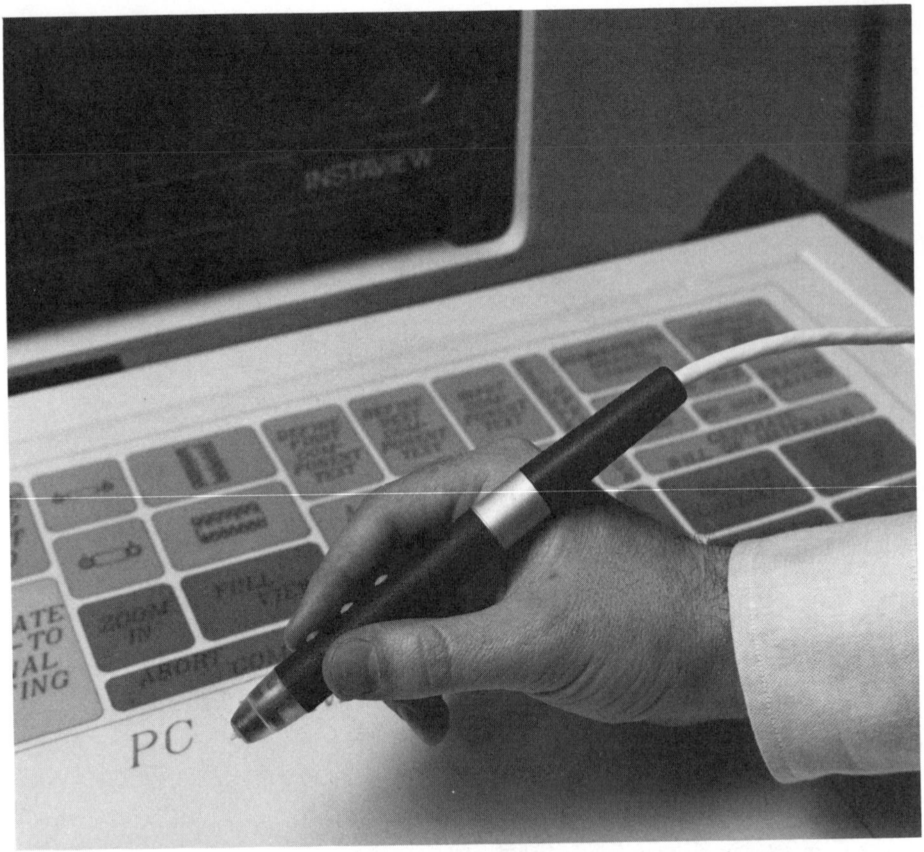

Figure 13 A designer menu tablet. (Reprinted with permission from Computervision Corporation, Bedford, MA.)

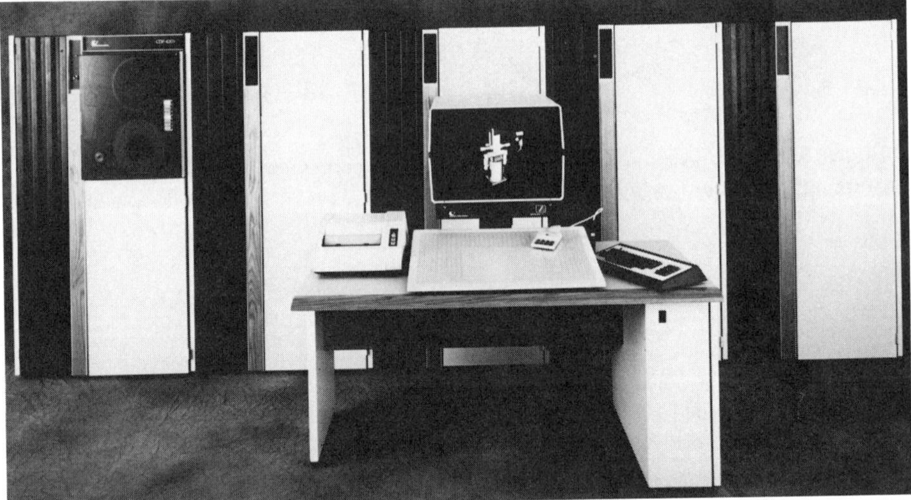

Figure 14 CDS 4201–32 bit CAD/CAM system. (Reprinted with permission from Computervision Corporation, Bedford, MA.)

Figure 15 CDS 4101–32 bit CAD/CAM system. (Reprinted with permission from Computervision Corporation, Bedford, MA.)

Figure 16 Electrical schematic capture. (Reprinted with permission from Computervision Corporation, Bedford, MA.)

Figure 17 High speed line printer. (Reprinted with permission from Computervision Corporation, Bedford, MA.)

Figure 18 Various hardware devices. (Reprinted with permission from Computervision Corporation, Bedford, MA.)

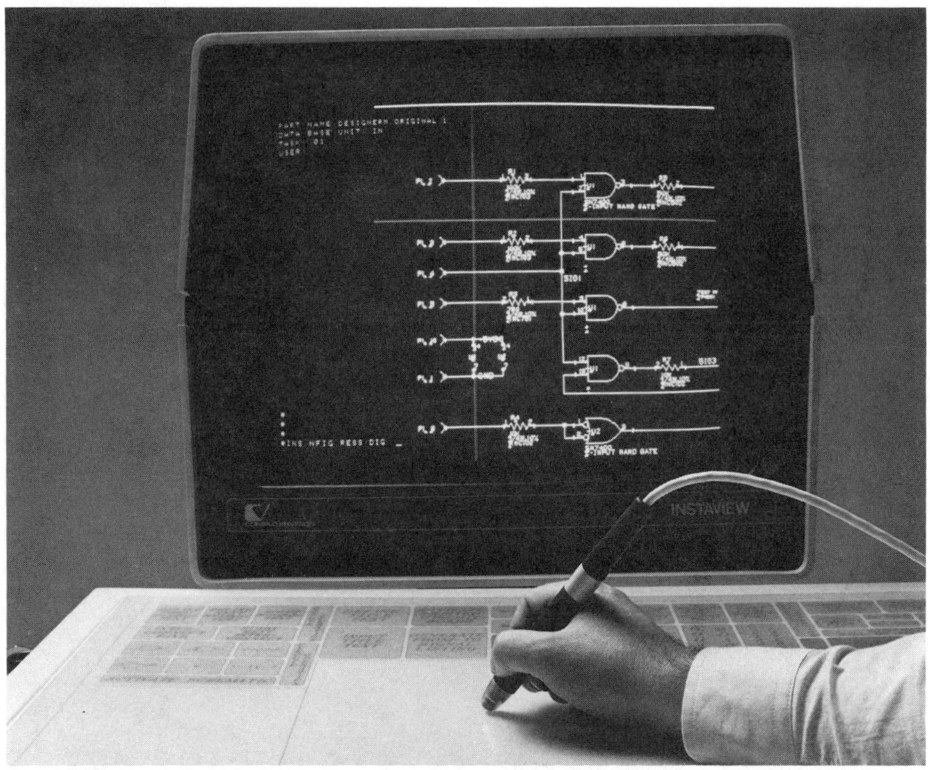

Figure 19 Designer Workstation and menu tablet. (Reprinted with permission from Computervision Corporation, Bedford, MA.)

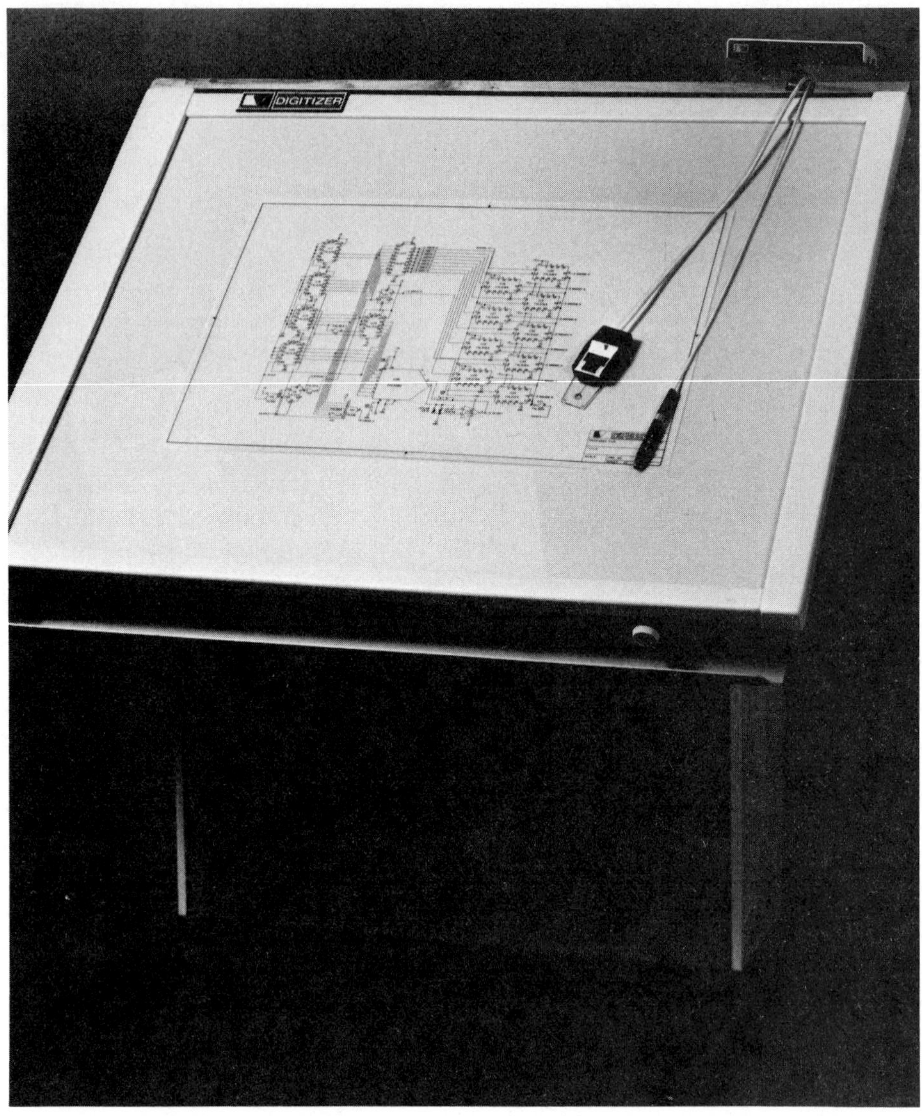

Figure 20 Digitizer for data capture. (Reprinted with permission from Computervision Corporation, Bedford, MA.)

Figure 21 Designer M-A 16 bit CAD/CAM system. (Reprinted with permission from Computervision Corporation, Bedford, MA.)

Figure 22 CDS 4001-32 bit CAD/CAM system. (Reprinted with permission from Computervision Corporation, Bedford, MA.)

Figure 23 Engineering and manufacturing application. (Reprinted with permission from Computervision Corporation, Bedford, MA.)

Figure 24 Designer work station. (Reprinted with permission from Computervision Corporation, Bedford, MA.)

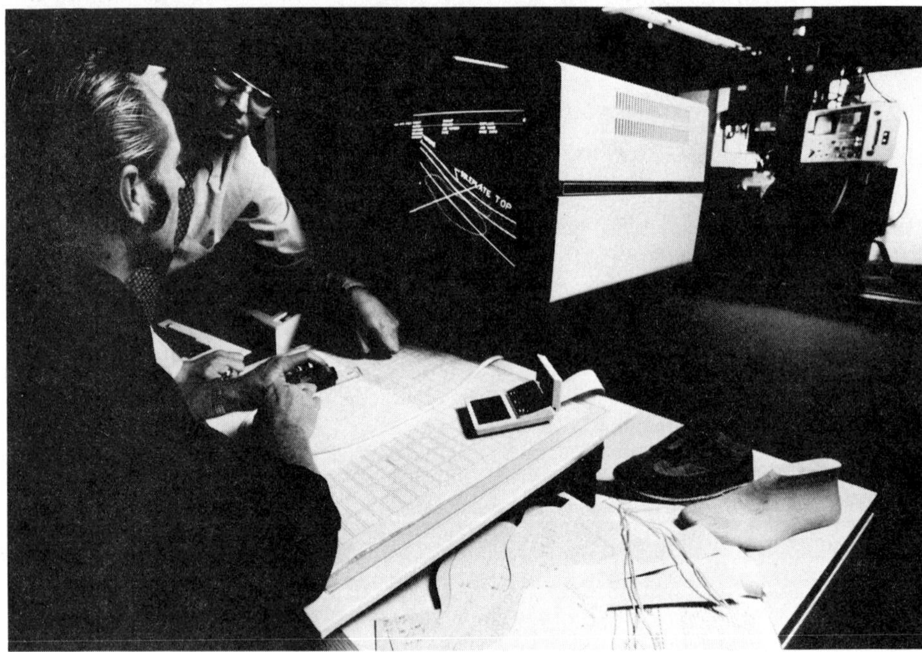

Figure 25 Three-dimensional design activity. (Reprinted with permission from Computervision Corporation, Bedford, MA.)

Figure 26 Design and drafting. (Reprinted with permission from Computervision Corporation, Bedford, MA.)

Figure 27 300 MB disk drive. (Reprinted with permission from Computervision Corporation, Bedford, MA.)

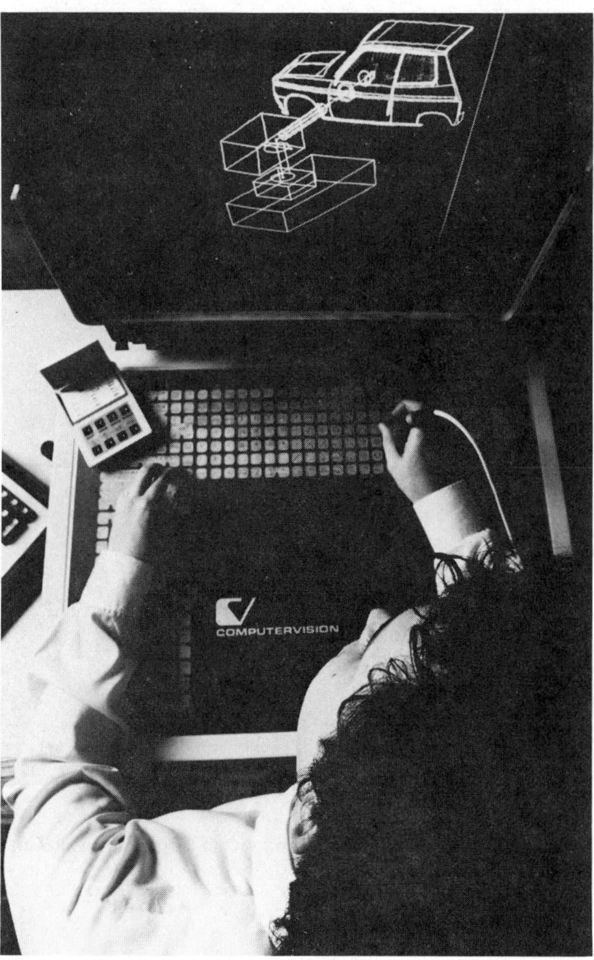

Figure 28 Three-dimensional design activity. (Reprinted with permission from Computervision Corporation, Bedford, MA.)

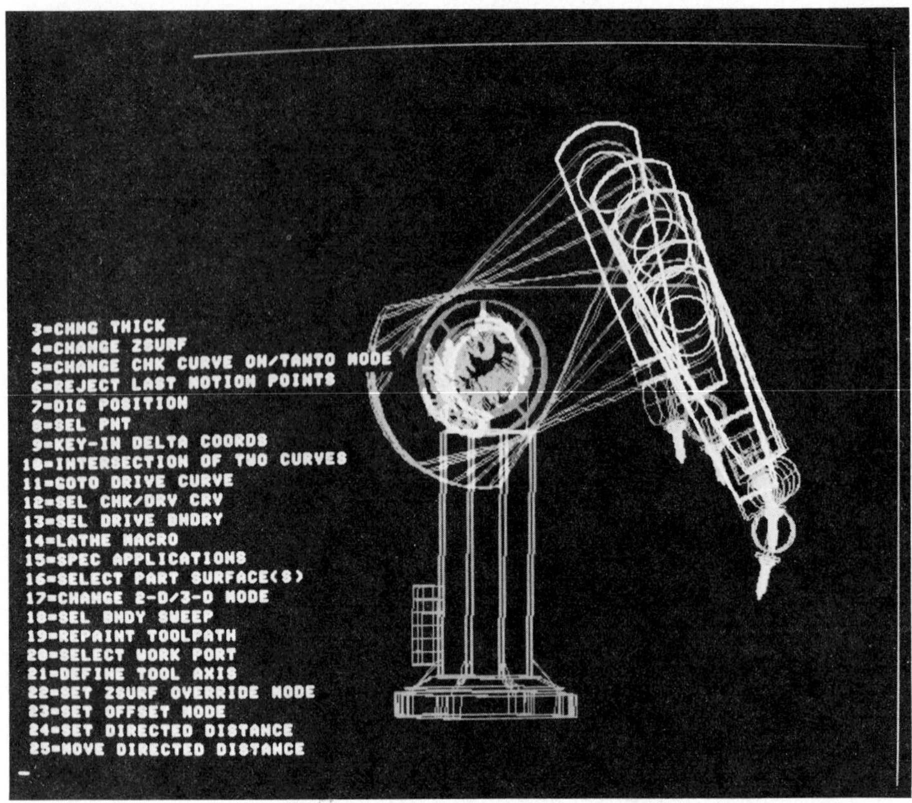

Figure 29 Kinematics software. (Reprinted with permission from Computervision Corporation, Bedford, MA.)

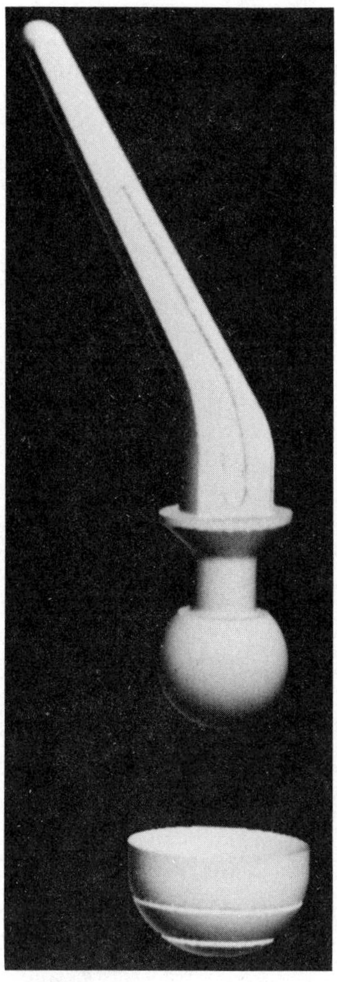

Figure 30 Solid modeling activity. (Reprinted with permission from Computervision Corporation, Bedford, MA.)

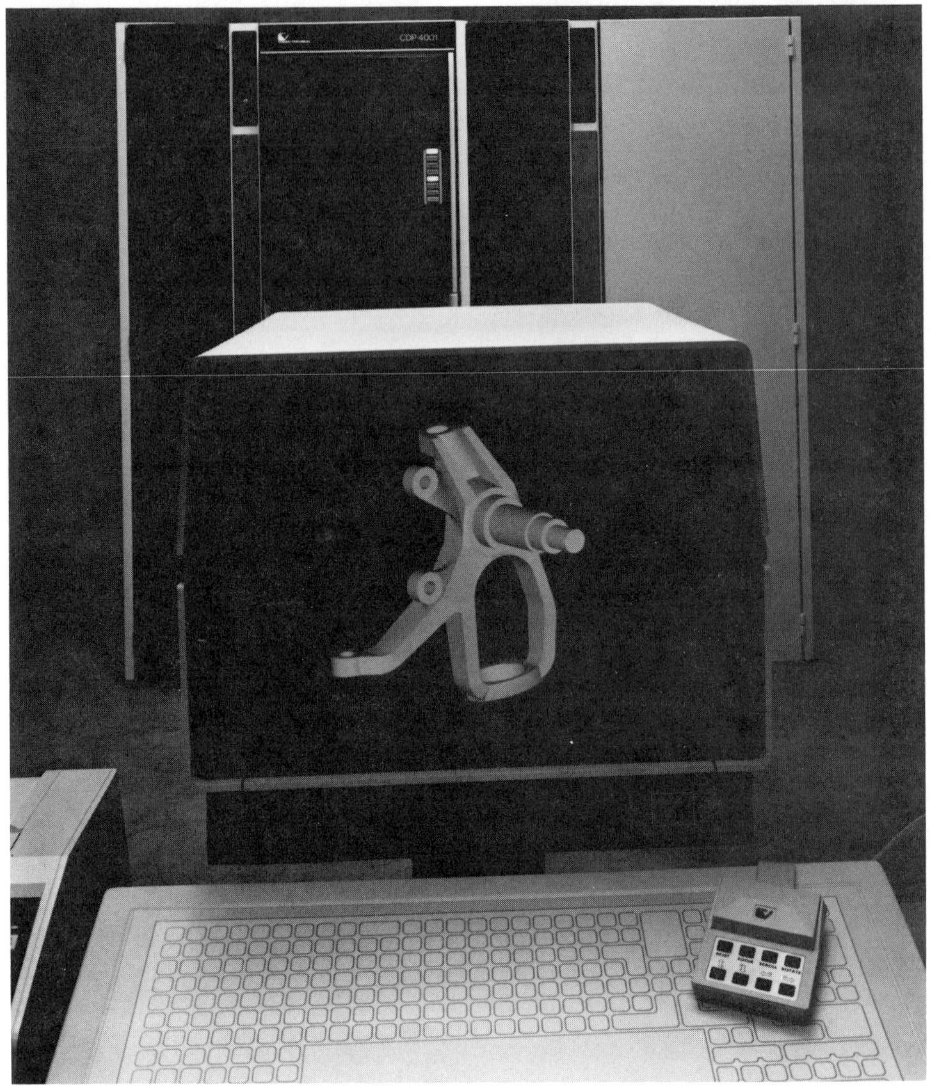

Figure 31 Solid modeling actvitity. (Reprinted with permission from Computervision Corporation, Bedford, MA.)

Figure 32 Solid modeling on a 32-bit computer. (Reprinted with permission from Computervision Corporation, Bedford, MA.)

Figure 33 P1000 pen plotter. (Reprinted with permission from Computervision Corporation, Bedford, MA).

3

Service Bureau Considerations

A good computer-aided design/computer-aided manufacturing (CAD/CAM) services organization can provide all the benefits of use without the risk of capital expenditure, staffing, training, start-up time, utilization of space, and resources. It is like renting a car before buying one, or dating before marriage. You should strongly consider using this tool before you decide to purchase, and very often continue to do so after the purchase.

A key to your consideration of using a CAD/CAM services organization, or CAD/CAM in general, is to compare it with the traditional way your drawings are done, manually. Competition against CAD/CAM is surprisingly not other CAD/CAM systems, but manual effort. Our research indicates that not over 5% of those organizations that should be using CAD/CAM, in fact, use it. And, of the organizations that either have systems or use services, on average less than 20% of their total workload that should go to CAD/CAM does so.

Therefore, comparing a services organization with a manual approach is important. Is it truly better than manual drafting for example? Based on 17 years experience in automated and computerized drafting, I am confident that the answer is a resounding yes! A CAD/CAM approach versus manual is like comparing a bulldozer to a shovel, or an airplane to walking. Even though there are bulldozers, there are certain times to use a shovel; and we often walk to and from airplanes. Later we will point out guidelines for when you should and should not got to the computer.

---

*This chapter reprinted courtesy of Paul W. M. Zeman, President of NPS Automation Services, Inc., Morris Plains, New Jersey.

Although there are tremendous differences between manual and automated approaches, in order to put them into perspective, let us consider some of the strengths of the CAD/CAM approach. A computer does not forget; it can be called upon to rapidly repeat, rotate, scale, or otherwise modify all things which are symmetrical, similar, or repetitive. These items can be as simple as a schematic symbol or as complex as an entire machine or process plant. Think of your drafter, designer, or engineer as having an unlimited number of unlimited complexity two- and three-dimensional templates with associative data at his finger tips. Think about this person's ability to orchestrate and conduct rather than just playing one instrument. CAD/CAM services is the first necessary step in the process of freeing you to use a powerful alternative tool to traditional manual effort.

Will using a CAD/CAM services organization totally replace the need for manual drafting? No. Not now, but in 10 years, purely manual drafting should be the oddity. I predict, however, that this will take 20–40 years to happen. It is not really a competition of man and machine; it is man being smart enough to use the machine. The machine is ready. It awaits.

Photographic approaches, scissors drafting, pin-bar drafting, washoffs, reductions, and the like are all based on the correct concept, to rapidly and relatively accurately reproduce or otherwise take advantage of previously created graphics; and, in some cases, to take advantage of an ability to combine layers of independent data into a whole or complex subset of a greater whole. But whatever you have read about the benefits of a photographic approach, or whatever benefits you have experienced by using one, can easily be eclipsed by what a CAD/CAM services organization can do for you.

In simplest terms, in order to use a photographic approach, the graphic data, drawings or discipline layers would have to have been created first anyway. And if they were created on CAD/CAM, a photographic approach for layering, repeating, and scaling is not needed. Even the crudest CAD/CAM systems can instantaneously change scale, or command a plotter to general original ink quality at 30 inches per second. Also, CAD/CAM can scale data up or down without having line weights grow or shrink (an advantage particularly when scaling up and you do not want poor line edge resolution). In summary, on the comparison of CAD/CAM versus photographic approaches for drawing creation as compared with "pin-bar" approaches, it is vastly superior. On the other end of the spectrum, it is normally cheaper, faster, and more effective to run a blueline print of an original, than it is to call for or buy a second plot. However, if you do need multiple originals, and the data is in the computer, CAD/CAM is your best choice based on criteria of quality, speed, accuracy and low cost.

Until recently, CAD/CAM services organizations have not competed with reprographic service companies, but now they are doing so and numerous repro firms and departments have found out that they are not the only game in town, and they are nervous because they see CAD/CAM services taking an increasing share of what they considered to be traditional and new photographic applications.

How does a CAD/CAM services organization differ from an equipment vendor? Having an accurate answer to this question can be very important to your company. In the simplest analysis, a vendor wants to sell you equipment. A CAD/CAM services organization peforms work for you on a continuing basis, without any capital investment on your part; he makes his money only if you continue to use his services. You have the freedom to turn on and turn off a services company.

A CAD/CAM services organization has not sold you the "be all, end all, world's best and final combination of steel, plastic, and software." They just continually meet your needs in a way which satisfies you. They know that you always have options, and therefore they are under real pressure to always come through for you. It is impossible for any CAD/CAM services organization that wants to be in business six months from now to let their level of client satisfaction drop. In summary, a CAD/CAM services organization must continually meet with your satisfaction not only to make money, but just to survive.

What are the products of a CAD/CAM services organization? They are wide and varied. For instance, some specialize in one area such as engineering or numerical control tape generation. Others provide a wide range of design and drafting services.

Suffice it to say that there are CAD/CAM services organizations for almost any application you are interested in, in engineering, design, drafting, and even as a front end to computerized manufacturing.

Important questions are, when and how should I use a CAD/CAM services organization and which of their products should I need before I consider using them? The answer to all these questions starts with understanding where you are now. Experience has constantly demonstrated that the majority of companies have no firm handle on what their independent activities are costing them now. They might know the hourly wage of their drafters plus overhead; but not how long it takes the person to do his work. Before you consider using a CAD/CAM services organization find out what equivalent work is costing you now, whether it is done manually, photographically, or subcontracted.

Once you have a firm handle on your costs, send a production job out to a CAD/CAM services organization, and see what the result is. If it compares favorably with alternate methods, you know you have a winner. If it does not, there might be other benefits for you to consider such as quality, accuracy, fast turnaround time, or a digital data base for fast future changes that more than make up for the same or slightly higher costs.

Regarding which of their products to use, you are frankly quite safe to try a small quantity of whatever they propose. After all, without any capital expenditure or continuing commitment on your part, you can turn them off whenever you do not have workload or are not satisfied. And, they cannot "low-ball" you; they cannot lose money on every job and make it up in volume. You know that the second job and subsequent work you send to them must cost you the same or less than the first job did, or you turn off the valve, and go to another source.

Find out what services are available from a CAD/CAM services organization; study your current and anticipated applications, and try them out.

The volume of your in-house workload is a factor to consider when employing a CAD/CAM or any services organization. While you must have a significant ongoing volume to consider buying your own system, a CAD/CAM services organization will do as little as one drawing or project, or depending on their capabilities, hundreds or thousands. Normally, clients are smart not to put all their eggs in one basket; a sophisticated user will always maintain his own in-house capability to meet at least 25–50% of anticipated workload. What often happens is that organizations will aim for a lean, mean, permanent staff, and although some use a CAD/CAM services organization on a regular basis, it is most often used to meet peak workload periods that their lean, mean staff just cannot handle.

As a guideline, regardless of your workload volume, start small with a CAD/CAM services organization. As you get to know them, and they you, and depending on your workload, increase the volume and number of applications until you consider them a reliable tool that you can depend on, as you would your own staff. Regarding when to start work with them if you have not already, now is the best time. Do not wait until you absolutely and urgently need a tool to start learning how it works and what its strong and weak points are.

Do not get caught in a "catch 22" situation, rationalizing not using a CAD/CAM services organization because you are either too busy, or do not have enough work.

Once you are using a CAD/CAM services organization, when should you stop? When should you turn the valve off? We have already addressed one answer, and that is whenever you want to if you are not satisfied, for any reason. Other times include when your workload drops off, and you have to maintain work for the core of your own valued employees who must keep on staff for anticipated future situations. Another reason, is when you finally decide to buy your own system.

There is a point at which you should. Once you are confident that you know which system to buy (there are about 30 on the market), once you have tested your applications with a CAD/CAM services organization, and once you are sure that you will have both continuing workload and top management support for one, you should have one, at least one. Then, your primary workload will go to your own system, and the CAD/CAM services organization will be there for peak workloads, building data bases, and training or staffing. By the way, anyone who tells you that you will be efficiently producing drawings after two or three weeks training is either kidding you or does not know what he is talking about. When you buy your own system, your best friend will be the CAD/CAM services organization. Contracting with them for at least 90 days prior to and after system delivery will allow you to have your new system hit the floor running, with symbols, procedures, and trained people. You can either do this or risk a 6–12 month startup, during which the vice president or president who authorized the purchase keeps asking you what you have done with the system; and you will have nothing to show except the same canned demo and a game or two. The people who drive cars in races are not the same people who build the cars. Once you get your own system, and as mentioned earlier, even for a few months before, it is the racing drivers, the CAD/CAM services organizations, who will save your bacon, not the vendor.

Once you learn to use the tool called a CAD/CAM services organization, there are other times when you will know to turn it off. For instance, as you become more knowledgeable, you will want to fine tune your applications and procedures, and since you know your business best, the CAD/CAM services organization at some point might not have a sufficient level of expertise to satisfy your more sophisticated requirements. For instance, your personnel and business life will go through stages; you will normally outgrow early interests and need greater levels of challenge and accomplishment. If an existing tool cannot keep pace, it should be replaced.

A final point regarding when to stop using a CAD/CAM services bureau is based on a pure business decision. Once you have used one and truly know what they can and cannot do, they must continue to be your best alternative, but also, think about futures. Surprisingly few people balance alternatives against requirements on a regular basis. Success is most often measured in millimeters, not miles, and an ongoing evaluation of alternatives, with subsequent action can make the difference between success and failure. Evaluation of alternatives can occur on multiple levels; anywhere from a basic simple cost analysis of the price performance of manual effort versus a CAD/CAM services organization, to a more psychologically oriented analysis. For instance, if your in-house drafting staff thinks that they are the only game in town, they will not perform as well for you as they would if they knew that a CAD/CAM services organization will pick up the ball if they drop it. In other words, competition builds a higher level of performance all around, and you can plug this factor into your analysis of alternatives.

It is interesting to consider how a CAD/CAM services organization meets the requirements of a large number of clients, with an even larger range of applications. First of all, in order to be successful, they must have excellent organization and recordkeeping. They must use the correct standards and specifications, they must know how to rapidly locate the latest digital files relating to your current work, and they must have the right specialists, familiar with your disciplines, to do your work. Once these resources, logistics, equipment, and people have been established, their large number of clients and applications is a super advantage to them as compared with less challenged groups. The technology transfer that is served to their managers and operators, and always functioning under pressure, make them tigers. For instance, they might develop a method or procedure for doing structural drawings that with minor modifications applies to something as extremely different as printed circuits; or architectural work experience might help in tool design. Nowhere else but at a services organization is there this variety of work, challenge, and transfer of ideas between disciplines. Anyone can buy a CAD/CAM system; the real key to how a CAD/CAM services organization does it, is based on its organization, procedures, and people.

It takes a special services organization, however, to handle high technology applications. Never assume that they can do integrated circuit design because they can do drafting, and vice versa. Never assume they can do five-axis numerical control in the format you want just because they can do two-axis in a different format. Find out what they can do by testing them on small jobs. Go for a demo at their facilities. See your work being done.

The word computer is an inadequate word. There are hundreds of different computers, and thousands of different software packages. It takes a special CAD/CAM services organization to handle a specialized high technology application. They must have the right computer or computers, software, peripherals, people, and procedures aimed at meeting your needs. You must test them to see if they can help you.

You might also be concerned about distance from your location to a services organization. When you provide work to them a block away or across the country it is out of your hands. But it would be anyway if, for example, it would take a week to turn around in-house. The key is procedures. It really does not matter if they are next door or across the country; Federal Express can absolutely, positively have it there next day; most CAD/CAM services organizations work multiple shifts, and generally whatever they do for you can be done faster than by manual means. If the procedures for transmitting work, including specs and standards, are set up right and completely at the front end of a job, distance does not matter.

But suppose you are the type of person who insists that the work be done locally, or better yet, in-house at your location. A more advanced services organization will provide you with an intelligent workstation or complete system at your location. Of course, this type of offering from the services organization will call for a commitment on your part. Obviously, it would not make sense for them to provide you with a dedicated facility without one. But, this commitment would be much less than buying your own system and this option is available as an alternative. Here again, distance does not matter.

Typical work flows to and from a services organization vary in a key way from noncomputerized services. That key difference revolves around digital records.

Let us examine a typical work flow. The CAD/CAM services organization and your company should assign a primary and secondary project manager. You will define what your specs and standards are and provide input to them in a similar but perhaps simpler form than you would to a manual work force. The services project manager will provide suggestions regarding optimizing the company's performance for you, graphics communications rules, and a schedule of delivery.

The work, specs, standards, and any special instructions are entered in a client log book and production schedule. Here all similarities with a manual approach end. It is the digital record that becomes primary. Your output product, whether it is an ink on mylar drawing, a numerical control tape, or a printed circuit board is really incidental, because without such accurate and complete digital record, you would neither have a finished product, nor a means to change or modify it at electronic speeds in future. Although a CAD/CAM services organization will most probably save you money and provide other benefits on one-pass work, modifications and future variations will provide you with a quantum more, all because of the digital data base.

When your work is completed, it is plotted, checked, and delivered back to you under the responsibility of the CAD/CAM services project manager. (Great care is given to filing and protecting your digital records.)

When we talk about specs and standards, a good services organization can be of real value to you. If you don't have standards established at your company, starting up with services can give you a reason to put them in place. You can tell the foot-draggers that the services organization needs them; further, if you do not have them, the CAD/CAM services organization can help you to rapidly create standards. After all, they have probably done work for dozens of companies just like yours and have generic symbols, layering, associative data, and text rules that will fit the majority of your needs. These could become your standards. But perhaps you do not like five or six of a hundred symbols to be used on your work. Fine. These can be built or modified very quickly at negligible costs, and voilá, you have a set of your company's new symbols, and your standardization program is underway.

A CAD/CAM services organization, its equipment and software also provide extra human capabilities. Quality for reproduction and microfilming will be better than ever before, allowing you to tighten up on text size, while still being able to read it and fit much more data on one drawing. These are just two examples of how a services organization can help not only tighten up on specifications, but also to establish standards.

On the other hand, if you have existing standards and specs, a services organization will truly welcome hearing about what they are. This comprehensive definition enables them to create your log book more quickly and get on with the work at hand. Once your symbols, standards, and other rules become a part of a library to which an operator has access, the CAD/CAM system will not forget them, and barring human error, they will be honored, completely and forever.

We have discussed numerous factors regarding a services organization. You must ask yourself what you want it to do for you. What are your goals? Perhaps you are looking for a willing and competent tool to perform an ongoing service as part of your normal course of business. Maybe you just have a one-time redraw project that has to be done fast, in high quality and at low cost. And, it could be that you want to use CAD/CAM services as a vehicle toward getting your own system, safely, but as soon as possible. A CAD/CAM services organization is, and must be, flexible; they can respond to a broad range of your needs. But it is you, and only you, that must ultimately set the direction you want to go. Perhaps you are not clear right now about this. But understand, that you must have goals in order to achieve them.

Do not feel that you are alone if you do not totally understand your current status, or how a services organization can fit it. Few people and companies do. Normally what happens is that a vice president or president reads an article about how great CAD/CAM is and then writes a memo asking the manager of design and drafting or vice president of engineering "why we don't have it yet, or what we're doing about it." Then all sorts of random activity is generated for two reasons, to answer the president because he is the president, and because his memo is correct in its implication that you should be doing something about CAD/CAM.

Dealing with a services organization can position you correctly to provide a valid answer to Mr. Executive. By researching your applications to see how CAD/CAM services can help you, you will be well on your way to understanding your current and even your future status. By setting down or working to establish your goals for use of a services company you will rapidly and clearly establish to your satisfaction, and to that of your company, how they can help, in which areas, with what volumes, to what extent, and for how long. The only factor that you have to plug into these theoretical conclusions to achieve virtual certainty is workload. As recommended earlier, send some work out to a CAD/CAM services organization, test your assumptions, be they positive or negative. Their performance for you, speed, quality, cost, and other factors relating to their work are hard data which will prove or disprove CAD/CAM's value and answer the question of how a services organization fits your needs.

We believe the services business is based on benefits. In establishing your goals and criteria for evaluating alternatives, it will be helpful to take a look at some typical benefits that a good CAD/CAM services organization can provide. While the following benefits are geared toward drafting services, they can also be extrapolated to computer-aided engineering, design, and manufacturing.

The big one that everyone thinks of first is the real potential to achieve lower net costs on your finished work. But, the ability to dissect and manipulate drawings is often equally important. As well as providing a supplemental drafting capability, CAD/CAM services can often eliminate duplication of work with features as simple as changing scales, mirroring, repeating, and rotating. Earlier we mentioned digital storage of your work, high output quality, and reproducibility, but think about what layering of disciplines and three-dimensional rotation and projection can add. Output will be legible, uniform, and conform to your specs. Accuracy will be extreme, the work will be done faster than it could be done manually, and you will probably even experience reduced checking time on CAD/CAM output because it is so legible and your QA people will learn to safely skim modules repeated by the computer. Design time can be shortened too. Remember, the computer can accurately recall complex subroutines, whether they are graphic, alphanumeric, or a combination thereof. If the services organization provides you with a catalog of complex entities that they have created for you in the past, your designer could call for something like "X84 at column line intersect A7," rather than sketching the whole thing out.

Be careful of a system or organization that claims that it does all types of design and drafting. Although drafting can be a generalized function, design cannot. Design requires focus and in-depth specialized features and expertise.

There are numerous intangible benefits inherent in dealing with a CAD/CAM services organization. We have already mentioned the use of one as a psychological motivator for your full-time staff or systems people. There are many others. Use of a services organization will conserve your capital. This is particularly important in times of tight credit and high interest rates. Not only can you conserve your captial or credit that would otherwise be committed to buying a system, but there is a much more expensive factor, people. A CAD/CAM services organization will relieve you of costly hiring expenses, whether you have a temporary project or are considering long-term use of a CAD/CAM system.

People will be your greatest expense. When you hire someone, you have made not only a business but also a moral commitment to that person. As long as an employee does a good job, he or she should continue in your employ and advance with your company to the level of his or her ability. You cannot just turn people on and off, or, not only will you get ulcers, but your company will get a poor reputation and high quality people will stay away from you. You should be prepared to make a commitment when you hire people.

Earlier we mentioned how a CAD/CAM service bureau can help you have a system "hit the floor running," with symbols, trained people, procedures, and a data base. While an economic value could be assigned to this, the intangible benefits of fast start-up and executive satisfaction are significant.

And what is it worth to have a way to try computer graphics without having to make a career risking major capital purchase? Quite a lot; maybe even the value you place on your career.

Other intangible benefits are related to a services organization's tangible benefits. For instance, although presentation quality and fast turn around time are byproducts of their work for you, these features can be critical on proposal drawings that must be more presentable visually than your competitor's, and submitted on time. All other factors being equal, such as engineering content and concept, a computer-produced drawing package or presentation will be chosen over manual effort. Having a service organization do your proposal drawings, will increase your chances of getting the job. What is this worth?

By working with a services organization, you can justify the charges by receiving work done better, faster, or less expensively than any other alternative. But the education and hard data that will come to you as another byproduct can be of potentially greater value. You will learn which applications should be handled first, which applications or disciplines are best and have the highest return and benefits for you. You will learn which are easiest from your viewpoint and theirs, and perhaps most importantly which applications just will not work.

If you hire a consultant to help you through the jungle of systems, to study your applications, workload, and future needs, this is probably better than not seeking advice before you embark on an odyssey into CAD/CAM. But your typical consultant does not have hands-on experience; his solutions are theoretical, and he is expensive, not so much as related to his high fee, but probably more so based on what his conclusions could cost you. I wonder if there are any consultants good enough, brave enough, or rich enough, to offer to share in the success or failure of what they propose for you. There are some you know. They are called service organizations. If what they propose for you works, satisfies you, and continues to be your best alternative, they will make some money. If not, you can and will turn them off.

So, if you want to hire a consultant, fine, but do not miss out on getting a better one for free. Hands-on people know what works. My father-in-law used to say "in vitro and in vivo," implying that what happens in the laboratory does not necessarily happen in life. Listen to the theorists, but pay most attention to the hard data available to you from a services organization.

Another consideration is procedures, your own existing in-house, and those of the CAD/CAM services organization. Do you have to change? The answer is no with minor exceptions. If the services organization is good, they will be used to adjusting to their client's needs with minimum fuss and bother. The best tools are those that are easy to use. The only exceptions for internal procedural changes are those which will improve or optimize their performance for you, that you learn about when working with them, and as mentioned earlier, not having immediate access to the work while they are doing it. This, in fact, could be an advantage. An imposed cutoff date often serves to speed up a project, and lends discipline to what might otherwise drag on seemingly forever.

Certain companies buy a CAD/CAM system to maintain up-to-date drawings and digital records of a project, product, or facility. These people are in tremendous need of a services organization, because they have the toughest job to do first, and that is to build a digital data base. In order to work, it must be well organized, logical, complete, and accurate. A novice user is in no position to have this capability. A services organization is, and, the work to create the data base can be done at your place or his. The key ingredients you will get are experience, high volume production capability, and suggestions to organize your data base and how to maximize its future usefulness.

This point brings us to an interesting question. Are services organizations system independent? For instance, if they are good, but have a "brand X" system and you have a "brand Y" system, can they help you? The answer is yes on multiple levels. Although it would be desirable to have the same system you do, the procedures and experience are practical and malleable to almost any system. Further, data can be translated between another system and yours by using any number of input and output formatters available to communicate data between dissimilar systems. Although the data may not have all the bells and whistles, associative data, and the like, it will still be most adequate to transfer digital graphic files. Vendors and special interest groups are working on comprehensive format translators such as IGES. These communication mediums are designed to accept data at the highest level that a particular system can provide it, maintain its integrity to a great extent, and let another system of dissimilar manufacture, read the data to the extent of its intelligence. Although relatively complex, such an approach will pretty well handle two- and three-dimensional geometry, including solids and surfaces. More complex however will be the task of interpreting associative data such as tolerances, finishes, or understanding system-dependent user-level routines which vary widely from system to system. In my opinion, it will be at least 10 years before the vendors can all read and write to IGES, as well as adequately interpret what the other vendors' systems are talking about. Therefore, for the foreseeable future, the basic graphic file transfer packages available from most vendors and services organizations will be the most adequate means available which is practical.

A more important factor to consider than digital files is a CAD/CAM service company's level of experience and success in doing your type of work. Of course, a new company entering the business might be able to succeed for you, but your greatest safety and insurance for a fast start-up and a successful outcome will be to go with an experienced CAD/CAM services company.

What are some of the ways that you can help to optimize the performance of a services organization in your best interest? First, listen to their suggestions. After they have surveyed your needs and scope of work, do those things that make sense to you. For instance, the greater the volume of similar repeating work that you can provide to them, the more efficient and cost effective they will be. They will dedicate a project team to your needs who will do a good job up front, and a better job as they fine tune their performance for you. Another way to help optimize, is to strive to provide them simpler and simpler input. This will save you design time and relieve them of extraneous or redundant detail. This will also result in lower costs and faster turn around time for you.

Services organizations have various ways of structuring a contract to meet your needs and the situation. The most common and fair for both parties is on a time and materials basis. Most work is generative and involves changes and modifications. This calls for a time and materials approach. Most CAD/CAM services organizations will provide you with an itemized charge for each scope of work. Your protection in doing work on this basis is to turn them off if their price performance is not reasonable or competitive. Some clients like fixed price or hard money jobs. This can only be done when the scope of work is well defined and does not include or involve multiple changes and modifications.

There are alternatives to these standard contracts. One is unit pricing. Instead of time and materials for instance, you could base a contract on a different unit than time, like square feet of drafting, at a particular scale, in a particular discipline, or for example, price per average "D" size electrical drawing. Another alternative which is sometimes used is a time and materials contract with an up-side estimate. If it appears that the estimate will be exceeded, the client is notified of why and by how much. Then he can decide whether to proceed.

Special situations and contracts are also available from a CAD/CAM services organization. These might include a short-term training and workstation rental at his location, or a longer term at yours. Also, remember staffing, first, second, or third shift if you already have a system which you want to produce more for you. Further, you will not find a services organization to be "head up and locked," or inflexible. If you have a need that they can serve, there will usually be a way to work it out.

Let us begin to summarize. The best way to approach almost any situation is to balance the benefits against the risks. I would like to compare the risks of doing nothing about CAD/CAM to that of buying your own system, and to using a CAD/CAM services organization. If you do nothing you may think that you have no risks. Putting a decision off falls in the same category. But, be advised, your competitors may not be waiting or delaying a decision. They could be getting a head start on you that you will never recover from. Burying your head in the sand could bury you and your company. There is no standing still. You must move ahead with this well proven and available tool or you will go the way of the buggy whip and butter churn. If people are kind, they will remember you as quaint.

Finally, what are your risks of using a services organization? Compared to doing nothing, delaying a decision, or buying a vendor's system before you are educated, they are so miniscule as to be negligible. After all, CAD/CAM works; you can get into it right now without any capital commitment; and, you have got to be consistently satisfied with the services organization you choose, or you turn them off, just like that. You cannot lose, it is a win/win situation for you and your company.

4

Cost Justifying a CAD/CAM System

The computer-aided design/computer-aided manufacturing (CAD/CAM) industry fully understands the importance and magnitude of an investment in CAD/CAM. The various vendors recognize a customer's need for reassurance that such a capital purchase can be cost justified. In these very tight economic times, the justification issue becomes paramount. Very often, customers will want this area of evaluation satisfactorily addressed *before* the capability (adequate hardware/software) is fully answered. To this end, most vendors have developed marketing programs that are specifically designed to remove any doubts you may have with regard to the cost-effectiveness of the purchase.

What you see in Figure 1 is the outline of the responsibilities and capabilities of a CAD/CAM vendor's productivity consultant (supplied by Computervision Corporation). It is his job to find out "what it is you do and how you are currently doing it." (See discussion on business plan and product cycle in Chap. 1.) The normal cycle time from start to finish for an in depth productivity analysis is usually 4–7 weeks.

We would now like to explain in detail an industry tested and accepted approach in the cost justification of CAD/CAM systems. We begin with a very basic formula (Fig. 2).

It is the vendor's hope, at the conclusion of any productivity study, to have larger numbers associated with the benefits column than those that will be with the cost column.

If they are successful in this endeavor you will have the supportive documentation necessary for your Capital Authorization Request. The productivity pay back analysis should be of tremendous help in that most CAD/CAM select committee

Product cycle investigation
- Survey site(s)
- Uncover bottlenecks
- Collect measurable work samples

Productivity analysis
- Time trialing of customers work on CAD/CAM systems
- Compare manual vs. automated efforts
- System operator proficiencies defined
- Additional visit(s) to site possible
- Prepare analysis

Present findings

Figure 1 Presale productivity consultation.

members have never (separately) purchased anything as expensive as CAD/CAM technology and, therefore, usually come up short on ways to illustrate the worth/value of the system.

In a presale environment, it is not difficult for the vendor to quantify the costs associated with CAD/CAM, be it for a single or multishift environment on a yearly basis. Let us look at Figure 3 to examine some of the glaring costs that customers should consider when purchasing a CAD/CAM system.

You will have ample opportunity to develop these costs with your vendor representative. Not surprisingly, a thorough needs analysis (see Business Plans and Product Cycle) can result in a very close calling on the total costs for your system.

The problem for the vendor in a presale situation is that most of the benefits associated with their product are qualitative in nature, that is to say, until a meaningful three-dimensional data base has been established, most of the benefits derived are hard to report on with quantitative evidence (Fig. 4). There are too many variables associated with the implementation of a CAD/CAM system for us to point out convincingly that all of these areas will render quantitative benefits to you within the first 3–6 months of operation. We would rather talk about them in a *qualitative* sense and have you tell us, as time passes, that each of these have moved over to the quantitative side of the benefits column.

Looking at some of these benefits in the qualitative column, we first see the design issue. What we would like to say about pure conceptual design is the following: if we have two designers with the same task to complete in the same time frame, one of whom is working on a CAD/CAM workstation and the other at a

Benefits − costs = net gain

Figure 2

All *quantifiable*
- Amortization
- Interest
- Labor
- Maintenance agreement
- Room preparation
- Additional hard/software (over and above net investment)

Other
1. In house training costs
2. Dedicated/experienced systems manager

Service bureaus assistance (some customers allocate monies for the creation of symbol and part libraries before receiving their system)

Figure 3 Costs.

conventional design/drafting table, it is our contention the person on the system will, through alternatives, finish the design sooner by catching his mistakes quicker, rendering a more complete, error-free design than his counterpart on the drafting table. With regard to the accuracy question, we know that seven significant places of accuracy will have an impact on your design/drafting staff. Many CAD/CAM installations have reported that the accuracy translates to approximately 15–20% savings in time for the checking operation. That is to say, the checker can now do something else with this 15–20% extra time, or be able to check 15–20% more work. The reason for this is that the checker need not now measure line lengths with any conventional measuring device. Seven places of accuracy preclude such mundane time-consuming tasks. Another large segment of the engineering/manufacturing user base is telling us that by interrogating the three-dimensional math model, with finite-element modeling and analysis programs, the need to build the physical prototype now has been either reduced in full or in part. Tremendous savings will await you if this computer-aided

---

Design
Accuracy
Prototypes
Morale
Standardization
ECO/ECN
Technical publication/illustrations

Figure 4 Qualitative benefits.

engineering aspect is part of your product cycle with CAD/CAM. We know that since your designer/engineer/drafting staff will be utilizing state-of-the-art equipment, they quickly become state-of-the-art individuals. There is a new found enthusiasm toward their work and a true belief that they are assisting your company in manufacturing and marketing your product before your competition. We also strongly feel that the introduction of a CAD/CAM system to your operation will attract very professional, highly motivated engineers/designers/draftsmen who will want to join a company that is truly progressive and truly state-of-the-art. This list of qualitative benefits associated with CAD could certainly go on and on and certainly you might have ideas of your own to add to this list. The intent here is for us to convey to you that vendors should be the first ones to admit the quantification of all benefits associated with CAD/CAM is really a very hard chore to do, in that this is a presales situation and no system exists. The acquisition of this designer system should also be looked at as a *sales tool* for yourself. After all, you will be able to pass on savings to your customers because of the increased productivity this technology will provide.

You will be very proud to relate to your existing customers that *their* product is being engineered, designed, and machined via ''state-of-the-art'' technology.

It will also undoubtedly assist in securing *new* customers for the same reason.

There is something, however, that the CAD/CAM industry has developed to *quantify* the worth/value of the system—that is the document throughput itself. By working with a ''time-trialing'' operation and/or archival research, vendors have the ability to develop meaningful productivity improvement factors by comparing projected automated efforts against your fixed manual effort (Fig. 5).

Of course, the intent of both types of benefits, quantitative and qualitative, is to *shorten* your *product* cycle (Fig. 6).

What you are looking at now is a typical product cycle we see time and time again that portrays true engineering/manufacturing responsibilities (Fig. 7). This may or may not be exactly yours. The intent of it is to get you to think how yours varies from this example. The job of the productivity consultant is to understand this cycle and to determine how their system will impact each iteration, both in a quantitative and qualitative fashion. By this I mean, it is the CAD/CAM vendor's

Drawing/design throughput comparisons (manual vs. automated)

Figure 5 Quantitative benefits.

Qualitative benefits and quantitative benefits = shortened product cycle

Figure 6 Shortened product cycle.

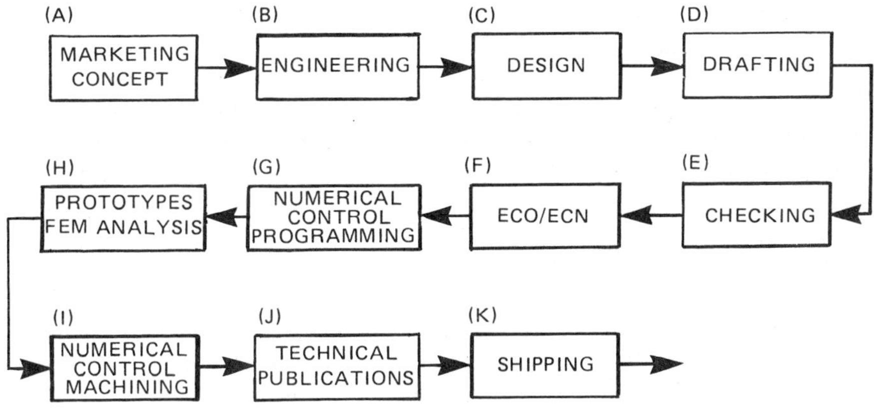

Figure 7 Product cycle.

responsibility to understand what the engineer does with documentation/product, what he passes on to the design team, what they do with that documentation/product, what they pass on to the drafting group, and so on, all the way through the cycle. This figure illustrates the 3-D data base theme that we hear talked about. It also reinforces the idea that each and every organization within the company can access, utilize, and draw benefits from this 3-D data base. It is within the *design* and *drafting* blocks of this cycle that we will attempt to calculate the worth of the system for you quantitatively.

Before we start the analysis, let us review some assumptions for this case study (Fig. 8). We are going to hypothesize that the system engineer is dedicated, that he or she is "productive" at the terminal 6–7.5 hours per day and that it is a closed-shop environment. By that we mean, work being done on CAD is truly from the engineering/design group and not from the marketing organization who

---

Assumptions
  Dedicated system engineer
  Design/drafting only
  Prep work done off-line
95% system up time

Figure 8 Productivity analysis.

are desirous of having bar charts established on CAD/CAM. We are looking at all work preparation being done offline. We are referring to all catalog research, all interaction with lead engineers, with design managers, having been done either by this person before he sat down at the system or by a system set-up person. Lastly, that this CAD/CAM system is operational at least 95% of the time.

We think it might be helpful at this point to review the system configuration we will be using for this case study (Fig. 9).

We will now begin the task of calculating the productivity values for this proposed system. This first of two approaches that we will examine was developed by Computervision Corporation. Our first step in this process is to work-up the productivity increase ratio for each measurable task that the productivity consultant has collected from your engineering/manufacturing staff. Normally, customers are asked to dissect their product or products by their generic drawing types (Fig. 10). That is to say, if we focus on an overhead projector as an example we know that there will be many detail drawings, there will be many pages of bills of material, wiring diagrams, layouts, assemblies, subassemblies, schematics, and so on.

The vendor will ask you to provide him with one representative sample drawing of average complexity from each generic type that goes into this product. What we are looking at in Figure 11 is the time trialing of a layout drawing. The manual column on this chart/graph is illustrating the fixed manual effort it is currently taking this company to generate this layout drawing using conventional means. The automated column is showing the *projected* effort it would take, along the learning curve, to do this same task on a CAD/CAM system. The third column refers to the milestones of learning associated with a CAD/CAM system (Fig. 12). The fourth column illustrates the % Δ that will be experienced from completing this task on a CAD/CAM system.

Let us go back to the second column, automated hours, and explain, in detail, how they are derived. There are two distinct ways in which these automated efforts are generated. The first way this can occur is through a "time-trialing" operation of your representative work on a CAD/CAM system. The vendors will have CAD specialists, who represent different levels of expertise, duplicate in part your representative work on their system four times. By doing this, they are then able to calculate the numbers residing in the fourth column, projected Δ.

Computer processing unit
Three workstations
Plotter
300 MB disk drive
Mechanical design and manufacturing engineering software packages

Figure 9 System analyzed.

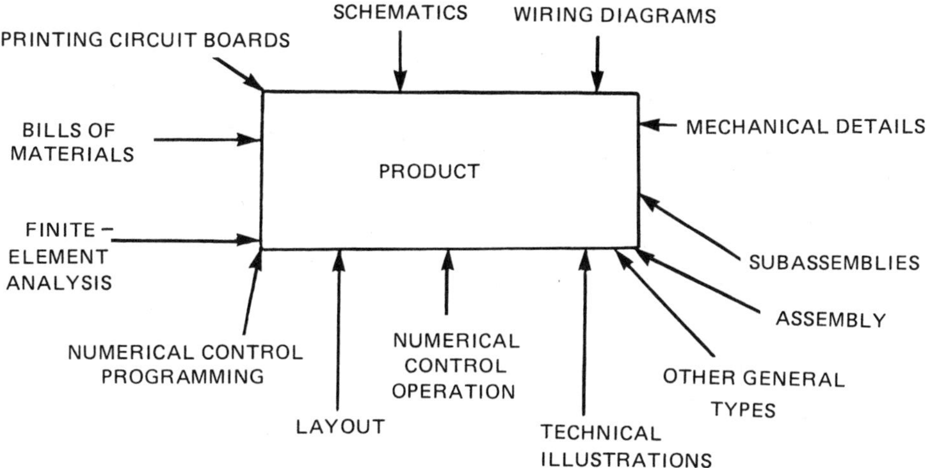

Figure 10 Components of products.

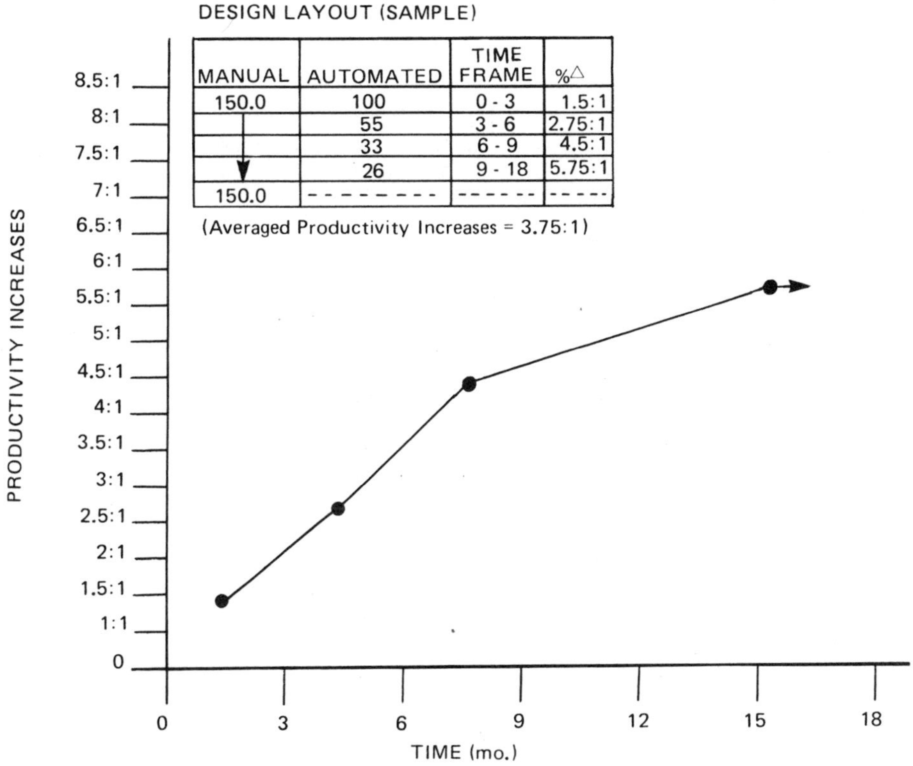

DESIGN LAYOUT (SAMPLE)

MANUAL	AUTOMATED	TIME FRAME	%△
150.0	100	0 - 3	1.5:1
	55	3 - 6	2.75:1
	33	6 - 9	4.5:1
↓	26	9 - 18	5.75:1
150.0	- - - - - - - -	- - - - - -	- - - -

(Averaged Productivity Increases = 3.75:1)

PRODUCTIVITY INCREASES

TIME (mo.)

Figure 11 Linear growth on CAD/CAM.

0–3 Months. In this period, symbol libraries are built and operators are familiarizing themselves with the equipment. With the exception of extremely gifted or previously trained operators, no productivity increases should be expected.

3–6 Months. The symbol libraries should now be built and operators should be reasonably familiar with the command language of the system. A modest savings in design/drafting time of previous techniques should be evident.

6–9 Months. By now, operators should be completely familiar with all commands and their uses. Shortcuts to production are being learned, such as PEP, a graphics language that allows operators to develop special-purpose functions for their use without learning FORTRAN. Dramatic productivity increase should occur now.

9–18 Months. Operators should be close to top speed, and completing even the most complex drawings with relative ease. A further increase in productivity can be expected, although not as dramatic as during the 6–9 month period.

Over 18 Months. Further acceleration of turnaround time will occur, not so much from increased operator speed and efficiency, but from improvements in system utilization, task prioritizing, and staff reorganization.

Figure 12 Learning curve milestones.

The second approach used in projecting these efforts is through archival research. By this we mean, if work has been done in the past on a system and is similar enough in nature and complexity to yours, the vendor will use those efforts to supply the automated column. The basic intent of this exercise is to remove the guesswork as to how much faster a CAD/CAM system can do your work for you. They will then do this exercise for each measurable task they have collected from you. A clear benefit you will gain from this exercise is that you will know which work will render the higher yield the fastest on CAD/CAM.

The next phase of the analysis will be to calculate the number of *extra hours* per annum our proposed system will be worth. We are going to format this analysis in a couple of different ways: we are going to show its worth when the system is being used either for a one-, one-and-a-half-, or two-shift operation. (It should be pointed out that the overwhelming number of CAD/CAM installations are currently running at least 1½ shifts per day.) Three workstations on a one-shift basis will be worth approximately 6000 labor hours per annum (Fig. 13). This is found by multiplying three terminals times 40 hours per week times 50 weeks. From the 6000 hours, we take off 15%. This 15% reflects system nonproductivity, such as in-house training programs, routine system maintenance, file archiving, and certainly in-house demonstrations that will be requested of you from your own sales force. This variable can be controlled by you. We can easily increase it to reflect higher "prep time." A default condition that is widely used by vendors is that the person working at the CAD workstation will be productive in a truly

6000 System hr available/yr
– 15% (maintenance, archiving, in-house training, demonstrations)
5100 Net system hr available/yr

Application	Hours		% Time dedicated to CAD/CAM		Averaged productivity increase		Additional production hours
Assembly	5100	×	.20	×	4.25:1	=	4,335
Design							
layout	5100	×	.60	×	3.75:1	=	11,475
Details	5100	×	.20	×	4.00:1	=	4.080
			100%				19,890 Additional production hr/annum

Figure 13 System capacity calculations for 3 workstations, 1 shift.

measurable sense. That is to say, and this was stated earlier, all necessary prep time, that is, interfacing with the lead engineer, making trips to manufacturing, catalog research, etc., have been done either by him or someone else for him. We now have the number of hours available to apply these projected increases against. Using a basic industrial engineering formula, we multiply the number of hours available times the weighted percentage that each of these tasks represents toward 100% of your total engineering workload times the projected increase for that task.

Multiplying these variables across will result in "extra" hours of productivity per annum you will derive. Customers then ask "How do we justify the extra hours that are projected for us?" We like to say that these hours can be applied against your attrition, retirements, job shoppers, outside service bureaus, hiring freezes, backlog, overtime, projects you cannot currently start, and perhaps products you cannot currently develop. All of these issues can be boiled down to labor shortages.

We can easily determine the impact from a 1½ shift operation. The 5100 hours would become 7650 gross hours. Using the same formula and replacing 7650 for 5100, the value of the system takes on a much more attractive look. The number of *additional production hours* per annum is 29,835, and a 2-shift day would be worth 39,780 additional hours. There is no mystery. The more you use the system, the quicker it will pay for itself!

We divide the number of additional production hours per annum, be it for one-, one-and-a-half-, or two-shift operations by 1700 hours (Fig. 14). (The 1700 hours refers to the number of hours that a draftsman would be productive per

1 Shift	19,890 additional production hr / 1,700 production hr/yr	=	11.7 equivalent designer/draftsman
1½ Shifts	29,835 / 1,700	=	17.5 equivalent designer/draftsman
2 Shifts	39,780 / 1,700	=	23.4 equivalent designer/draftsman

Figure 14 System capacity calculations (continued).

annum looking at it from an 85% of 2000 hours standpoint.) So these extra hours per annum that we are saying a CAD/CAM system will afford you, now become the worth of the extra people you currently do not have.

At this point, a brief recap of our methodology in the cost justification procedure would be helpful.

1. We have determined the productivity increase for your cross section of engineering work (Fig. 11)
2. We now have from that the additional production hours the system affords you because of this increase (Fig. 13)
3. Carrying it to its next logical phase, those hours now become the worth of equivalent designers/draftsmen (Fig. 14)

By multiplying the number of equivalent designers/draftsmen times a burdened rate per hour, times 2080 hours per year, we now see a number that can be thought of as the *projected gross savings* the system will provide (Fig. 15).

We will now start developing the anticipated costs associated with CAD/CAM implementation (Fig. 16). As you can see, we start off with a simple depreciation schedule of 7 years against our net investment. Next we apply the current prime interest rate against the net investment. We show labor with a system as a cost to you, be it for a single or multishift environment, and we also assume you would be taking out a full service maintenance contract with the vendor. We

11.7 Equivalent draftsmen	×	\$20/hr	×	2080 hr	=	\$486,720
17.5 Equivalent draftsmen	×	\$20/hr	×	2080 hr	=	728,000
23.4 Equivalent draftsmen	×	\$20/hr	×	2080 hr	×	973,440

Figure 15 Projected gross savings (1 shift).

1. 7 year depreciation schedule (straight line)		$ 57,142
2. $\frac{\$400,000}{2}$ × 17% interest		34,000 (averaged)
3. Labor on CAD/CAM		
1 shift	3 × $20/hr × 2080 hr =	124,800
1½ shifts	4.5 × $20/hr × 2080 hr =	187,200
2 shifts	6 × $20/hr × 2080 hr =	249,600
4. Maintenance contract at 12% (estimated)		48,000
5. Room preparation (first year only)		20,000
6. Additional training over and above factory training (six weeks) per person before he/she is back at 1:1 productivity 4.5 operators will be used here		21,600
1 shift		$305,542
1½ shifts		367,942
2 shifts		430,342

Figure 16 Annual CAD/CAM costs. Assumes $400,000 net investment.

will use six weeks per operator as a cost to you that will be lost until he or she is back at 1:1 productivity over manual means.

Lastly, since you probably already have an environmentally controlled room for your current computing system, we will be adding $20,000 for additional room preparation. This method has been used for sometime now with a great deal of success. Vendors also use a net present value-discounted cash flow model for their prospects. This approach will also be shown.

We now have both sides of the justification analysis. We developed "gross savings" (starting with productivity improvements as cornerstones), as well as "anticipated yearly costs." Our next formula (Fig. 17) will illustrate "net savings" that should be derived.

1 Shift	$ 486,720	(cost of 11.7 equivalent designers)
	− 305,542	(cost of CAD/CAM system/year)
	$ 181,178	(average net savings/year)
1½ Shifts	$ 728,000	(cost of 17.5 equivalent designers)
	367,942	(cost of CAD/CAM system/year)
	$ 360,058	
2 Shifts	$ 973,440	(cost of 23.4 equivalent designers)
	430,342	(cost of CAD/CAM system/year)
	$ 543,098	

Figure 17 Costs vs. savings.

1 Shift	$400,000 (net investment) / 181,178	=	2.2 years
1½ Shifts	$400,000 (net investment) / 360,058	=	1.1 years
2 Shifts	$400,000 (net investment) / 543,098	=	.73 years (8 months)

Figure 18 Payback periods.

Using simple payback formulation (Fig. 18), we divide the projected net savings per annum into the known investment cost, rendering the payback periods, or, to put it another way, the number of years it will take for the system to pay for itself. Again, by illustrating this payback period with a variety of shift applications, you readily see the attractiveness of multishift operation.

Using a reciprocal formula (Fig. 19), net investment into net savings, we now are able to calculate the return on investment (ROI) this proposed system will offer, or, how much money your money has made by making this investment. You can see on the bottom on this graph a very important statement. All projections regarding productivity, payback, ROI, net savings, are based upon design/drafting comparisons only! If we think back to the beginning of this presentation and we look at the benefits − costs = net gain, we know with the reasonable passage of time all of those benefits that we look at *qualitatively* now render hard savings to you.

Reporting to customers this kind of possible success was at first uncomfortable for me. Not owning a system myself, I found it awkward projecting such astonishing figures. However, the CAD/CAM user community that has kept good bookkeeping principles with their custom will attest to this potential.

1 Shift	$181,178 (net savings) / 400,000 (net investment)	=	45%
1½ Shifts	$360,058 (net savings) / 400,000 (net investment)	=	90%
2 Shifts	$543,098 (net savings) / 400,000 (net investment)	=	135%

Figure 19 Return on investment. Formulation is based solely on design/drafting comparisons.

I would like to point out the importance of tracking what this purchase has done for your company. I feel it is essential to know what amount of effort was necessary to do the task *before* the system gets installed, as well as the effort *with* the system. Without this information, requests by yourself for additional hardware and software cannot be convincingly argued. Your management will be asking the question "What has the system saved me in time and money since it was installed?" You should be prepared to present this information in a concise manner. More on this in the Evaluation section.

If you are strongly considering the purchase of a CAD/CAM system you would do well to request the different vendors to support you with the preparation of a productivity/payback analysis. They can provide you with information you would otherwise find next to impossible to generate. The benefits your organization will derive are numerous (Fig. 20). This material could then be integrated into your already started justification. You would then have a solid hybrid product that should be quite convincing when it is reviewed by senior management. The respective vendors should be on standby to copresent this story with you if you feel it appropriate. I, myself, have on many occasions done this with the select committee chairman.

I would like to mention two additional benefits that can be derived from such an analysis (Fig. 21). If the CAD/CAM vendor reports to you a variety of productivity improvements ranging from a low of 1.5:1 to a high of 5.0:1, we think this exercise might be useful in helping you decide *what* should be put on the system. That is to say, if you know next year that your drafters will be responsible for 10,000 D-size wiring programs and the vendor is projecting very high yield for them, it might be best to dedicate the entire system to this one endeavor. If you do, certainly the payback picture will improve. Earlier we said the vendor will ask you to supply them with "one of everything" in order for them to prepare a study. What we were suggesting is that it is *your decision* as to what exactly should be implemented on CAD/CAM. If it will help you select the work most

Cost effective solutions
- Quantifiable
- Qualitative

Learning curve breakdown
System capacity calculations
Payback projections
Return on investment projections
Glossary of CAD/CAM terminology
Implementation plan (suggested)

Figure 20 Productivity analysis benefits.

Guide for selection of work best suited for CAD/CAM
Guide for selection of system engineer best suited for CAD/CAM

Figure 21 "Extra" analysis benefits.

suitable, then we feel it will also help you decide *who* should work on the equipment. If you decided to go with the repetitive, highly symbolic wiring diagrams, you probably would be wise not to put on your most valued engineer. An analogy might be made of driving in a thumb tack with a sledge hammer. Rather, you would probably be better off to put on your less expensive novice designer/draftsperson.

Likewise, if it is heavy three-dimensional modeling that is important, you most likely would want your more senior technical employee.

The two previously mentioned areas are ones that customers find extreme difficulty in getting direction from the vendors. Very often it is an emotional decision. You feel somewhat obligated to let your senior people have first crack at the system, or possibly you are being pressured to put on a project that will make a particular organization look good. This kind of implementation can have serious effects on the whole productivity picture. "Backing in" to what is best for the system in terms of operation and work selection should be considered totally objective and, thereby, the best approach.

I would like to discuss some of the reinforcements that make this particular approach to cost justification a very conservative one (Fig. 22). Number one, this was mainly an engineering study. This methodology attempts to quantify improvement for your work primarily in the design/drafting department in that this is where 99% of all CAD/CAM systems get installed and where data bases get established. Since manufacturing will be called upon to access, utilize, and draw benefits from said data base after a period of time has passed (possibly in as little as six months), we chose not to include manufacturing operations from a *quantitiative* standpoint.

Engineering only!
Productivity improvements are averaged.
Portion of benefits against *all costs*.
Assume no hardware/software development.

Figure 22 Conservative criteria.

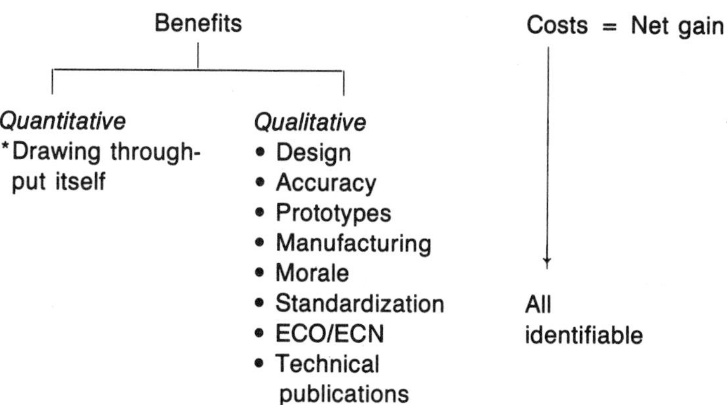

Figure 23 CAD/CAM cost justification.

Number two, we are comparing only a portion of all the benefits against all of the known costs.

Three, we have put a working freeze on all software and hardware development. The CAD/CAM companies have no way to accurately forecast what software/hardware enhancements will be forthcoming from their respective research and development centers two years into the future. Because of this limitation, they are really taking a ''snapshot'' of current capabilities when they go through the time-trialing operation on your work (refer to Fig. 11.)

Lastly, we are going to use *averaged* productivity improvement factors in calculating the system's capacity rather than using the much higher ratio that would be achieved after 12 to 12 months or so. We think, in addition, that *your* future CAD/CAM system engineers will surpass any projections that a vendor's system engineers might make because of *their* intimacy with *your* work process. The CAD/CAM user base is advising us that the learning curve is really closer to 10 to 12 months before a designer/drafter is fully trained (refer to Fig. 12).

As we had stated earlier, there would be two different approaches used to justify the purchase of CAD/CAM equipment. The following model uses a discounted cash flow-net present value of money technique. Here we will be focusing on the printed circuit board application. Let us assume this is an 8 × 10 in. analogue-to-digital PC board which contains 35 integrated circuits (ICs) and 150 components. Also, there are 25 new designs and 75 design revisions annually. There are many approaches to the justification issue. Perhaps some will feel more comfortable with this style.

CAD/CAM Cost Savings Analysis
New Designs
Labor-Hours Saved per Sample Board

Function	Manual labor-hours	System labor-hours	CAD system time
Layout	80	80	—
Tape up	48	—	—
Digitize, checkplot, edit, photoplot	—	8	12
Checking	20	15	—
Assembly	16	—	1
Detail drawing	4	—	.5
Silk screen drawing	16	—	1
Solder mask	4	—	.5
Engineering changes	8	2	2
Bill of materials	4	—	.5
Total	200	105	17.5
Labor-hours saved: 95			

CAD/CAM Cost Savings Analysis
Revised Designs
Labor-Hours Saved per Sample Board

Function	Manual labor-hours	System labor-hours	CAD system time
Revise artwork (retape)	25	—	—
Edit design, check plot, and photoplot	—	4	8
Checking	8	6	—
Assembly drawing	8	—	1
Detail drawing	2	—	.5
Silkscreen drawing	2	—	1
Solder mask	2	—	.5
Engineering changes	1	—	.5
Bill of materials	1	—	.5
Total	50	10.5	12
Labor-hours saved: 39.5			

CAD/CAM Cost Savings Analysis

Assume: $22/hr burdened overhead rate, increasing at 7%/yr
22 new designs/yr
75 revisions/yr

Manual system: labor-hour costs (first year)

25 designs	× 200 hr/design	=	5000 hr
75 revisions ×	50 hr/revision	=	3750 hr
Total design/drafting hr/yr			8750

$22/hr × 8750 hr – $192,500 first year personnel expenditure

Photography costs (first year)

25 designs	× $240/design	=	$6000
75 revisions	× $120/revision	=	9000

Total first year photography costs $15,000

CAD/CAM system: labor-hour costs (first year)

25 designs	× 105 hr/design	=	2625.0 hr
75 revisions	× 10.5 hr/revision	=	787.5 hr
Total			3412.5 hr

$22/hr × 3412.5 hr = $75,075 first year personnel expenditure

CAD/CAM system time

25 designs	× 17.5 hr/design	=	437.5 hr
75 revisions	× 12 hr/revision	=	900.0 hr
Total			1337.5 hr

CAD/CAM System versus Manual System

First year dollar savings
($192,500 + 15,000) – 75,075 = $132,425

First year labor-hour savings
8750.0 – 3412.5 = 5337.5 hours

CAD/CAM system utilization

$$\frac{1337.5 \text{ hr}}{2080.0 \text{ hr}} = 64\%$$

(Note: 2080 hr represents 52 weeks at 40 hr/week)

CAD/CAM Financial Analysis
($000s) Prepared for: XYZ Corporation

	Year 1	Year 2	Year 3	Year 4	Year 5
CAD/CAM					
Net cash outflow	129.8	40.9	43.8	46.9	50.3
Cum. cash outflow	129.8	170.7	214.5	261.5	311.7
Present value of cash outflow	126.9	32.6	31.2	29.8	28.5
Cum. present value of cash outflow	126.9	159.5	190.7	220.5	249.0
Manual system					
Net cash outflow	103.8	111.0	118.8	127.1	136.0
Cum. cash outflow	103.8	214.8	333.5	460.6	596.6
Present value of cash outflow	92.7	88.5	84.6	80.8	77.2
Cum. present value of cash outflow	92.7	181.2	265.8	346.6	423.8
CAD/CAM financial advantage					
Positive values indicate CAD/CAM financial advantage					
Net cash outflow	(26.0)	70.1	75.0	80.2	85.7
Cum. cash outflow	(26.0)	44.0	119.1	199.1	284.9
Present value of cash outflow	(23.1)	55.9	53.4	51.0	48.7
Cum. present value of cash outflow	(23.1)	32.8	86.2	137.2	185.9

To Summarize:
Total capital outlay ($000s): 102
Design/drafting labor-hour savings: from 8750 hours to 3411.5 hours
System utilization: 64%
Cumulative net savings ($000s)
  Year 1: (26.0)
  Year 2: 44.0
  Year 3: 119.0
  Year 4: 199.1
  Year 5: 284.9
Return on investment: 76%
Payback period: 16 months

5

Request for Proposal

A very important phase of your justification process is the generation and submission of your request for proposal (RFP). This document is issued to the different computer-aided design/computer-aided manufacturing (CAD/CAM) vendors and should contain relevant points you consider of importance in *your* CAD/CAM selection process. This is your opportunity to convey an overview of your business, a description of your product, and how you see a CAD/CAM system integrating into it.

It usually addresses hardware, software, training, maintenance, communications, programming support, data-base management, terms and conditions, and warranty.

The following example should hopefully guide you in the preparation of your request for proposal. The sample request for proposal on the followng pages will provide the reader with a good idea as to how far-reaching a CAD/CAM system can be in an organizations. For the sake of brevity, only the most important *excerpts* are presented in full. Your own request for proposal should be as complete as possible expanding on all the points listed in the sample.

1.0 SCOPE

1.1 PROJECTED SYSTEMS USE

This specification details the requirements for a turnkey, stand-alone, interactive computer-aided design and computer-aided manufacture (CAD/CAM) system. The system shall be utilized to increase productivity in the areas of:

1. Mechanical design and drafting
2. Numerical control tape preparation
3. Printed circuit board design
4. Wiring diagram construction
5. Facilities design and management

1.2 BASIC OBJECTIVES

The interactive graphics system shall allow this company to fulfill the following objectives:

- A general increase in efficiency and productivity in design, engineering, manufacturing, and administrative operations.
- A general improvement in the quality and consistency in the design, drawings, bills of material, schedules, manufactured items, and other products.
- An improvement in the overall workload balance within the organization through the more effective utilization of available manpower and special skills.
- An improvement in communications between all engineering groups.
- The development and maintenance of a comprehensive, flexible, computerized data base, which utilizes computer files on magnetic media and can be shared by the various departments and disciplines within the organization.

2.0 GENERAL REQUIREMENTS

This specification shall describe in complete detail the general requirements for an interactive graphics system highlighted in this section.

2.1 MINICOMPUTER FUNCTIONS

The system shall be a true three-dimensional, multitask, multiapplication, FORTRAN-based, self-contained system.

2.1.1 Multitask

The system shall be a combination of specialized hardware and software that may be configured from a single to a 10-task system. Each task shall function independently from other tasks and shall be able to acquire its own dedicated peripherals as appropriate to conduct any type of processing, including software modification and graphics display, without interfering with other tasks.

2.1.2 Multiapplication

All two- and three-dimensional applications shall run simultaneously, using the same command system, with the result being a common data base.

2.1.3 FORTRAN-Based

The system software shall be written in FORTRAN to facilitate convenient extensions of applications features, including the incorporation of user-written programs and modifications.

2.2 HUMAN ENGINEERING

The system shall be built on a philosophy of human engineering, accommodating users' physical comfort, individual preferences, and abilities.

2.2.1 Comfort

2.2.2 User-System Interface

Language utilities
Menuing
On-line documentation
Error messages

2.3 DATA BASE REQUIREMENTS

2.3.1 Associativity

2.3.2 Precision

2.4 COMMUNICATION

2.5 UPWARD COMPATIBILITY

3.0 HARDWARE REQUIREMENTS

3.1 PROCESSOR

The interactive graphic system processor shall consist of a distributed processing system that combines a general purpose 16-bit computational unit with a memory protection and mapping unit, a special purpose floating point unit, and a special purpose graphics computational unit. All processors shall run in parallel. It shall be configured to operate in a stand-alone environment and shall support all the software contained in this specification. The following requirements shall be included:

- Operational support for concurrent execution of multiple tasks/applications; simultaneous graphics and general purpose execution
- 512K bytes of dedicated graphics memory; 172K bytes of dedicated memory for operating system and graphics system support; dual-ported memory for a maximum of 1280K bytes; memory parity checking

- Single/double precision floating point processor; hardware integer multiply/divide
- Speed:
  Memory read/write time: 400 nanoseconds
  Microinstruction cycle time: 300 nanoseconds
  Memory cycle time: 600 nanoseconds
- Graphics processor with microprogrammed instruction set to implement graphics directly and provide:
  Transformations in 2-D and 3-D
  Data searches
  Entity and layer discrimination
  Line font selection
  Nested subfiguring
  Programmable text
  Mixed 16-bit and 24-bit precision data types
- Priority interrupts, write/execution protection interrupts
- Built-in diagnostics/remote maintenance
- Real-time clock
- Cold-start capabilities

3.1.1 Processor Expansion

An optional expansion of the processor capabilities shall provide enhanced instruction set, call, and return procedures, and double integer instruction with superior diagnostics support. This expanded-capability processor shall operate in a stand-alone capacity or shall act in an input/output (I/O) mode for the 32-bit processor. Improved memory functions include:

- 8-Megabyte physical memory capacity
- Ability to support 8 disk drives
- 128K bytes logical address space
- Simultaneous data access by two tasks through increased data channel

3.1.2 Disk Drive

The disk drive shall be a random-access disk storage device with a storage capacity of 300 megabytes unformatted. The interactive graphics system shall support up to 1.2 billion bytes of on-line storage capacity. Disk drive specifications shall include:

- Removable disk packs
- Four disk drives per controller
- Overlap seek availability
- Transfer rate: 1.2 megabytes/sec
- Track-to-track positioning time: 6 ms
- Average positioning time: 30 ms

- Average rotational latency: 8.33 ms
- Spindle speed: 3600 rpm
- Recording surfaces: 19

3.1.3 Magnetic Tape Drive

3.2 ANALYTIC PROCESSOR

3.3 SYSTEM CONSOLE

3.4 ALPHANUMERIC PROGRAMMING TERMINAL

3.5 INTERACTIVE GRAPHICS TERMINAL

3.5.1 CRT Screen Display
3.5.1.1 Monochromatic graphic CRT screen
3.5.1.2 Color graphic CRT screen display

3.5.2 Image Controller
3.5.3 Alphanumeric Keyboard
3.5.4 Command Menu Tablet/Digitizer
3.5.5 Hard Copy Unit
3.5.6 Reference Table and Chair

3.6 LARGE TABLET DIGITIZER WORK STATION
Digitizing tablet
Interactive CRT screen display
Options

3.7 PLOTTERS

3.7.1 High-Speed Roll Plotter
3.7.2 High-Speed Pen Plotter
3.7.3 Electrostatic Printer/Plotter

3.8 PHOTOPLOTTER

3.9 LINE PRINTER

3.10 PAPER TAPE PUNCH/READER

3.10.1 Paper Tape Punch
3.10.1 Paper Tape Reader

4.0 OPERATING SYSTEM SOFTWARE

4.1 GENERAL DESCRIPTION

4.2 OPERATING SYSTEM CAPABILITIES

4.2.1 Multiuser Support
4.2.1.1 Priority allocation
4.2.1.2 Batching and spooling

4.2.2 File Management
4.2.2.1 Multivolume file system
4.2.2.2 File protection
4.2.2.3 Working directory support

4.2.3 Input/Output System
4.2.4 System Command Processing
4.2.5 Job Accounting
4.2.6 Hardware Error Logging

4.3 PROGRAMMING SUPPORT

4.3.1 Editors

4.3.2 Programming Languages
4.3.2.1 FORTRAN
4.3.2.2 Additional languages
4.3.2.3 High-level system implementation language

4.3.3 Loader
4.3.4 Debugging Support

4.4 COMMUNICATION

4.4.1 Communication Lines
4.4.1.1 Communication with nonvendor systems
4.4.1.2 Communication between vendor systems
4.4.1.3 Message and file transfer

4.4.2 Networking
4.4.2.1 Multitask configuration
4.4.2.2 Flexibility of operation
4.4.2.3 Peripheral device use

4.4.2.4 File access

4.4.2.5 Physical interface characteristics

4.4.3 Offline Media

4.4.4 IGES Data Format

5.0 APPLICATIONS SOFTWARE

5.1 FUNDAMENTAL CAPABILITIES

5.1.1 Introduction

The fundamental capabilities described below must be inherent in the graphics software system and applicable across all applications.

5.1.2 General Description

The graphics system shall be a true engineering design, drafting, and manufacturing system to answer the needs of all aspects of the engineering and manufacturing environment. It shall be designed to facilitate the design, drafting, and production cycles by automating, as much as possible, these processes.

One geometric data base shall be used to store all information pertaining to individual development projects so that a model may be designed, and drawings of the model may be easily produced. The model shall not have to be reconstructed for each drawing. Rather, the user shall be able to tailor the existing model to suit the needs of each drawing without having an effect on the underlying model definition.

The graphics software shall enable the user to automatically present different views of the model during design operations. Once the model is completed in model mode, the user shall be able to go into drawing mode to produce drawings to present and detail the model. The graphics software shall automate the layout process needed to produce attractive and informative drawings.

The operator shall be able to create and arrange different views of the model in one of several drawings. There shall be a dependent relationship between the model description and all drawings so that, when a change is made to the model, all drawings shall be automatically updated to reflect the change.

All designing and drafting operations shall be performed through the graphics languages. The languages shall use normal English spelling so that they are easily understood by the first-time user. On-line documentation shall enable the user to receive pertinent command information without referring to a manual.

5.1.3 Data Base Structure

The part data base structure shall clearly delineate between drafting information (i.e., dimensions, labels, notes, sheet borders, views), and information that describes the piece or model as an object in two- or three-dimensional space.

5.1.3.1 Operational modes

To distinguish between design and drafting operations, two operational modes shall be provided, model (design) mode and drawing (drafting) mode. Operations performed within model mode shall affect the data base description of the model. Operations performed within the drawing mode shall affect the presentation of the model within that drawing only; the underlying data base description of the model shall not be affected.

5.1.3.2 Parts, models, drawings

A part shall consist of a data base description of the model and any reasonable number of drawings necessary to describe the model. The model and its associated drawings shall be stored under the part name.

A model shall be the data base description of the abstract object or project being designed or produced. All geometry and data required to define the model shall be stored automatically by the system. Models may be two- or three-dimensional.

Drawings shall be the means by which the model is presented and detailed. A drawing shall contain one or more independent views of the model, each tailored to express some particular quality of the model. The representation of the model shall be editable within a drawing without changing the data base description of the model. Drawings shall use a copy of the data base description of the model, eliminating the need to recreate the model for each drawing. Drawings shall be dependent upon the data base description of the model so that all changes and revisions made to the model data base geometric description in model mode shall be reflected, where appropriate, in all drawings.

5.1.3.3 Coordinate systems

Model space
Construction or view space
Drawing space

5.1.3.4 Views

5.1.3.4.1 Construction planes

5.1.3.5 Associativity of data base
5.1.3.6 Data base units

5.1.3.7 Basic geometric entities
5.1.3.7.1 Point
5.1.3.7.2 Line
5.1.3.7.3 String
5.1.3.7.4 Circle/arc
5.1.3.7.5 Fillet
5.1.3.7.6 Chamfer

5.1.3.7.7 Conic
5.1.3.7.7.1 Hyperbola
5.1.3.7.7.2 Parabola
5.1.3.7.7.3 Ellipse

5.1.3.7.8 B-spline
5.1.3.7.9 Offset construction

5.1.3.7.10 Surfaces
- Tabulated cylinder
- Surface of revolution
- Ruled surface
- B-spline surface
- Fillet surfaces
- Offset surfaces
- Surface intersection
  - Plane cut
  - Surface-to-surface intersection
  - Face/holes

5.1.3.7.11 Solids

5.1.3.8 Connective entities
5.1.3.8.1 Connect node
5.1.3.8.2 Nodal line
5.1.3.8.3 Nodal text
5.1.3.8.4 Nodal figures

5.1.3.9 Library capabilities
5.1.3.9.1 Standard drawing formats
5.1.3.9.2 Standard parts library
5.1.3.9.3 Figure library

5.1.3.9.4 Family of parts

Parametric parts

The user shall be able to store variable two- (2-D) or three-dimensional (3-D) geometric constructions (parametric parts) as programs on disk or magnetic tape. Variations on the design of these parts shall be accomplished simply by changing the parameter values.

Group technology

A capability shall be provided to classify and code parts based on shape and manufacturing characteristics so that the user may retrieve drawings of parts that are the same or similar to the part being worked on. This capability shall take advantage of all past design efforts by providing a fast, efficient means to access these existing designs. Using group technology, the user shall determine whether the same part or a similar part has previously been designed, retrieve that design, make the modifications necessary to meet the needs of the specific part, and then produce a hard copy of the part drawing, if desired.

The manufacturing engineer shall be able to utilize this same technique to retrieve information on similar jigs, fixtures, tooling, numerical control cutting paths, or in-process drawings which can then be used in the manufacture of the new part design.

5.1.3.10 Parts protection
To preserve model descriptions in the data base, model information shall be capable of password protection. A multilevel security facility shall be provided to restrict the operations performed by various users.

5.1.4 User/System Interface

5.1.4.1 Language utilities

5.1.4.1.1 Graphics command language
5.1.4.1.1.1 User-translatable language

5.1.4.1.2 High-level graphics command language
5.1.4.1.2.1 Control constructs
5.1.4.1.2.2 Symbolic variable administrator
5.1.4.1.2.3 Expression evaluation
5.1.4.1.2.4 Calculator capabilities

5.1.4.1.2.5 FORTRAN callability
5.1.4.1.2.6 Macro capability

5.1.4.1.3 Graphics construction language
5.1.4.1.3.1 Variables and expressions
5.1.4.1.3.2 Statements

5.1.4.1.4 Macros

5.1.4.2 Input capabilities
5.1.4.2.1 Command entry
5.1.4.2.2 Entity identification
5.1.4.2.3 Coordinate input
5.1.4.2.4 Stream digitizing

5.1.4.2.5 Menuing
Digitizing tablet menuing
Dynamic menu

5.1.4.3 Command entry support
5.1.4.4 On-line documentation
5.1.4.5 User-definable error messages

5.1.5 Construction Capabilities

5.1.5.1 Appearance control
5.1.5.1.1 Color
5.1.5.1.2 Line fonts
5.1.5.1.3 Highlight
5.1.5.1.4 Intervals
5.1.5.1.5 Plot weight
5.1.5.1.6 Cross hatch
5.1.5.1.7 Pattern hatch
5.1.5.1.8 Shape fill

5.1.5.2 Dynamics
5.1.5.2.1 Zoom
5.1.5.2.2 Scroll
5.1.5.2.3 Rotate
5.1.5.2.4 Drag
5.1.5.2.5 Revision
5.1.5.2.6 Rubberband

5.1.5.2.7 Mirror
5.1.5.2.8 Snap
5.1.5.2.9 Rigid body motion

5.1.5.3 Graphics controls
5.1.5.3.1 File
5.1.5.3.2 Exit
5.1.5.3.3 Blank
5.1.5.3.4 Erase
5.1.5.3.5 Save
5.1.5.3.6 Restore

5.1.5.4 Design capabilities
5.1.5.4.1 Insert
5.1.5.4.2 Change
5.1.5.4.3 Copy
5.1.5.4.4 Join
5.1.5.4.5 Remove

5.1.5.5 Construction aids
5.1.5.5.1 Layers
5.1.5.5.2 Grids
5.1.5.5.3 Centerline
5.1.5.5.4 Windows
  Clipping
  Sectioning

5.1.5.5.5 Multiple views
5.1.5.5.6 Groups
5.1.5.5.7 Default parameters
5.1.5.5.8 Tags
5.1.5.5.9 Flags

5.1.5.5.10 Symbols
  Feature control symbols

5.1.5.5.11 Labels
5.1.5.6 Text
5.1.5.6.1 Text fonts
5.1.5.6.2 Graphical text editor
5.1.5.6.3 Text insertion

5.1.6 Nongraphic Information Management

5.1.6.1 List
5.1.6.2 Verify

5.1.6.3 Measurement
Distance
Angle
Area
Length

5.1.6.4 Dimensioning
5.1.6.4.1 Semiautomatic dimension
Automatic dimension

5.1.6.4.2 Associative dimension

5.1.6.4.3 Specific dimensions
Linear dimension
Ordinate dimension
Radial dimension
Diameter dimension
Angular dimension

5.1.6.5 Tolerance capabilities
Tolerance stack-up

5.1.6.6 Report generation/back annotation

5.1.7 Output and Postprocessing Options

5.1.7.1 Plotters
5.1.7.2 Storage
5.1.7.3 Interface capabilities

5.2 MECHANICAL DESIGN AND DRAFTING

5.2.1 Introduction

The system shall provide specialized applications of the fundamental capabilities (Sec. 5.1) to serve the specific needs of the mechanical design and drafting process. The mechanical design and drafting (MDD) software shall allow the user to produce, change, update, and store drawings and to move through production cycles automatically.

5.2.2 General Description

The drafting and design capabilities of the system shall allow creation of a data base of information about a mechanical part. By implementing the basic and complex geometric entities available in the system, the model and drawings of the model shall be drafted. At the same time, the user shall be able to select and store nongraphic properties of the part (e.g., dimensions, materials, costs, names, etc.).

The nongraphic information shall be associated with the graphic data, allowing changes in one to be automatically reflected in the other. The system shall provide display of the nongraphic information in label and report form.

Features of the software that facilitate the mechanical design and drafting process shall include:

- Dynamic motion, allowing the user to move entities or parts around the cathode ray tube (CRT) screen.
- ANSI Y14.5-compatible dimensions in manual and associative models.
- Construction facilities, including tangent, perpendicular, parallel, intersection, horizontal, vertical, and angle specification.
- Text and line font functions, providing virtually unlimited choice of appearances.
- Family of parts, permitting the creation, storage, and recall of similar or parametric parts.
- Fast, convenient user-definable input facilities, including English commands, menuing, and macros.
- Direct output to FEM, NC, plotters, printers, and storage.

5.2.3 Data Base Structure

5.2.3.1 Mechanical design and drafting data base

5.2.3.2 Basic geometric entities
5.2.3.2.1 Tubes

5.2.3.3 Connective entities
5.2.3.4 Library capabilities

5.2.4 User/System Interface
Language utilities
Input capabilities
Commands entry support

5.2.5 Construction Capabilities

5.2.5.1 Appearance control
5.2.5.2 Dynamics
5.2.5.3 Graphics controls

5.2.5.4 Design capabilities
5.2.5.4.1 Flat pattern generation
5.2.5.4.2 Hidden line removal
5.2.5.4.3 Entity projection
5.2.5.4.4 Entity division

5.2.5.5 Construction aids
5.2.5.6 Text

5.2.6 Nongraphic Information Management

5.2.6.1 Basic functions

5.2.6.2 Mass properties
5.2.6.2.1 Volumetric properties
5.2.6.2.2 Sectional properties
5.2.6.2.3 Mass point

5.2.6.3 Report generation

5.2.7 Output/Postprocessing Applications

5.2.8 Finite-Element Modeling

5.2.8.1 Information types

5.2.8.2 Mesh generation
5.2.8.2.1 Automatic mesh generation
5.2.8.2.2 Semiautomatic mesh generation

5.2.8.3 Finite-element analysis

5.3 NUMERICAL CONTROL

5.3.1 Introduction

The numerical control (NC) applications package shall be a multiuser, multiapplication manufacturing tool. Toolpaths and subsequent numerical control tapes shall be interactively generated by the system with accuracy, speed, and applications versatility. The package shall support from two- through five-axis machining capabilities in manufacturing operations such as punching, milling, drilling, turning, electronic discharge machining, flame-cutting, and fully integrated surface machining, including complex B-spline.

The system shall offer the following features and capabilities:

- Elimination of unnecessary labor-hours wasted on the obsolete task of manual parts programming.
- Dramatic savings in a broad spectrum of manufacturing requirements, including program debugging, test machining, and machine setup.
- Easy-to-use English command language common to all the vendor's other software.
- Menuing capability.
- Virtually unlimited 3-D visualization of the toolpath (thereby reducing the scrapping of parts cut by trial and error).
- 3-D display of a tool at any point on the toolpath from any view orientation. Optional dynamic tool motion display.
- Verification of input parameters and commands used to create the toolpath. Statement on the tool to be used.
- Edit modes allowing modification to toolpath points and of postprocessor statements embedded within the path after a toolpath has been created.
- "Look-ahead" analysis to prevent part gouging (e.g., recognition and automatic pass-over of a slot too narrow for the tool being used).
- Free-form APT (ADAPT or UNIAPT), COMPACT II, and SPLIT statement input capability in order to indicate such parameters as feedrate, spindle or coolant changes, print statements, etc.
- Generation of NC tapes for subsequent off-line use, of APT or COMPACT II source output for later off-line postprocessing, or of IBM 360 APT compatible CL file output.

The capabilities described here shall extend and specialize the fundamental graphic capabilities (Sec. 5.1) to meet specific NC applications requirements.

5.3.2 General Description of Toolpath Creation

5.3.2.1 Operation modes
5.3.2.2 Toolpath generation

5.3.3 Data Base Structure

5.3.3.1 Associativity

5.3.3.2 Library capabilities
5.3.3.2.1 Optional user interface
5.3.3.2.2 Tool library

5.3.4 User System Interface
Language utilities
Input capabilities
Commands entry support

5.3.4.1 Command language organization
5.3.4.1.1 Command languages
5.3.4.1.2 NC graphic construction language

5.3.5 NC Generation Capabilities

5.3.5.1 Automatic tool motion mode

5.3.5.1.1 Profiling and pocketing
Cycle statements
Retract coordinate mode
Cutting depth coordinate mode
Surface bottom pocketing
Base rough cut
Side rough cut
Look-ahead analysis
Clearance point
Retract plane
Finish tolerance
Front approach/end retraction
Tool side of boundary
Reverse finish path
Thick offset distance
Limiting line

5.3.5.1.2 Point-to-point
- Two-and-a-half axis
- Four- and five-axis

5.3.5.1.3 Surface machining
5.3.5.1.3.1 Three-axis surface machining
- Multiple surfaces
- Rough cuts
- Tolerance
- Sweep
- Lace cutting
- Nonlace cutting
- Regional surface milling
- Machining interior/exterior
- Number of cuts/scallop height
- Start and end positions

5.3.5.1.3.2 Four-axis surface machining
5.3.5.1.3.3 Five-axis surface machining

5.3.5.1.4 Surface intersection machining
- Rough cuts
- Tool start and end positions
- Tool side/surface positions

5.3.5.1.5 Multiaxis positioning

5.3.5.2 Absolute tool motion mode
5.3.5.2.1 Toolpath creation procedure
5.3.5.2.2 Axis capabilities
5.3.5.2.3 Tools
5.3.5.2.4 Tool boundary display
5.3.5.2.5 Insertion and addition of commands
5.3.5.2.6 Macros

5.3.5.2.7 Menu functions
5.3.5.2.7.1 General commands
5.3.5.2.7.2 Tool positioning
5.3.5.2.7.3 Tool movement
5.3.5.2.7.4 Command modifiers
5.3.5.2.7.5 Other

5.3.5.3 Toolpath modification

5.3.5.3.1 Postprocessor or offline
Language statement

5.3.5.3.2 Toolpath point edit
5.3.5.3.3 Toolpath regeneration
5.3.5.3.4 Toolpath linking
5.3.5.3.5 Ordered collection of toolpaths

5.3.6 Toolpath Information Management

5.3.6.1 Toolpath verification
5.3.6.2 Tool display
5.3.6.3 Cost calculation

5.3.7 Output Features

5.3.7.1 General output
5.3.7.2 Numerical control output

5.4 PRINTED CIRCUIT/ELECTRICAL SCHEMATIC

5.4.1 Introduction
The printed circuit/electrical schematic (PC/ES) applications software package shall facilitate creation of schematics and printed circuit boards, display and editing of drawings, automatic board routing, automated component placement and packaging, verification and checking capabilities, report generation, and postprocessor interfaces to other systems.

5.4.2 General Description
The system shall provide the designer with an interactive, automated means of creating final printed circuit board drawings and associated documentation, starting from an existing schematic or one created on the system.

The system shall feature the following capabilities:

Standard library of PC symbols, complete with graphic representation and associated properties.

Easy, flexible, user-definable command language.

Dynamic placement, rubberbanding and snapping to grid/symbols/pins for efficient figure insertion.

Automatic interconnection routing, figure insertion.

Multiple layer (up to 20) PC board support.

Multiple report generation capabilities, including bills of material, subfigure name extraction, and net, component, and wire lists.

Engineering analysis, including net list compare, design rules checking, and clearance checking.

Full range of postprocessing options for NC production, PC board testing, plotting, and storage.

5.4.3 Data Base Structure

The PC/ES software shall meet all the data base structure requirements defined in Sec. 5.1.3.

5.4.3.1 Associativity of data base entities

Data stored in the data base shall be logically associated. Graphic symbols stored in the data base shall exist as separate entities, but shall relate to other graphic symbols in the data base. The system shall easily identify which pins of several different components are tied together by the same logical name. Text shall be related to graphics.

This associativity shall facilitate interactive editing functions, engineering analysis, and engineering/manufacturing postprocesses, including bill of materials preparation, interface to automatic test equipment, etc.

5.4.3.2 Basic entities

The primitive graphic elements of PC design shall be lines, circles, arcs, and nodes. From these primitive elements, higher level figures shall be constructed.

A variety of data base entities shall exist for the creation of the printed circuit board data base. These shall include figures for components, strings for interconnects, text for annotation, connect nodes for the connection points of interconnects, text nodes for text, and special figure for pad flashes.

5.4.3.3 Library capabilities

The user shall be able to implement the library capabilities (described in Sec. 5.1.3.9) to create:

- Standard drawing formats
- Standard parts
- Standard subfigures
- Family of parts
  - Parametric parts
  - Group technology

5.4.3.3.1 Standard PC parts library

The system shall support a library of standard logic symbols and PC parts. The user shall be able to create common figures, components, or basic PC board designs, which shall be stored in a library for easy, standard insertion in later drawings and PC boards.

5.4.3.4 Parts protection

To preserve standard PC boards, drawing formats, components, and symbols, etc., libraries and models shall be password protected. A multilevel security system shall be provided to restrict the operations performed by various users.

5.4.4 User/System Interface

- Language utilities
- Input capabilities
- Commands entry support

5.4.5 Construction Capabilities

5.4.5.1 Appearance control

5.4.5.2 Dynamics
5.4.5.2.1 Rubberband
5.4.5.2.2 Snap

5.4.5.3 Graphics controls

5.4.5.4 Design capabilities
5.4.5.4.1 Stitch interconnect
5.4.5.4.2 Automatic PCB component insertion
5.4.5.4.3 Automatic interconnection routing
5.4.5.4.4 Printed circuit general editing

5.4.5.5 Construction aids
5.4.5.5.1 Layers

5.4.4.6 Text

5.4.6 Nongraphic Information Management

5.4.6.1 Properties
5.4.6.2 Data extraction
5.4.6.3 Net list verification
5.4.6.4 Design rules checking
5.4.6.5 Signal highlighting
5.4.6.6 Signal net identification

5.4.7 Output and Postprocessing Applications

5.4.7.1 Plotters
5.4.7.2 Storage
5.4.7.3 Postprocessors

5.5 WIRING DIAGRAM

5.5.1 Introduction

The system shall allow the user to create and maintain an orderly intelligent data base of graphic and nongraphic information relating to wiring diagrams. Nongraphic related information shall include properties such as cost, quantity, size, color, and material, as well as associations between different elements of the diagram. The user shall have the capacity to modify, add, or delete both graphic and nongraphic data in order to easily design and manufacture wiring diagrams. The capabilities described here shall extend and apply the fundamental graphic capabilities (Sec. 5.1) to meet specific wiring diagram design needs.

5.5.2 General Description

5.5.2.1 Wiring diagram definition

A wiring diagram shall be a graphical presentation showing all circuits and the device elements of an electrical system and its associated apparatus, or any clearly defined functional portion of the system. Such a diagram shall emphasize the device elements and their interconnectivity (internal and/or external) with each other, as distinguished from physical arrangement of the devices, conductors, or device elements. A wiring diagram shall show physical wires and wire runs and their ordered point-to-point connections. A wiring diagram may consist of one or more sheets of diagrams.

An elementary wiring diagram (wiring elementary or elementary) shall be a logic diagram showing wire nets. There shall be no physical ordering implied by the connection order within the nets. An elementary shall consist of one or multiple sheets.

5.5.2.2 Wiring diagram process

The wiring diagram process shall be divided into two phases:

1. Diagram creation and editing. This process shall create the data base. This data base shall contain drafting, engineering, and even manufacturing information. The information shall be edited by the user, either to correct errors or to add additional data. Once the data capture is complete, then phase 2 shall begin.
2. Data extraction and reporting. This process shall extract information from the data base and translate it into either user-readable form or postprocess it into a form readable by other devices (magnetic tape for off-line plotters, etc.).

Intermixing of these two phases shall be available to create an interactive design cycle leading to final drawing completion.

5.5.2.3 Features of the wiring diagram package

While the system shall offer many tools and capabilities which can be used in these two phases, the features which are specifically oriented to wiring diagram products shall be:

Diagram creation and editing
- Drawing duplication
- Drawing standard options
- Graphical text editor
- Global/default properties

Data extraction and reporting
- Drawing tally
- Split equipment cross-reference
- Split equipment report
- Split equipment rules check
- Wire lists and net lists
- Bills of material and component lists

These capabilities shall be detailed in the following sections.

5.5.3 Data Base Structure

5.5.3.1 Wiring diagram data base
5.5.3.2 Associativity of data base

5.5.3.3 Data base entities
5.5.3.3.1 Basic geometric entities
5.5.3.3.1 Connective entities

5.5.3.4 Library capabilities
5.5.3.4.1 Standard drawing formats
5.5.3.4.1.1 Title block part
5.5.3.4.1.2 Diagram map part

5.5.3.4.2 Standard parts library
Internal connections
Wire trunk symbols

5.5.4 User/System Interface
Language utilities
Input capabilities
Commands entry support

5.5.4.1 Graphics commands entry
Manual digitizing

5.5.5 Construction Capabilities

5.5.5.1 Specific wiring diagram
Construction capabilities

5.5.5.1.1 Default properties
5.5.5.1.2 Disconnects and busbars
5.5.5.1.3 Wire constructions

5.5.5.2 Diagram editing

5.5.5.3 Text editing
5.5.5.4 Bulk annotation

5.5.6 Nongraphic Information Access

5.5.6.1 Report generation
5.5.6.1.1 Wire list, logic net list
5.5.6.1.2 Bills of material

5.5.6.1.3 Split equipment processing
Contact/coil cross reference
Contact/coil back annotation
Network cross reference
Contact/coil rules check

5.5.7 Output/Postprocessing Applications

5.6 PLANT DESIGN

5.6.1 Introduction

5.6.2 General Description

5.6.3 Data Base Structure

5.6.3.1 Models and drawings
5.6.3.2 Views
5.6.3.3 Associativity

5.6.3.4 Data base entities
5.6.3.4.1 Connective entities
5.6.3.4.2 Piping entities

5.6.3.5 Data base units

5.6.3.6 Library capabilities
5.6.3.6.1 Major equipment
5.6.3.6.2 Solids

5.6.3.6.3 Fittings libraries

Stock numbers file
Parameters file
Description file
Automatic selection file

5.6.4 User/System Interface
Language utilities
Input capabilities
Commands entry support

5.6.5 Construction Capabilities

5.6.5.1 Appearance control
5.6.5.1.1 Pattern patch

5.6.5.2 Dynamics
5.6.5.2.1 Rotation

5.6.5.3 Graphics controls

5.6.5.4 Design capabilities
5.6.5.4.1 Pipe routing
5.6.5.4.1.1 Semiautomatic line routing
5.6.5.4.1.2 Pipeline entry specification
5.6.5.4.1.3 Locations referencing
5.6.5.4.1.4 Branches and continuations
5.6.5.4.1.5 Attachment
5.6.5.4.1.6 Alignment
5.6.5.4.1.7 Elbow room
5.6.5.4.1.8 Inclinations
5.6.5.4.1.9 Out-of-sequence routing
5.6.5.4.1.10 Rubout

5.6.5.4.2 Fittings insertion
5.6.5.4.2.1 Automatic orientation
5.6.5.4.2.2 Fitting placement options
5.6.5.4.2.3 Automatic component selection
5.6.5.4.2.4 Automatic flange/gasket insertion
5.6.5.4.2.5 Assembly insertion
5.6.5.4.2.6 Reducing fittings

5.6.5.4.2.7 Fitting deletion
5.6.5.4.2.8 Modifier selection options
5.6.5.4.3 Detailing
5.6.5.4.3.1 Appearance procedures
5.6.5.4.3.2 Automatic detail generation
5.6.5.4.3.3 Hidden line removal
5.6.5.4.3.4 Model editing after detail generation
5.6.5.4.4 Piping isometrics and spools
5.6.5.4.4.1 Model decomposition
5.6.5.4.4.2 Stand-alone mode
5.6.5.4.4.3 Dimension protection
5.6.5.4.4.4 Isometric dimensioning
5.6.5.4.4.5 Automatic vs. interactive descaling

5.6.5.5 Construction aids
5.6.5.5.1 Grids
5.6.5.5.2 Multiple views
5.6.5.5.3 Labels

5.6.5.6 Text

5.6.6 Nongraphic Information Management

5.6.6.1 Nongraphic properties
5.6.6.2 Lists
5.6.6.3 Verification
5.6.6.4 Interference checking
5.6.6.5 Dimensioning

5.6.6.6 Report generation
From-to reports
Bill of materials
Back annotation

5.6.7 Output and Postprocessing Options

5.6.7.1 Related programs

5.6.7.2 Finite-element modeling

5.6.7.2.1 Information types

5.6.7.2.2 Mesh generation
5.6.7.2.2.1 Automatic mesh generation
5.6.7.2.2.2 Semiautomatic mesh generation

5.6.7.2.3 Finite-element analysis

5.6.7.3 Pipe stress analysis
Programs interface

5.6.7.4 Output

5.7 FACILITIES DESIGN AND MANAGEMENT

5.7.1 Introduction

The facilities design and management software package shall directly address the interdisciplinary demands of building design and management. The system shall provide the means to coordinate the various tasks associated with architecture, architectural, engineering, and facilities management. On a macro scale, the system shall support the functional relationships between applications to facilitate the design-management-redesign evolutionary cycle of a facility.

5.7.2 General Description

The system shall facilitate in the design and management of buildings. The software shall support architectural engineering and facilities design and management. Command and menu structures shall use vocabulary and work sequences common to architects, engineers, and facilities planners.

The system shall be capable of creating two and/or three-dimensional models and quality drawings in the same data base. This data base shall be accessible to architectural and structural analysis programs and to dimensioning, scaling, dynamic motion, and editing functions. The data base shall also be the basis for working drawings, material takeoffs, and reports, including construction, environmental, economic feasibility, etc. All information shall be available to other departments for ordering, billing, etc. The facilities design and management package shall provide an interface for the following disciplines:

- Architectural design
- Site planning
- Space planning
- Structural design
- Electrical design
- Mechanical equipment placement
- Piping/plumbing
- Heating, ventilation, and air conditioning (HVAC)
- Interior design
- Facilities management
- Environmental planning

5.7.3 Data Base Structure

The building design software shall build upon the fundamental data base structure described in Sec. 5.1.3.

5.7.3.1 Operational modes

Two operational modes shall be provided. In the model mode, two and three-dimensional drawings and designs shall be created. In the drawing mode, all drafting procedures shall be carried out. Any modifications applicable to all drawings and designs shall be made in model mode and shall be reflected in the data base. All changes pertaining to a single drawing (in particular, drafting, annotation, documentation, etc.) shall be made in drawing mode and shall not affect other drawings.

5.7.3.2 Data base units

Dimensions of the design shall be entered at actual size. Scaling changes shall be supported as needed during subsequent design stages. The designer shall have the use of all data base units described in Sec. 5.1.3.6. The user shall be able to create a drawing at a different scale from the model. For example, if the model is designed in feet, the user shall be able to draft one drawing at 1/8 inch equals 1 foot and another drawing at 3 centimeters equals 1 meter.

5.7.3.3 Basic geometric entities

All the entities described in Sec. 5.1.3.7 and listed below shall be supported in the facilities design and management software:

- Point
- Line
- Arc
- Circle

- Fillet
- Spline
- Chamfer

5.7.3.4 Connective entities

5.7.3.5 Library capabilities
5.7.3.5.1 Standard drawing formats
5.7.3.5.2 Standard construction/equipment library
5.7.3.5.3 Appearance libraries
5.7.3.5.4 Parametric parts
  Parametric parts
  Group technology

5.7.3.6 Design protection capabilities

5.7.4 User/System Interface
  Language utilities
  Input capabilities
  Commands entry support

5.7.5 Construction Capabilities

5.7.5.1 Appearance control
5.7.5.2 Dynamics
5.7.5.3 Graphics controls

5.7.5.4 Design capabilities
5.7.5.4.1 Interference checking
5.7.5.4.2 Hidden line removal

5.7.5.5 Construction aids
5.7.5.6 Text

5.7.6 Nongraphic Information Management

5.7.7 Output/Postprocessing Options

5.7.7.1 Related programs
5.7.7.2 Interface to constructional analysis programs

5.7.7.3 Finite-element modeling
5.7.7.4 Output

5.8 ENGINEERING CARTOGRAPHY

5.8.1 Introduction

5.8.2 General Description

5.8.3 Data Base Structure

5.8.3.1 Mapping-specific data base structure
5.8.3.2 Mapping-specific coordinates
5.8.3.3 Views and construction planes
5.8.3.4 Associativity
5.8.3.5 Units of measurement

5.8.3.6 Graphic entities
5.8.3.6.1 Polygons

5.8.3.7 Connective entities

5.8.3.8 Library capabilities
5.8.3.8.1 Figure library
  Point symbols
  Line symbols
  Area symbols

5.8.4 User/System Interface
  Language utilities
  Input capabilities
  Commands entry support

5.8.4.1 Input capabilities
5.8.4.1.1 Digitize modes
5.8.4.1.2 Data transfer capabilities

5.8.5 Construction Capabilities

5.8.5.1 Appearance control
5.8.5.1.1 Line fonts

5.8.5.2 Dynamics
5.8.5.2.1 Scroll

5.8.5.3 Graphics controls

5.8.5.4 Design capabilities
5.8.5.4.1 Geometric relationships calculation
5.8.5.4.2 Traverse adjustment
5.8.5.4.3 Edge matching
5.8.5.4.4 Calibration
5.8.5.4.5 Rectification
5.8.5.4.6 Map generalization

5.8.5.5 Construction aids
5.8.5.5.1 Layers
5.8.5.5.2 Windows
5.8.5.5.3 Multiple views

5.8.5.6 Text
5.8.5.6.1 Text fonts
5.8.5.6.2 Text insertion

5.8.6 Nongraphic Information Management

5.8.6.1 Vectors
5.8.6.2 Data search and highlight
5.8.6.3 Polygon highlight

5.8.7 Postprocessing and Output Capabilities

5.8.7.1 Related programs

6.0 VENDOR COMMITMENT

6.1 BENCHMARK

6.2 TERMS AND CONDITIONS

6.3 WARRANTY

7.0 SUPPORT SPECTRUM

7.1 TRAINING

7.1.1 Basic Operator/Designer Courses

7.1.2 Programming Courses

7.1.3 Management Courses

7.1.4 Supplemental Training
7.1.4.1 Media services
7.1.4.2 Train-the-trainer
7.1.4.3 On-site training

7.2 DOCUMENTATION

7.3 MAINTENANCE

7.3.1 Software Maintenance

7.3.2 Hardware Maintenance
7.3.2.1 Maximum service
7.3.2.2 Fundamental service

7.4 VENDOR SUPPORT CENTERS

7.4.1 Response Center

7.4.2 Logistics Network

7.5 ON-SITE SERVICES

7.5.1 On-Site Applications Assistance

7.5.2 Postinstallation Evaluation

7.6 ACCEPTANCE TESTS

7.6.1 Preshipment Acceptance Test

7.6.2 Installation Site Acceptance Test

8.0 SHIPMENT AND INSTALLATION

8.1 SHIPMENT

8.2 INSTALLATION

8.2.1 Environment

8.2.1.1 Power

8.2.1.2 Temperature and humidity

6
Benchmarking

Benchmarking. A point of reference from which measurements of any sort can be made. (*Source: Webster's Third New International Dictionary.*)

As your computer-aided design/computer-aided manufacturing (CAD/CAM) committee gets deeper into the evaluation, a point will be reached where you will want to benchmark one of your typical designs on each of the vendors' systems. By doing this you are insuring that they

1. Possess the necessary hardware/software to do your job
2. That it can be done more productively than it is currently being done

These basically are the two major rationales for this test procedure. I am sure, however, that there could be other less important rationales.

Usually, this means your entire CAD/CAM select committee commutes between vendor locations and spends anywhere from one to five days in determining who scores the highest in the test you have prepared.

This would seem, on the surface, to be an ideal way to select. After all, speed and capability are critical factors.

But, if you really think about it, all vendors will shorten the time for you. Assuming all are equally capable, the differences *between the vendors* can be quite small. (See Figure 1.)

A very dangerous situation is now staring at us. Some committee members will argue that vendor B should be selected hands down, and quite frankly, some vendors have probably both won and lost orders because of this approach.

Manual effort	—	20.0 hours
Vendor A	—	8.0 hours
Vendor B	—	7.5 hours
Vendor C	—	7.75 hours

Figure 1 Scenario — E size wiring diagram of average density.

We can carry this a step further and determine the savings between the three vendors by examining a hypothetical workload. Your output for 1984 is:

1000 new E-size wiring diagrams
5000 revised E-size wiring diagrams

Manual	1000 × 20 hours	=	20,000 hours
	5000 × 10 hours	=	50,000 hours
			70,000 total hours needed
Vendor A	1000 × 8 hours	=	8000
	5000 × 1.5 hours	=	7500
			15,000 total CAD/CAM hours needed
Vendor B	1000 × 7.5 hours	=	7500
	5000 × 1.0 hours	=	5000
			12,500 total CAD/CAM hours needed
Vendor C	1000 × 7.75 hours	=	7750
	5000 × 1.25 hours	=	6250
			14,000 total CAD/CAM hours needed

On the surface, vendor B will provide 1500 additional production hours/per annum over vendor C and: 2500 additional production hours/per annum over vendor A.

However, let us discuss some of the possibilities that may have afforded vendor B the best time on the test. These items are exactly the ones that confirm my belief that benchmarking to this detail is an unnecessary waste of your time and money. A thorough demonstration of the vendors hardware and software, coupled with user testimony should be used as the deciding factors. Vendor B might have:

1. Been using nonreleasable hardware and software to do your test. That is to say, it could be capabilities that will not be releasable for as much as a year. Saying it another way, the capabilities are *demonstrable*, not releasable.
2. Been using their "star" systems engineer. This is probably the most dangerous facet of benchmarking. Invariably, the benchmark committee rate the *operator* and not the *system*. What this means is that vendor B could win if they were able to man the workstation with a person who is more experienced than his counterparts from vendors A and C. More importantly, your group of design engineers and draftsman would not be able to come close to even the slowest star supplied by the vendors. Remember there is a learning curve associated with the technology! The benchmarks engineer has long since passed his.
3. Not configured the system the way in which you invented it. System speed is clearly associated with the size of the configuration or the number of workstations that access the central processing unit. So, a two-station environment should be more responsive than a six-workstation system. If you are buying a six-station system, make sure each vendor is in fact running a six-station system at the time of your test. If they say it is six, and only two are being used, you will definitely get misleading information.

IMPLEMENTATION

7
Introduction

With the preliminary process of justification complete, you now approach the next phase of actually implementing the new system. At this point, the vendor that will supply your computer-aided design/computer-aided manufacturing (CAD/CAM) system has been selected, the hardware/software mix has been determined, and a purchase order has been written. A lot of hard work and long hours has brought your selection team to this point, but still more needs to be done to insure a successful installation at your site.

The purpose of this section is to present a comprehensive guide to implementing a CAD/CAM system which includes:

Preparation of the system site
Selection of the type of operation
Staff selection
Training of operators
Establishment of standards and procedures
Procurement of materials and supplies

and even how to call for help if it is needed.

A number of chapters in this section were greatly influenced by sections of a publication available from Computervision entitled *Introduction to CAD/CAM Systems*. It should be a prime reference source for you and your selection team.

8
Facility Planning

Every major interactive graphics vendor can supply you with an installation guide (e.g., site preparation guide or an installation guide). These guides provide detailed vendor-specific information needed for planning and preparing your site for the graphics equipment that you have selected. This includes information on site considerations, environmental conditions, electrical requirements, and even helpful hints.

As shown in Figure 1, the most useful portion of the guide is the hardware module templates that can be cut out or duplicated and cut out and placed on a guided outline representative of your available floor space. Examples of several layout plans are included in Figure 1 and elsewhere in this chapter.

Since the information required to plan the successful site installation is so vendor-specific, the purpose of this chapter is to present in general terms facility planning for your site. Make as much use of your vendors' expertise and publications as possible. You will avoid many potential problems.

PLANNING THE INSTALLATION

Every well-planned graphics installation is summarized at some point in its planning by a chronological history of the major highlights of the installation in a milestone chart. This is normally done for facility planning by developing a schedule showing all the necessary operations in the order in which they will occur and then assigning both a start and completion date for each operation. In this way, holes in the schedule can be found, progress can be reviewed and appropriate action taken to ensure an orderly, timely, and successful graphics system installation.

Figure 1 Installation guide and hardware module templates.

At a minimum, the milestone chart should summarize the following events:

Finalize space and power requirements
Survey site requirements
Construct necessary facilities
Review completed facilities
Proposed system delivery date
Install graphics system
Perform system acceptance tests
Train personnel
Start production

The milestone events are normally referenced to system delivery. In other words, all construction and support systems such as power and air conditioning are completed and checked out before the system arrives.

There are generally three major phases that the milestone chart is divided into the months before delivery:

Phase I (4–6 Months Before Delivery)

1. Site selection
2. Define and locate structural constraints
3. Determine power requirements
4. Site layout
5. Prepare facilities drawings
6. Request and award construction bids
7. Start facilities construction

Phase II (2–4 Months Before Delivery)

1. Start major site construction
2. Install electrical systems
3. Install air conditioning
4. Order all site-related durables such as furniture

	Phase I	Phase II	Phase III
Site selection	X—X		
Define and locate structural constraints	X—X		
Determine power requirements	X—X		
Site layout	X—X		
Prepare facilities drawings	X—X		
Request and award construction bids	X—	——	—X
Start facilities construction		X——	—X
Start major site construction		X—X	
Install electrical systems		X—X	
Install air-conditioning		X—	—X
Order all site related durables such as furniture		X—	—X
Receive supplies			X
Complete construction			X
Check all electrical systems			X—X
Test and balance air-conditioning			X—X
Re-check everything			X—X
Delivery			X

Figure 2 Milestone chart.

Phase III (Final Month Before Delivery)

1. Complete construction
2. Check all electrical systems
3. Test and balance air conditioning

Although it is usually difficult to synchronize the three phases, you can arrange to have the system delivered on the very same day the facilities are ready. Proper planning and management of your plan will have definite effects on the costs associated with the installation. A typical milestone chart is included as Figure 2.

SYSTEM POWER REQUIREMENTS

Most computer-aided design/computer-aided manufacturing (CAD/CAM) systems are designed to run on a number of selectable levels of AC power for reliable operation. In addition, mass storage devices normally require 208 or 230 Vac. Reliable system operation requires stable, noise-free power. Since each device in your system has different characteristics, power requirements are generally classified in three classes.

Class I: Voltage-Sensitive and Noise-Sensitive Devices

The computer system and plotters must provide sustained, error-free operation over long periods of time. Therefore, these devices require voltage regulation and noise suppression for optimum reliability. Class I power supplies must provide both voltage regulation and noise suppression in a single package.

Class II: Noise-Sensitive Hardware Devices

To provide reliability, mass storage devices require noise protection and isolation, but not a high degree of regulation. This is because of their built-in lack of sensitivity to voltage variations due to the inertia of the spinning platters. In addition, mass storage devices require extremely high starting currents, which would make an adequately regulated source very costly. For noise suppression and line isolation, a commercially available class II power transformer is recommended.

Class I and II devices must meet the following criteria

1. The power source must not be shared with large motors or other equipment that may produce voltage dips, surges, transients, or spikes.

2. The average voltage must remain within a set tolerance, usually +5%.
3. There must be freedom from voltage spikes. A line monitor placed on the source should not record an impulse or spike of 150% of nominal voltage during normal operating hours.
4. When the power source does not satisfy the regulation and/or noise requirements, or where brownouts are anticipated, the power will need special conditioning. Power conditioning module(s) or line filters will provide the required voltage stabilization and isolation.

Class III: Normal Electrical Hardware Devices

This category is included to clearly distinguish the interactive terminals from the rest of the system. However, the required voltage is normally the same as for the rest of the system.

SYSTEM ENVIRONMENT

A controlled and monitored environment for the CAD/CAM system is necessary to assure accurate and reliable flow of data and information among system components. Typically, CAD/CAM systems are made up from three major hardware groupings, each requiring a different set of environmental quality rules. Environmental quality is affected by:

Temperature range
Humidity range
Temperature/humidity changes

The first major grouping is the computer (Fig. 2). Here, temperature and humidity are critical and should be controlled and monitored continuously. This should also be a limited personnel access area to prevent rapid environmental changes caused by the presence of either large groups of people or by exposure of the room to outside-controlled temperatures and humidity through active doorways.

Temperature should be kept in a constant range given in the site preparation guide. Rapid variations in temperature, even within the acceptable constant range, should be avoided to prevent physical changes and stress to components, and expansion or contraction of recording media. Even though the actual CAD/CAM computer systems are relatively small, they still require effective temperature and humidity control.

The second major system grouping includes those components that are accuracy-dependent, such as photoplotters, drum plotters, flatbed plotters, and large-surface digitizers. Photoplotters, especially when used for integrated circuits (IC) and printed circuit board (PCB) artwork generation, require stringent temperature and humidity controls to prevent changes in film size and emulsion characteristics. Paper-on-drum and flatbed plotters are also susceptible to changes in the size of the holding surface and the plotting media.

Accuracy of large digitizers is affected by temperature and humidity because of the expansion/contraction qualities of the surface and the grid matrices used for digitizable points. Here again, wide temperature variations, even in the specified temperature range, will have adverse effects on accuracy-dependency devices.

The last major grouping is the interactive work station or cathode ray tube (CRT) terminal, which consists of electronic components, a viewing device, and even a local newspaper. Again, wide temperature variations should be avoided. More importantly, it is at this device that the operator spends the most time and comfort must be assured. A suitable office environment is 68 to 72°F with 40–60% relative humidity. This is also a good temperature differential between the inside and the outside of the cabinet to assure heat transfer.

In all of the above major CAD/CAM groupings, the main consideration is temperature variation or gradient. On any CAD/CAM equipment, the gradient should not exceed the level given in the site preparation guide, normally 10°F per hour.

If the manufacturer does not provide a table in the preparation guide, a good way to figure the required amount of cooling for the hardware in a given area is to use the formula:

3.4* (Sum of the watts of all modules) = BTU/hr
(rounded up to the nearest 1000).

This is a gross formula which provides a safety margin that includes people, lights, and average gradient due to change in area environment. For example, let us say there are eight design terminals and two plotters in an area. The manufacturing specifications are as follows:

1. Design terminal = 302 watts
2. Plotter = 1409 watts

Then using the formula

3.4* [8(302) + 2(1409)] = 17,796 BTU/hr

Rounding up to the nearest whole thousandth, the answer is 18,000 BTU/hr.

An air-conditioning unit capable of this amount of cooling is required for the terminals, plotters, and the other heat-sensitive equipment in the CAD/CAM area.

Air purity is another consideration in the CAD/CAM system environment. A good rule of thumb is that airborne particles in the form of dust, smoke, or grease should not exceed that of a normal office environment. Dust-coated electronic components retain heat, thereby impeding convection cooling. Excessive dust will clog equipment air filters and, in time, promote dehydration of motor bearing in disk drives, magnetic tapes drives, and plotters.

In summary, airborne particles of dust chemicals, and paper should never exceed those of a normal office environment. In most factories or areas of comparable cleanliness, air filtration is necessary to assure CAD/CAM system reliability and long life. See your note preparation guide for any additional recommendations.

Noise may also affect productivity because excessive noise is distracting. On the other hand, sound deadness may contribute to claustrophobia. Noise may consist of several audio frequencies or random frequencies that may vary in amplitude. The best solution is to physically divide the CAD/CAM system into two major sectors, as shown in Figure 3.

Figure 3 CAD/CAM system divided into noise sectors.

CAD/CAM system devices that generate noise are fans, drive motors, and mechanical functions that are erratic (disk drives and plotters). Normally, interactive design stations do not possess any of the common noise-generating components.

Noisy components should be placed away from other system components, in areas slightly quieter than an office environment. Normal sound-deadened materials such as carpeting, roughened flat ceiling tiles, wall drapes, and even flat paint on the walls help the problem but still allow some undistracting noise to occur, such as speech and ringing telephones. This is a natural atmosphere for most people.

High-performance sound-deadening may in some cases be desirable. However, sound-deadened rooms tend to stifle verbal communication and in some cases might make the operators overly cautious in actions necessary to complete their tasks. When sharp noise is generated in an overly quiet area, the distractions seem multiplied by the reactions of the individuals. In part, dropping a pencil or accidentally hitting an object with one's foot may have the same effect as an exploding bomb.

In summary, the CAD/CAM work stations/design terminals should be placed in an environment that allows the operators to concentrate on their work with reduced noise levels. It is also of prime importance that the operators be able to communicate with each other, especially in a new installation, without fear of magnified noise due to excessive sound-deadening.

SYSTEM LAYOUT

There are as many variations of system layout as there are business styles, and as many advantages to each layout as there are disadvantages. However, one fact is constant: the central processing unit (CPU), disk unit, and magnetic tape unit should normally be in a controlled environment removed or enclosed from the terminals in order to maintain controlled temperature and humdity, and to deaden or eliminate the noise associated with these devices.

The first major consideration is the location of the CAD/CAM system. Whether the system is centralized or the work stations are scattered in remote locations, they should be readily accessible to all users with a minimum of time and travel. Thus, the system and/or work stations should be placed in an easily accessible central location.

Initially, regardless of this final type of operation, work stations should be clustered until all of the original operators have achieved a high performance level. As the nucleus of persons with expertise reaches an acceptable number, it may be desirable to place the CAD/CAM work stations in the areas or departments utilizing them. Again, this strategy should be implemented, if at all, at some time—say a year or more after the start-up date—after the operators are well trained on the system. Most companies centralize their systems. The main advantages are:

1. Ease of maintenance
2. Better control over usage (where and when)
3. Limited duplication of effort
4. Standardized rules and regulations on projects and data base management
5. Single budget and cost control
6. Reduced installation costs
7. Less manpower to operate
8. More communication between operators
9. Faster and more effective formal training
10. Better control over integration of multiple applications

Before the actual placement of the CAD/CAM hardware, the general physical attributes of the room, windows, lighting, storage, and electrical requirements, must be evaluated.

There are three main criteria to consider in locating windows: (1) outside light, (2) work station environment, and (3) computer room environment.

Ideally no outside light should be allowed into the work station area or the computer room area because it is distracting to the operators; it may cause reflections, either directly or indirectly, onto the CRTs; it could cause the temperature of the units and general environment to increase sufficiently to cause system damage. If outside windows are present, they should be draped with metalized fabric or vertical venetian blinds, to reflect sunlight out of the room but allow very little light to filter in.

Windows surrounding the work station area are acceptable except that persons looking into the area, or tapping on the windows, can be distracting to operators operating in a closed-shop environment. Window placement around the work station area should be planned to prevent this potential problem.

On the other hand, windows in the computer room can be useful. They can be arranged so that the work station operators can observe the equipment, especially the tape-drive movements and the computer indicator lights, to ensure that the equipment is performing properly. In addition, maintenance people can observe the work station CRTs from the computer room for the same purpose.

Room lighting in the work station area is critical. Storage tube CRTs are inherently dimmer than raster scan tubes, so that sunlight shining on the tube face will nearly eliminate the image. The image of the operator is readily reflected on the tube and overhead lighting can cause glare. It is, therefore, important to illuminate the work station area in subdued light by using light intensity control.

This can be accomplished in several ways. Commercially available dimmers for incandescent lamps and fluorescent lamps are the most popular. Optimally, each work station should have a dimmer control and allow operation placement of the lights.

In Figure 4, all lighting is dimmer-controlled and movable. This arrangement negates glare and at the same time permits the operator to have a well-lighted work table. In this example, the lights are incandescent spotlights mounted on rails. There are also fixtures for flush-mounted spotlights that can be moved off center approximately ten degrees (see Fig. 5).

Lighting placement is of special importance. The work table area should be well lighted with the lights placed at least 14 feet from the floor. The only other lighting is above the work station, preventing any direct light from reflecting on the CRT face. This allows the work station area to be lighted but eliminates glare on the front of the CRT or on the operator's face.

There are many variations in the type and placement of lighting in work stations. Some general rules to consider are:

1. Work stations should be indirectly lighted
2. Work tables should be directly lighted
3. Ceiling lights should not be directly reflected on the CRT screen

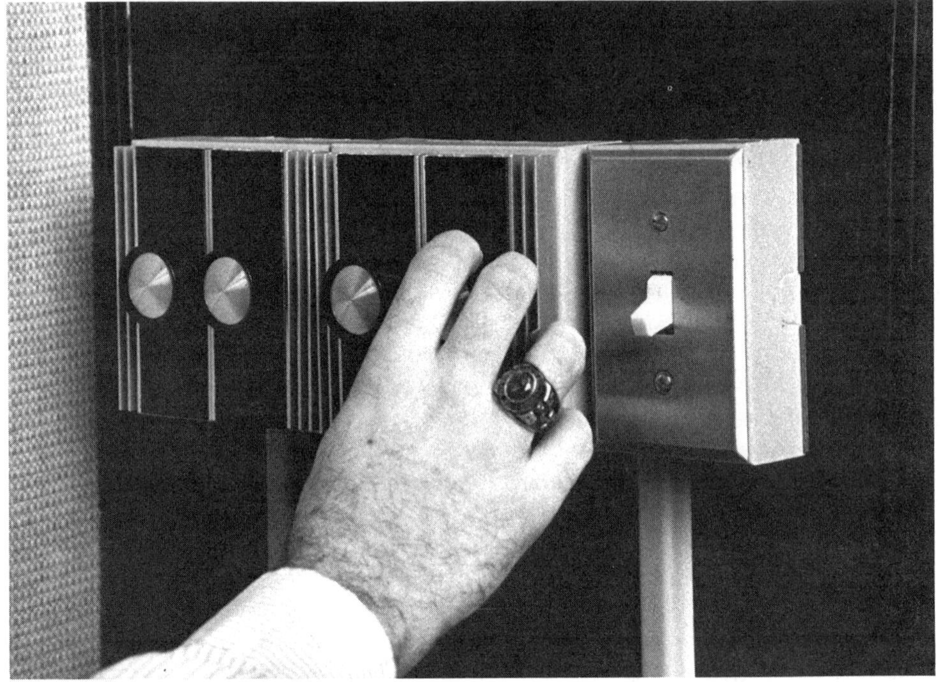

Figure 4 Dimmer-controlled movable lighting.

Figure 5 CAD/CAM lighting.

4. Fluorescent ceiling lights should not be shielded with light-polarizing plastic (refer to Fig. 6)
5. Dimmer controls should be handy to operators

Storage space requirements should also be considered. The work station area should be large enough to provide storage for general office supplies, a holding or central file for hardcopy drawings, and a records section. The computer room must have storage space for fireproof cabinets to house magnetic tapes, disk packs, and spare parts. Magnetic tapes and disk packs must be in a temperature and humidity stabilized area.

SYSTEM COMPONENT ARRANGEMENT

This arrangement of CAD/CAM hardware devices is dependent on many variables which can include centralized versus remote location, size of system versus floor space allocation and present versus future system usage. As previously discussed the work stations should be in an environment that meets the need of the

Figure 6 Fluorescent ceiling lights.

equipment and the user. The other components should be placed in an environmentally controlled area.

Initially, it is normally best to cluster the work stations. This enhances operator learning and promotes discussion-related learning. Assuming that initially the CAD/CAM system is centralized, room layout considerations are as follows (refer to Fig. 7):

1. Outside walls: floor to ceiling
2. Inside walls (work station cubicles): 4 × 5 ft
3. Work station cubicles floor area: 10 × 10 ft
4. Work station floor: tile
5. Computer room floor: (a) tile, (b) raised (optional)
6. Lighting for computer room: standard ceiling fixture
7. Lighting for work station: standard ceiling plus variable position and intensity control
8. Windows: thermopane or heavy plate glass
9. Personnel access: standard door
10. Equipment access: double doors

Figure 7 Room layout example with cubicles.

Figure 8 Room layout example without cubicles.

A slightly less than ideal arrangement would involve elimination of the cubicles (refer to Fig. 8). In this case, the varieties of work station arrangement are infinite. The only prerequisite would be to make sure there is adequate space for the service personnel.

Other considerations in the layout are: (1) telephone location, (2) cleaning facilities, (3) storage space, and (4) visual and physical access to plotters and the computer room. The final layout should be approved by both the users and the system vendor. Although all these considerations take time to finalize and require almost constant attention, they are well worth the effort in terms of the bottom line—increased productivity.

REFERENCE AND ACKNOWLEDGMENT

Much of this chapter was directly influenced by "How to Get Started," by Lawrence Edwards in *The CAD/CAM Handbook*, published by Computervision.

9

Facility Organization and Administration

The type of graphics system selected and the actual physical layout of the hardware for your system are important factors in achieving productivity from your new system, but to achieve efficient productivity, work organization is an equally important success factor for interactive graphic facilities that normally perform their work in a step-by-step manual process. This type of application is normally divided into functional or logical work movement steps that are dependent on the type of shop, either open or closed, single or multiple shifts, and so on, that has been implemented for the system.

OPEN OR CLOSED SHOP

The first of many problems facing the new graphics manager is what type of operation will be run; should it be an open shop where every user normally operates the terminal directly, but does not have to be an employee of the computer-aided design/computer-aided manufacturing (CAD/CAM) facility, or a closed shop where people bring work to the graphics facility and the facility sells the services provided by its full-time employees. This decision is normally related to the application to be performed but is not dependent on the graphics system because the system as delivered from the graphics vendor is flexible, allowing the manager to develop an open or closed operation with single or multiple shifts or varying numbers of terminals, or any combination.

The closed shop is normally used if the graphics operation is used to support conversion of graphic documents, such as integrated circuits, printed circuits, or mapping. Full-time terminal operators in a closed shop convert prepared layout documents to digital data by a digitizing process, and do so at a lower pay scale and with less experience or technical education. Minimal creativity is needed and desired to directly monitor the operation of the work unit. The monitoring process allows the productivity level of each unit of work to be varied for cost-effectiveness and maximum throughput.

In a closed shop, the manager's goal is to sell a cost-effective service for converting graphic information to digital data, accurately and on time. This requires an employment structure responsive to the many needs of the facility while providing career advancement for the employees. A typical set of work levels might include:

1. *An apprentice operator* who primarily operates a digitizer to convert documents to digital data. The apprentice operator also generates graphic plots for verification of digitizing effort. Technical education is not required.
2. *An operator* who primarily operates a cathode ray tube (CRT) terminal or work station and has experience as digitizer operator. Technical knowledge is necessary in order to operate other hardware such as plotters, punches, and printers. One year technical degree or equivalent experience is required.
3. *A senior operator* can use any of the system hardware efficiently and effectively. Senior operators should be able to communicate technical problems with the company's customers to resolve errors in work performed and give technical leadership to other operators. A two-year technical associate degree or equivalent experience is necessary.
4. *A designer* must have a comprehensive understanding of computer graphics technology to understand work applications thoroughly and develop library and data base parameters to support work activity. A 2–4 year technical degree and experience as a senior operator are prerequisites.

Chapter 11 discusses this subject in more detail.

Auditing or verification of the data base through manual checking is another important function in a closed shop. To maintain high levels of confidence and credibility with the facility's customers, auditing of system outputs is necessary. It is recognized that computer technology is providing more and more automatic audit checks. However, an evaluation is necessary to determine the present cost of computer-aided and manual auditing.

The closed shop with its controlled employee environment also simplifies the distribution of technical and operational information. Workflows or processes are usually developed and documented to assist the facility staff in their day-to-day activities as well as in training new employees.

The open shop is a direct contrast with the closed shop. It is manually selected for work applications that require direct design activity, such as mechanical design, numerical control (NC), and tool design. The major advantage of an open shop is that it allows the engineer, designer, or tool designer to operate the graphics terminal personally. Anyone with the direct need can use the computer capability to assist in the design and definition of a part or design.

In an open shop, the manager's primary task is to provide sufficient hardware and technical support for the graphics system to allow the users direct access to the terminals. Based on the number of terminals within the facility and the potential number of individuals who may need terminals, scheduling daily usage as well as long-term capacity needs can be a major problem. Complicating the problem is whether the request for terminal time takes into consideration necessary design "think" time; or is the purpose simply to construct a part that requires only detail definition from the design layout? Another significant task is to provide technical and operational information support to a group of intermittent system users. If the group is small, with frequent access to the system, the support can be minimal. If the access is infrequent, full-time user support people, in addition to the system managers, may be necessary.

SINGLE OR MULTIPLE SHIFTS

Multiple Shifts

Most interactive graphic installations are initially established as single-shift facilities. When growing work volume demands more capacity, management must evaluate the options of spending additional capital or implementing multiple shifts. This can be a difficult decision for an organization with little or no knowledge of multiple shifts.

The initial question to be answered is whether or not the applications performed lend themselves to multiple-shift operations. Open shop facilities may present a problem, since system users are technical employees unreceptive to the idea of night work.

Multiple-shift operations have basically two advantages. The first and most obvious is capital savings. With the rising cost of computerized systems, a single-shift installation, where hardware is idle for most of the night hours, is certainly a capital-intensive luxury. The other advantage is faster turnaround. A work unit that requires multiple steps within a process flow can be started and completed across shift boundaries much more conveniently and quickly than by starting and stopping single shifts until completion. The result is that the facility accomplishes its work much sooner in terms of throughput and user satisfaction.

Single Shifts

Single-shift facilities have several advantages. It is difficult to resolve a design definition problem with a user at 3:00 A.M. when the user is not available. Therefore, working the same hours as the user offers a better opportunity to coordinate the job. The technical and administrative communciations problems that exist between multiple shifts are eliminated. Single-shift operation permits an individual to perform his entire work unit without interruption, which can improve his job interest and attitude. It also simplifies system management and monitoring of work performance. Another advantage is related to employee hiring. As CAD/CAM technology grows more complex, so does the need for more technically oriented employees. It is difficult to recruit technical people to work night shifts. If working night shifts is a job requirement, make sure that the individuals are aware of that condition of employment before they are hired to be operators.

CENTRALIZATION OR DECENTRALIZATION OF SYSTEMS

Centralization or decentralization of graphics systems within a company or division is usually an economic decision. At a half million dollars or more per system, spending additional capital for separate installations can be very expensive. In addition, considerations of user convenience and functional control may affect the decision.

Locating two or more systems within the same graphics facility reduces capital investment, because expensive hardware items such as plotters can be shared as long as the work volume permits. Depending on the hardware mix, the savings per item can be significant. For example, sharing a photoplotter can save as much as $85,000. Centralization also simplifies the technical management of the data base. Often, more than one group, such as engineering and manufacturing, or engineering and technical support use the data base. This makes organization and utilization of the data base important in reducing the need for subsequent data processing.

Communicating and understanding data base needs can best be done when the systems are centralized. A centralized facility can better handle product throughput at peak times as well as smooth out peaks in the workflow. This can be an important advantage considering that many products do not have enough lead time to allow for planning level workloads. Centralized systems also reduce the impact of system or terminal downtime. Although decentralized facilities may function together, it may be difficult to off-load work from a facility that is totally down onto the existing workload of the functioning facility.

The problem of large, inefficient computer facilities has produced legitimate concerns about centralized graphic facilities. It is a recognized fact that the larger the facility, the more difficult it is to manage. Also, the user becomes very intolerant of minor computer-related errors that cannot be addressed because of more demanding work. Many of these concerns such as overhead costs, throughput efficiency, errors and user insensitivity, are serious enough to discourage potential users from interfacing with the graphics system. In that case, the facility manager must use some public relations through individual communications and "show-and-tell" demonstrations to groups outside the immediate graphics team. Finally, the facility must produce the required work as accurately as possible and within the time frame quoted. If this problem is not resolved, the effectiveness of the facility is reduced and productivity goals will not be realized.

Decentralization of systems significantly reduces the time expended commuting to centralized facilities. Since many of the commuters are engineering personnel, the cost for the lost time can be significant, especially if the user's building or building complex is large.

An advantage of decentralization is the reduction of managerial time spent prioritizing work from the different organizations using the facility. Most centralized facilities support more than one department/division/group so managerial action is frequently required to rank work requests. Given today's rapid business pace, work prioritizing is a must, especially during the facility's peak cycles.

If decentralization is followed throughout the company, communication between facilities will need to be developed. This can range from the transmission of data files for subsequent use by another facility to a simple review of data files for investigation of system problems. The process can be accomplished by either hand-carrying magnetic tapes or by installing a communications network. The advantages of a communications network are that it is easy to use, reduces tape-drive workload, eliminates occasional read/write incompatibility between different drives, and eliminates the need for transferring magnetic tapes. One advantage of using magnetic tapes for data file transfer is that the user avoids the capital investment for each central processing unit (CPU) and for transmission hardware. In addition, the magnetic tapes can be used for system backup.

Much of what has been said about centralization and decentralization of CAD/CAM systems also applies to terminals within a system, with one exception. As the user community becomes more aware of computer graphics, most users request terminals to be located in their particular working areas.

The added capability of individualizing each terminal by adding significant terminal capability for local operations has enhanced the idea of decentralization significantly. This new terminal capability seems to be the new graphics terminal "wave of the future." However, the need for reading and writing data files to magnetic tapes as well as system administration still exists. Therefore, a thorough evaluation should be made before planning to decentralize terminals.

FACILITY MANAGER

One of the most important factors and sometimes the easiest to overlook in developing a CAD/CAM facility is the selection of supervisory staff. System evaluation terms typically assume that if the system is purchased as a "turnkey" system it will generally develop and operate itself. This assumption has had disastrous results in existing facilities. The interactive has demanded and will continue to demand innovative, forward-looking management that can readily accept continual change. The growth from two- to three-dimensional to solids software systems in the past several years is typical. The continually broadening capability spectrum challenges the system manager to cope with each new innovation. These constant challenges may involve anything from simple instructions, to system uses, to local integration into special work applications.

Newly acquired graphics hardware requires continual attention if the facility expects to keep pace with graphics technology. The size of the facility and related demands determine whether or not the manager can manage without support. In the case of a single-system installation, the manager with designated lead operators can probably handle it. In a larger facility (3–4 systems), a full-time support commitment and staff is necessary.

Many facility managers are selected for their experience and knowledge of the intended applications rather than for their computer orientation. The reason is that the operation of a "turnkey" system requires immediate application involvement. There is very little need for computer knowledge at the system implementation stage. As a result, the individual with applications experience need only learn the system command structure, while the individual with computer experience must learn both the applications in detail and simultaneously the system command structure.

In time, most facilities expand to handle additional work volume and address new activities not originally considered. The staff may have little knowledge of the new work and require detailed familiarization before they can provide the desired output. For example, a facility might be expanding from simple CAD design to producing output for CAM applications. This not only requires additional learning effort, but can also present scheduling problems for the manager if the same hardware is used to address all needs.

A significant challenge for a facility manager is to provide a functional graphics facility with minimal change in the user community. In the past, computer technology required the user to adapt to the standards and limitations of the "system." Unless the manager has a thorough understanding of the application and a commitment to address the user's needs fully, the same result can happen in a graphics facility. The facility needs to perform for the user and not require the user to work for it. For example, if the user must operate as a programmer to use the system instead of using his conventional design methodology, he will not become an enthusiastic user. There are many people who still resist computer graphics technology if it changes their daily tools. This attitude can seriously affect the facility's productivity.

REFERENCE AND ACKNOWLEDGMENTS

Similar ideas are presented in "How to Organize and Manage a CAD/CAM Facility," by Donald Earll in *The CAD/CAM Handbook*, published by Computervision.

10
Personnel Planning

For your upper level management, the most important benefit of the installation of a graphics system is increased productivity and quality of the products your division produces through reduced task-cycle time. A graphics system will directly impact original design, analysis, detail design, documentation, and manufacture of your products. Even though reduced task-cycle time is the main goal of the graphics system, it takes people to make it work.

At some point during the acquisition of the graphics system, your upper management will make the following statement: "With the installation of a graphics system there should be an immediate reduction of personnel because the same number of people will be able to do more design work than our current work load needs." In practice, it is normally found that even though the same number of persons can perform their customary design tasks in a shorter time, a measurable amount of additional time is spent in designing a better product. In addition, there is a measurable or even marked increase in company or division profits. This usually means that the product line can be expanded and new products can be introduced. Designs can be refined to yield better product quality and lower costs. All this contributes to a better competitive position for the company and more job stability for its employees. The net results for both personnel and company profits after the installation of a graphics system are positive.

Increased task throughput and reduced task cycle times profoundly affect job content and status. Job content visibly changes because a cathode ray tube (CRT), an intelligent tablet, and an electronic pen replace the drawing board. Lower-level repetitive tasks previously done by a designer are now done by the system. The designer has more time for creative thinking. Previously unstructured and undefined design processes are simplified and standardized.

Two major problems must be resolved. First, the introduction of a graphics system changes the interface between designers and engineers in a company. Previously, the engineers made all major decisions on configuration of parts. That responsibility is now given to the designers, thus increasing their responsibility and elevating their status.

Secondly, normal opposition to the introduction of a graphics system needs to be overcome. In many cases this is a generational question—the inability or reluctance of older or highly trained designers to adjust to new methods. Often, it involves fear of losing a privileged position due to special experience and skill if everything is made generally accessible and shared equally by anyone who uses the computer system.

A sound approach here is to promote a sense of personal involvement by inviting the advice and collaboration of such personnel by documenting their techniques and approaches. They can be assigned the responsibility of checking or amending design programs. The point is, age should not be a deterent to system usage. Experienced designers possess a real knowledge of the process of designing acquired over many years of effort. This knowledge can and must be captured in the graphics system data base. Too often, the living "walking data bases" are lost at retirement. Many pitfalls and obstacles, sociological and psychological, have to be overcome when implementing a graphics system. The bottom line is that education, training, participation, and understanding must be considered when introducing computer-aided design/computer-aided manufacturing (CAD/CAM) into any company.

The most common obstacles and misconceptions encountered are that:

1. CAD/CAM limits creativity
2. Skills are fragmented
3. CAD/CAM reduces jobs and job security
4. System prompting and fast decision making create fatigue
5. Traditional work methods are changed
6. Designers may lose protected positions and skills developed with experience

Some of these points are completely false, and some have positive implications for the company and the individual. To present them in their true light, sound educational programs must be in place before, during, and after system implementation. Training on system usage must be results-oriented. In addition, users should participate in task-related decisions because it is the graphics users who ultimately make the system work.

Another major problem encountered when introducing a graphics system is job status. Normally, status and added responsibility have a positive effect. However, it may have a negative effect in some situations. To illustrate how and why a crisis can sometimes develop, consider a typical design process:

New designs start out on the conceptual level from ideas, requirements, and other related criteria. This conceptual data is translated into a rough visual depiction of the design. Then the initial design is made by manually translating ideas into graphical form.

Next, and here the problem starts, the design is translated into a mathematical model and converted to discrete digital data for computer analysis. This manually keypunched data is batch-fed into a computer for design analysis. The computer outputs massive amounts of discrete data, which must be converted back into graphic form. This is a manual process that is error-prone, time-consuming, and above all, uninspiring.

The design engineer is not designing; he is a data processor or a number-sifting clerk. He may rightly figure that the computer is forcing him to do clerical work. This is obviously not the case with our interactive graphics system. A point worth stressing. Today, the design engineer can start at the idea stage, simultaneously creating the graphics and seeing them. He can create a mathematical model, analyze the design, reduce the design data to graphics, automatically perform several iterations of design modification and reanalysis, and even plot the work prints and generate a numerical control (NC) tape for the manufacturing process. Granted, this is simplistic but the main point is that the designer can see, modify, and manipulate his design with relative ease. No longer does the designer have to work in the data reduction mode. The system does it faster and better. Better for both the designer and the company.

When these common psychological and sociological problems have been overcome, you need to fuse the problem of who should be assigned to use the graphics system. The system must be used by the draftsperson, designer, and engineer. The system and its operators should be a compatible, close-working team. The human is intuitive, creative, and innovative; present systems are none of these. Sometimes the human can be unreliable and inconsistent, the system is always reliable and consistent. Working as a team, the human and the system can each compensate for the weaknesses of the other.

The proper education of new CAD/CAM operators is of prime importance. A logical question at this point is: Since the systems are computer-based, wouldn't normal procedure dictate selecting a programmer or computer operator as the graphics system operator? For these systems the answer is quite the contrary. If only computer-educated persons could operate the system, it would indicate poor human engineering. If the command syntax, the operating procedures, and the method of visualization were abstract or computer-oriented, then only a programmer could use the system. That is seldom the case. More likely, the designers, draftspersons, and engineers have not been properly educated on system operation.

What should you look for in selecting operator personnel?

1. A computer-system-oriented engineer, designer, or draftsperson. They are much easier to teach system usage and computer disciplines than programmers.

2. A person new to the industry but with related engineering education and computer orientation.
3. A professionally mature design/engineering person, not necessarily to be an operator, but as an advisor to the operator.

Additional criteria are given in Table 1.

With these general guidelines in mind, the last crucial step is to actually select the operators. The criteria for selection should be those you would apply to a person seeking a new position, or upgrading a present position. A person who has, in part, assumed the new position by dressing, acting, or in fact,

Table 1 Operator Selection Criteria

1. Knows your drafting and design rules:
   Formats
   Set-up specifications
   Standards of parts
   Overall end-product standards

2. Good conceptual designer:
   Visualizes the end product before it is started
   Formulates a planned approach quickly
   Is able to succinctly describe a plan of attack and the result it will achieve
   Is able to define time frames even with distractions, and interruptions

3. Can exhibit good motor skills:
   Gross motor skills
   Fine motor skills
   Observing an equality between fine and gross motor skills
   Speed of execution of movements

4. Attitude and motivation:
   He or she likes him or herself and likes what he or she does
   Enjoys challenges
   Serious but friendly
   Extrovert/introvert

5. Outside interests:
   Recreational likes and dislikes
      Related vs. unrelated
      Music: listener vs. performer
      Crafts
   Educational

performing in some way conducive to his newly perceived position or goal. Candidates should have been educated or have educated themselves, either partially or wholly, to be able to perform in this new position. Eventually they should have a position that fulfills their goals—if their attitude and motivation are right. When the new position is made known, an application is filled out, the applicant is interviewed, and in effect, makes a verbal or written contract with the new management to perform the new job to the satisfaction of both parties.

Using the general procedures and criteria previously outlined, how should you go about selecting your CAD/CAM operators?

1. Inform and educate prospective operators about the system. The educational material and the instructor should be supplied by the system vendor, or by other educational means.
2. Have each prospect fill out a brief questionnaire on why they are interested in being a CAD/CAM operator. The questions should relate to the person's individual goals, creativeness, and adaptability to new skills and ideas. A typical questionnaire is included at the end of this chapter.

From the first questionnaire, a determination can be made as to the potential of the CAD/CAM operator's attitudes and motivation. Look for the following traits in the person's answers:

1. The person promotes a positive image and likes what is being produced.
2. The person enjoys challenge.
3. The prospect wants to improve his or her worth to your company and on a personal level, and has set his or her sights on higher achievement.

At this point the prospect has made out an application for employment.

In the next phase, the interview process begins. Some general attributes to look for are:

1. The person will be able to work in close harmony with the other operators.
2. The person knows company procedures, pecking order, product-related specification, department standards, and so on. This list is determined by the interviewer.

The quality of the interview will yield persons who will work together and share ideas with one another. In addition, the interview phase should yield information that verifies and even amplifies the applicant's answers to the questionnaire.

QUESTIONNAIRE FOR DRAFTING AND DESIGN PERSONNEL

We are embarking on a pilot project to determine the usefulness of an interactive graphics system.

We will need a number of drafters and designers to participate in the pilot project. The success or failure of this development project will depend heavily on the attitude and abilities of the people who will be using the equipment. The selection of the drafting members for the development team will be made by drafting management and the selection of desired members by engineering management.

The following questionnaire was prepared in order to give you an idea of the requirements of this project as we see them now and to provide us with information to help select a team:

- Why are you interested in the graphics system?

  ____

  ____

  ____

- In order to use the system successfully, the drafters and designers will have to be enthusiastic, adaptable, creative, open to new ideas, and capable of working with a minimum of supervision.
  - Do you feel you fit this description? __________

    Why?

  ____

  ____

  ____

- One of the objectives of developing a graphics system is to improve our drafting and design productivity.
  - Are you willing to work under this pressure?
  - Are you willing to have your productivity measured on this system?
  - Are you willing to accept your removal from the development team for productivity related reasons? __________

- Introduction to this system will require several weeks of training, both here and at the supplier's sites. Typically, each user will spend one week at the supplier's factory site, one week here, and possibly seve two - five day periods at the supplier's local office. The first users of the system will be expected to help the training of later users and conducting system demonstrations, should the need arise.
  - Are you willing to travel for as much as a week at a time for training purposes? __________
  - Are you willing to accept your removal from the development team, during training, based on the recommendation of the supplier? __________
  - Are you willing to train others? __________
  - Are you willing to travel occasionally to attend user group meetings, if asked? __________

- Since this is a pilot system, we have little experience in how the users should approach their work. Much of the organization of the project and the procedures will be undefined at the start, and will have to be developed by the development team.
  - Are you willing to work with a group to help solve problems, resolve conflicts and develop graphic standards and procedures? __________

- Initially, the working conditions may also be ill-defined. We are looking for a place which will house the system. We are also considering several alternative working schedules, with an eye toward maximizing the utilization of the system.
  - Are you willing to be located away from the drafting or design department? __________

- Are you willing to work shifts other than first shift? __________
  Preferred Shift (1, 2, or 3)? __________
  2nd Preference? __________
- Within any shift, are you willing to be flexible about your starting and ending times? __________

• As mentioned previously, the success of this system will depend heavily on the dedication of the members of the development team. Part of this dedication includes a commitment to staying with the project to minimize turnover. Note that participation in this project will not restrict your normal promotional prospects within the Drafting Department.
  - Are you willing to stay with this project for at least two years or until the termination of the project, whichever occurs first? __________

Next is a contract, not a binding legal contract, but a reaffirmation of the individual's integrity, attitudes, motivation, and skills. The questions do not paint a picture of things to come, but provide a reference point portraying what the person and the company can expect from each other. If the answers to all of the questions are favorable and the person shows every intention of doing what was stated, you have a prospect likely to contribute to the successful operation of your graphics system.

REFERENCE AND ACKNOWLEDGMENTS

The general outline and the examples used in this chapter were freely abstracted from "How to Get Started," by Lawrence Edwards, and the questionnaire at the end of the chapter was adapted from an original by Kenneth Durham. Both are in *The CAD/CAM Handbook*, and are used by permission of the copyright holder, Computervision.

11

Personnel Development and Organization

PERSONNEL CAREER DEVELOPMENT

I know what you are thinking at this point: "Why spend time looking at a whole chapter on personnel development and organization?" But, as manager of an Interactive Graphics Facility, you cannot forget about development of the people that work for you because most people allow chance happenings to shape their careers in an organization. If most people never plan their careers, why should you take the responsibility to do it for them? The simple answer is that you want to insure the survival of both yourself as a manager and your graphics facility as a viable organization.

An organization or manager should never overtly take over career planning from the affected employees, but should create an environment that both stimulates and encourages them to do their own planning. The task can be interactive if the partnership between you and the people who work for you is recognized.

You may have never realized it, but in many cases the only time interest is expressed in an employee is when a job vacancy needs to be filled. This need triggers a search that may result in a career move for some person in your department. Some departments do not even spend time to search inside for a qualified candidate, but recruit from the outside, ignoring the resources already available and in place.

In addition to career planning and development, any organization needs to make certain that everyone understands its basic purpose. It needs to show how the organizational structure will assist in carrying out those objectives and how each department within this structure contributes to reaching company objectives. To achieve this goal, you need to look at the following areas:

1. How are objectives and functions developed for your graphics department?
2. What is the most effective way to develop a career path network that not only accomplishes the department's objectives, but also stimulates and motivates employees?
3. What framework or process is necessary to help employees plan their careers?

To find real answers for these questions, all management must be committed to employee development and achievement. Management must believe a real payoff will result when people understand what job opportunities are available to them and what they need to do to prepare for those jobs.

As a general rule, graphic systems retain their usefulness for about five years, and then are made obsolete by new technology. Because of this quick turnover in technology, you need to be responsive to your organization's needs. You can start this process by completing your own analysis, describing your department's needs in detail, and then setting objectives to fulfill these needs. The process should include the following items:

1. Identifying the graphical information needs of your entire division, factoring those needs into discrete elements and prioritizing them. Think big. Develop long-range plan elements that look at graphical data transfer between groups.
2. Thinking of how you can improve the work environment to attract and retain people who can implement the long-range plan.
3. Developing a long-range plan element based on company objectives by reviewing the company's strategic plan and interviewing higher-level management to determine graphical information requirements. This long-range element can provide much of the basis needed for a career path development progam.
4. Developing a career path program for all interactive graphics systems personnel. The program should allow technicians to remain in that function, but permit growth without requiring a switch to professional or management positions.
5. Providing training for supervisory personnel and their subordinates to improve communications and establish a support network that allows people to cope with a rapidly changing environment.
6. Improving the communications process beween the interactive graphics group and all other groups that use the developed information by clearly identifying the responsibilities of each group and by specifying the documentation requirements needed by each group.

HUMAN RESOURCES PLAN AND POSITION DESCRIPTIONS

When a new technology is introduced in a work place, every upper management team wants to see a *human resource plan* and several levels of *position descriptions* that will aid in fitting the new technology into the existing process.

This section will aid you in producing the needed documents for your location. The sequel presents first a human resources plan for a multishift interactive graphics facility and then five levels of operator position descriptions.

INTERACTIVE GRAPHICS HUMAN RESOURCES PLAN

The personnel affected by the installation of the interactive graphics system represent a significant investment in technical skill and knowledge of this division's product. Based on this, the division will pursue a policy of continued employment opportunity for all personnel displaced because of present or future technological advancement programs based on the interactive graphics system.

The Plan

The plan is laid out over an 18-month period with major communication points and tasks strategically sequenced in line with the interactive graphics implementation schedule. The milestones for the interactive graphic human resources plan are shown schematically in Figure 1.

Job Descriptions

Job descriptions for drafting will be rewritten to include the use of interactive graphics equipment. Graphics will be a major portion of the drafting activities and requires a whole new approach in the method used in developing drawings.

New Hiring

New hiring in drafting must be for temporary positions only until full implementation and productive work has started using the interactive graphics equipment. Permanent hiring can then be administered in line with normal engineering load levels.

New Job Classifications

New job classifications will be established for the drafting function. Bidding or transfer into the new classifications will be based on the most senior qualified. Technical competence and compliance with the new job descriptions will be

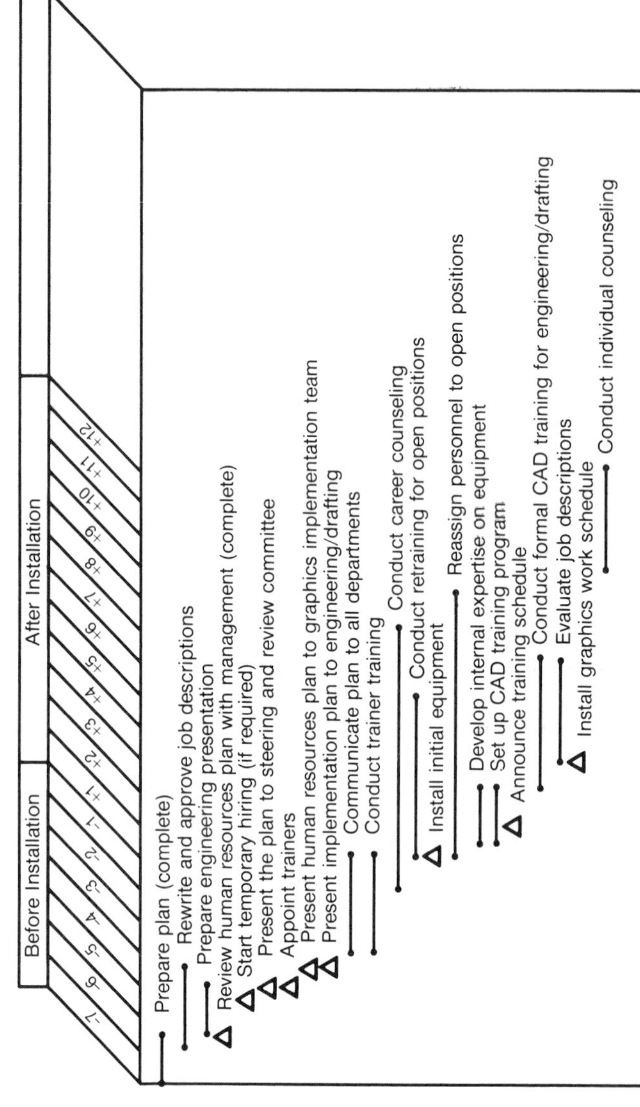

Figure 1 Human resources plan milestones.

for the drafting and design applications of interactive graphics. Code levels will be determined by personnel relations for the new positions in drafting and design.

During the position-filling process for the new job classification positions in drafting and design, counseling will be provided for personnel to assure proper qualification and placement in the new positions.

The Bid/Transfer Process

Bidding on or transfer to the new graphics positions will be based on the most senior qualified. Each person who is deemed technically qualified will be interviewed and ranked by seniority. Positions will be placed in line with the projected engineering load determined at that particular time. Monitoring of each selected individual will continue after selection to determine the person's adaptability to the graphics system.

Management Training for Career Counseling

Engineering management personnel will undergo training for career counseling. Personnel relations has had previous training in this area. This training will prepare management for career counseling which will be provided throughout implementation. The objectives will be to determine interest areas, develop career paths, and assist in job placement.

Off-Site Training

Training will be conducted off-site in varying degrees. It will be the primary concern to adequately prepare the key operating personnel before equipment is installed. "Beta Division," with already installed hardware, will be used for hands-on experience and consultation.

Formal courses will be considered for developing basic skills.

Other off-site training will be provided for the graphics coordinator and engineering/drafting management normally at the interactive graphic systems vendors' training facility.

Retraining

Personnel who do not want to operate the interactive graphics system and who desire relocation within "Alpha Division" will be retrained in an attempt to achieve the required qualifications in applying for open positions. The retraining approach will be given preference over seeking qualified personnel from outside the division.

Internal Relocation

After the bidding/transfer process and qualification counseling, personnel will be given the option of moving to other open positions within Alpha Division.

Qualifications for these positions will be posted. Retraining possibilities will be considered as a possibility to gain these qualifications.

Open positions may include management, professional, nonexempt, and hourly classifications. Open positions may be higher or lower codes, depending on the open position at that particular time. Provided the present salary rate fits within the open position rate range, the person's salary will remain the same for all relocation. Otherwise, it will be adjusted upward or downward. Personnel accepting these positions will be eligible to bid on new open positions at they occur. If open positions do not exist, personnel will be retained at the present rate until such time as these positions become available.

Internal Graphics Expertise

Prior to formal training, the key graphic system operators and the graphics coordinator will attempt to gain expertise on initial skills in the use of the graphics system after installation of the equipment. Loading, retrieval, and data manipulation will be attained as well as setting up and experimenting with various graphic aids.

The Training Program

The formal training program will be set up by the graphics coordinator in conjunction with the key graphics system operators. The formal graphics training schedule will be conducted over three 4-week sessions covering two shifts. Each session will involve 16 students and 2 trainers. Four graphics terminals will be available for the training, thus two students per shift per terminal will be utilized. This allows sufficient ''hands-on'' and observation time. The daily formal training schedule is shown in Figure 2.

The formal training schedule will be announced one month prior to the first session. Productive work will start following each session.

Drafting/Design Work Schedule

After the formal training period, a different work schedule will be used. The drafting/design work schedule will consist of two 8-hour overlapping shifts. This is intended to maximize the equipment usage each day. Preference to shift selection will be based on seniority for specified job requirements. To assure a proper mixture, imbalances will be realigned by management. If ''no preference'' is indicated, the person will be assigned after the shift selection process.

The work schedule allows ample interaction with engineers and other personnel on either shift and is in compliance with other site schedules. Two possible work schedules are shown in Figure 3.

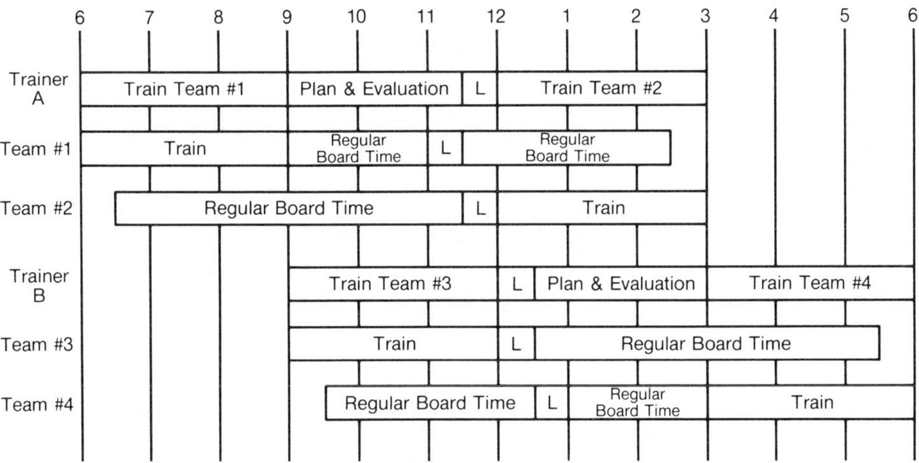

Figure 2 Daily training schedule.

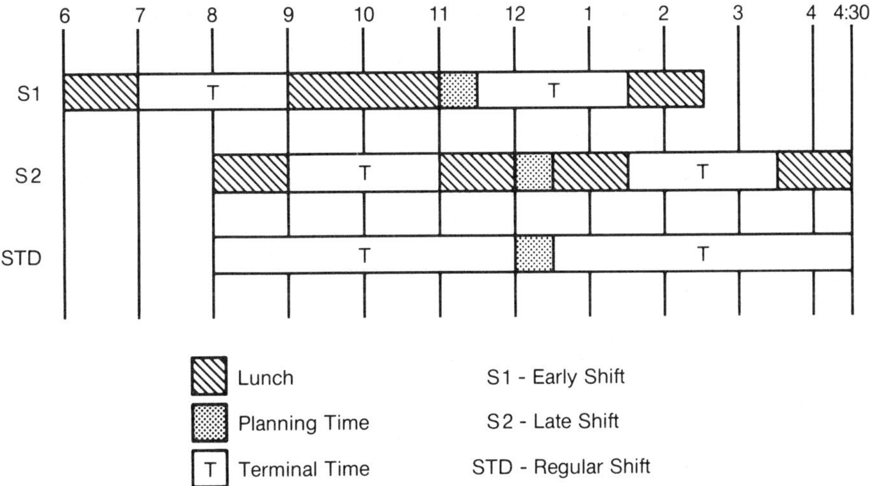

Figure 3a 10½-hour work schedule.

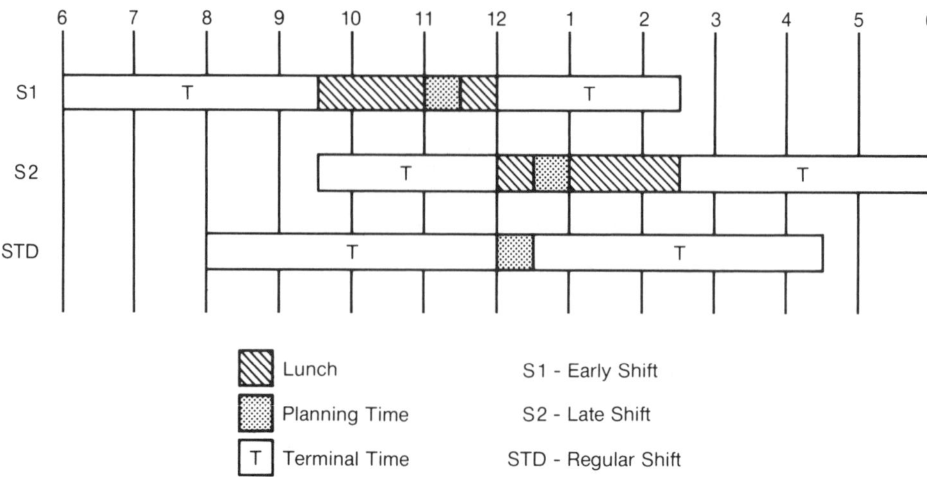

Figure 3b 12-hour work schedule.

Individual Counseling

Counseling will be provided for displaced personnel not selecting open position options or training. Efforts will be made for reassignment outside the division. Contacts will be maintained as open positions occur.

Communications

The Interactive Graphics Human Resources Plan will be presented in the following sequence:

1. Division Manager
2. Interactive Graphics System Steering and Review Committees
3. Interactive Graphics System Implementation Team
4. Engineering and Drafting

Other division personnel will be communicated to via group, divisional and company newsletters, and divisional news. This process will continue throughout implementation.

POSITION DESCRIPTIONS

Title: Interactive Graphics Design Operator (Level 0–Entry Level)

Basic Function. Under the general supervision of the department supervisor or manager, provide assistance to department personnel in performing various data management routines and producing final interactive graphics outputs through the various data plotting media.

Scope: This position involves logging, handling, and compiling information on department procedures to insure proper data management and configuration, and the operation of various operator-controlled, computer-assisted controlled-data output devices to produce final engineering documentation.

Work Performed

1. Perform minor daily maintenance and test plots on equipment.
2. Maintain integrity of magnetic tape data bank by assuring proper numbers of tapes and maintaining reconditioning specifications.
3. Convert interactive graphics data format to plotter format via plot form request.
4. Perform limited testing and analyze results of new plotter media.
5. Assure completeness of final documentation plots.
6. Maintenance of department work measurement system logs and reports.
7. Perform manual drafting tasks in support of other product design or engineering disciplines.
8. Perform related tasks as assigned.

Supervision Exercised

A. Positions directly supervised: None
B. Positions indirectly supervised: None

Supervision Received

A. Supervisor: Department supervisor and/or lead persons.
B. Supervision received: Observation to insure adherence to company and department working rules and operating procedures. Technical direction as required to assure proper performance of assigned duties and responsibilities.

Minimum Requirements

A. Equivalent education level required: High school or equivalent
B. Experience required: Minimum 1 year, job related.
C. Knowledge required: Knowledge of drafting standards similar to those used at this division.
D. Other: Must be willing to work second and/or third shifts.

Title: Senior Interactive Graphics Design Operator (Level 1)

Basic Function: Under the general supervision of the department supervisor or manager, provide assistance to department personnel in performing various data management routines and producing final interactive graphics outputs through the various data plotting media.

Scope: This position involves logging, handling and compiling information on department procedures to insure proper data management and configuration, and the operation of various computer-controlled data output devices to produce final engineering documentation.

Work Performed

1. Perform minor daily maintenance and test plots on equipment. Become familiar with hardware operations and major maintenance procedures.
2. Maintain integrity of magnetic tape data bank by assuring proper numbers or tapes and maintaining reconditioning specifications.
3. Convert interactive graphics data base format to plotter format via plot form request.
4. Interface with plotter media vendors. Be responsible for acquiring samples, testing and recording results of samples, and ordering of all plotter-related items.
5. Assure completeness of final documentation plots.
6. Provide training and guidance to lower-classified personnel.
7. Command a good working knowledge of interactive graphics drafting operations.
8. Maintenance of department work measurement system logs and reports.
9. Perform manual drafting tasks in support of other product design or engineering disciplines.
10. Procure microfilm of data using department operating procedure.
11. Procure printed circuit (PC) artwork photoplots using department operating procedure.
12. Basic operation of interactive graphics equipment to produce relatively simple drawings and effect minor updates.
13. Assist in the publication of interactive graphics data catalogs.
14. Perform related tasks as assigned.

Supervision Exercised

A. Positions directly supervised: None.
B. Positions indirectly supervised: None.

Supervision Received

A. Supervisor: Department supervisor and/or lead persons.
B. Supervision received: Observation to insure adherence to company and department working rules and operating procedures. Technical direction as required to assure proper performance of assigned duties and responsibilities.

Minimum requirements

A. Education level required: High school or equivalent.
B. Experience required: Minimum 2 years, job-related.
C. Knowledge required: Knowledge of drafting standards similar to those used at this division. Basic knowledge of automated drafting techniques.
D. Other: Must be willing to work second and/or third shifts.

Title: Assistant Interactive Graphics Product Designer (Level 2)

Basic Function: Under the general direction of the department supervisor and/or manager, perform design and documentation studies on new, varied, and complex problems as they relate to computer-aided/design, drafting, and manufacturing applications.

Scope: This position involves the operation of operator-controlled, computer-assisted automated design/drafting equipment and various computer peripheral hardware devices to create the interactive graphics data base to be used for final output of drafting/design documentation and numerical control tapes.

Work Performed

Automated Drafting System

1. Serve as back-up for department supervisor or lead person.
2. Using preferred interactive graphics techniques, generate documentation from "rough" layouts provided by other departments. These documents may include final electrical and mechanical production drawings as well as printed circuit card master layouts and various charts and graphs.
3. Perform necessary computer operations to facilitate everyday work routines and have a good knowledge of all hardware and software operations and minor trouble-shooting techniques.
4. Interface with interactive graphics supervisor or lead person on data base control, standardization, and library part preparation.

5. Provide direction to interactive graphics personnel to promote interactive graphics operating techniques, standardization, and smooth work flow.
6. Help interactive graphics supervisor status active programs and maintain schedule requirements.
7. Help in training of newly hired personnel.
8. Prepare layouts for other interactive graphics operating personnel from system engineering inputs.
9. Perform manual drafting tasks in support of other product design engineering disciplines.
10. Perform minor daily readiness and preventive maintenance routines as assigned.
11. Assist in the publication of interactive graphics data catalogs.
12. Check the incorporation of engineering change notices and keep interactive graphics shift leaders aware of any new requirements that would affect existing documentation.
13. Perform related tasks as assigned.

Automated Design System

1. Serve as back-up for department supervisor or lead person.
2. Using preferred interactive graphics techniques, perform detail design and documentation tasks from digitized design data base, from manually generated engineering layouts and from verbal instructions from senior interactive graphics designers.
3. Perform necessary computer operations to facilitate everyday work routines and have a good knowledge of all hardware and software operations and minor trouble-shooting techniques.
4. Interface with interactive graphics supervisor or lead person on data base control, standardization, and library part preparation.
5. Perform minor daily readiness and preventive maintenance routines as assigned.
6. Assist in the publication of interactive graphics data catalogs.
7. Check the incorporation of engineering change notices and keep interactive graphics shift leaders aware of any new requirements that would affect existing documentation.
8. Perform related tasks as assigned.

Supervision Exercised

A. Positions directly supervised:None
B. Positions indirectly supervised:Interactive graphics positions levels 0-2 when assigned as shift leader.

Supervision Received

A. Supervisor: Department supervisor and/or lead persons.
B. Supervision received: Observation to insure adherence to company and department working rules and operating procedures. Technical direction as required to assure proper performance of assigned duties and responsibilities.

Minimum Requirements

A. Education level required: Associate degree in an applicable discipline or equivalent.
B. Experience required: Minimum of 6 years job-related experience including 5 years producing engineering packaging designs and production drawings.
C. Knowledge required: Thorough working knowledge of design drafting technique similar to those used at this division. Basic knowledge of design and engineering fundamentals including:

    1. Mechanics
    2. Kinematics
    3. Strength of materials
    4. Machine design elements
    5. Reliability
    6. Maintainability
    7. Electrical/electronic packaging design
    8. Printed circuit design principles

   Good working knowledge of manufacturing processes. General knowledge of computer systems. Good knowledge of configuration control procedures.
D. Other: Must be willing to work second and/or third shifts.

Title: Interactive Graphics Product Designer (Level 3)

Basic Function: Under the general direction of the department section head, supervisor, or manager, perform design and documentation studies on new, varied, and complex problems as they relate to computer-aided design, drafting, and manufacturing applications.

Scope: This position involves the operation of operator-controlled, computer-assisted, automated design/drafting equipment and various computer peripheral hardware devices to create interactive graphics data base to be used for final output of documentation and numerical control tapes.

Work Performed

Automated Drafting System

1. Serve as department lead person or as back-up for the department supervisor or lead person when assigned.
2. Review and analyze all pertinent contract procurement specifications and program work instructions for design and data preparation requirements.
3. Using preferred interactive graphics techniques, generate documentation from "rough" layouts provided by other departments. These documents may include final electrical and mechanical production drawings as well as printed circuit card master layouts and various charts and graphs.
4. Perform necessary computer operations to facilitate everyday work routines and have a good knowledge of all hardware and software operations and minor trouble-shooting techniques.
5. Provide direction to interactive graphics personnel to promote interactive graphics operating techniques, standardization, and smooth work flow.
6. Help the interactive graphics supervisor status activate programs and maintain schedule requirements.
7. Conduct training sessions for newly hired interactive graphics operating personnel.
8. Perform minor daily readiness and preventive maintenance routines as assigned.
9. Participate to the extent required in the preparation and review of department bids.
10. Participate in periodic state-of-the-art reviews held to examine the department's technical and competitive posture regarding the latest technological advances of interactive graphics hardware/software manufacturers and other related manufacturing divisions.
11. Assist the department section head in the preparation of the interactive graphics department expansion plans including the resultant budgets and their justifications.
12. Participate in and/or conduct packaging design reviews.
13. Perform related tasks as assigned.

Automated Design System

1. Serve as department lead person or as back-up for the department supervisor or lead person when assigned.
2. Review and analyze all pertinent contract procurement specifications and program work instructions for design and data preparation requirements.
3. Using preferred interactive graphics techniques, perform detail design and documentation tasks from digitized design data base, from manually generated

engineering layouts and from verbal instructions of senior interactive graphics designers.

4. Perform necessary computer operations to facilitate everyday work routines and have a good knowledge of all hardware and software operations and minor trouble-shooting techniques.
5. Interface with interactive graphics supervisor or lead person on data base control, standardization, and library part preparation.
6. Perform minor daily readiness and preventive maintenance routines as assigned.
7. Conduct training sessions for newly hired interactive graphics operating personnel.
8. Participate to the extent required in the preparation and review of department bids.
9. Participate in periodic state-of-the-art reviews held to examine the department's technical and competitive posture regarding the latest technological advances of interactive graphics hardware/software manufacturers and other related manufacturing divisions.
10. Assist the department section head in the preparation of the interactive graphics department expansion plans including the resultant budgets and their justifications.
11. Participate in and/or conduct packaging design reviews.
12. Perform related tasks as assigned.

Supervision Exercised

A. Positions directly supervised: Interactive graphics positions levels 0-3 when assigned as department lead person.
B. Positions indirectly supervised: Interactive graphics positions levels 0-2 when assigned as shift leader.

Supervision Received

A. Supervisor: Department supervisor and/or lead persons.
B. Supervision received: Observation to insure adherence to company and department working rules and operating procedures. Technical direction as required to assure proper performance of assigned duties and responsibilities.

Minimum Requirements

A. Education level required: Associate degree in an applicable discipline or equivalent.

B. Experience required: Minimum of 8-10 years job-related experience including 6 years producing engineering designs and production drawings.
C. Knowledge required: Thorough working knowledge of design drafting techniques similar to those used at this division. Thorough knowledge of design and engineering fundamentals including:

   1. Mechanics
   2. Kinematics
   3. Strength of materials
   4. Machine design elements
   5. Reliability
   6. Maintainability
   7. Electrical/electronic packaging design
   8. Printed circuit design principles

   Good working knowledge of manufacturing processes. General knowledge of computer systems. Good knowledge of configuration control procedures.
D. Other: Must be willing to work second and/or third shifts.

Title: Senior Interactive Graphics Designer (Level 4)

Basic Function: Under the general direction of the department section head, supervisor, or manager, perform design and documentation studies on new, varied, and complex problems as they relate to computer-aided design, drafting, and manufacturing applications.

Scope: This position involves the operation of operator-controlled, computer-assisted, automated design/drafting equipment and various computer peripheral hardware devices to create an interactive graphics data base to be used for final output of documentation and numerical control tapes.

Work Performed

1. Serve as department lead person or as back-up for the department supervisor or lead person when assigned.
2. Review and analyze all pertinent contract procurement specifications and program work instructions for design and data preparation requirements.
3. Using preferred interactive graphics techniques, perform complex and sophisticated designs, detail designs and documentation from digitized design data base, from manually generated engineering layouts and from verbal instructions of design engineering or systems engineering personnel.
4. Perform necessary computer operations to facilitate everyday work routines and have a good knowledge of all hardware and software operations and minor trouble-shooting techniques.

5. Interface with interactive graphics supervisor or lead person on data base control, standardization and library part preparation.
6. Perform minor daily readiness and preventative maintenance routine as assigned.
7. Help in training of newly hired personnel.
8. Perform manual drafting tasks in support of other product design engineering disciplines.
9. Assist in the publication of interactive graphics data catalogs.
10. Check the incorporation of engineering change notices and keep interactive graphics shift leaders aware of any new requirements that would affect existing documentation.
11. Perform related tasks as assigned.

Supervision Exercised

A. Positions directly supervised: Interactive graphics positions levels 0-4 when assigned as department lead person.
B. Positions indirectly supervised: Interactive graphics positions levels 0-3 when assigned as shift leader.

Supervision Received

A. Supervisor: Department supervisor and/or lead persons.
B. Supervision received: Observation to insure adherence to company and department working rules and operating procedures. Technical direction as required to assure proper performance of assigned duties and responsibilities.

Minimum Requirements

A. Education level required: Associate degree in an applicable discipline or equivalent.
B. Experience required: Minimum of 10 years job-related experience including 8 years producing engineering designs and production drawings.
C. Knowledge required: Thorough working knowledge of design drafting techniques similar to those used at this division. Thorough knowledge of design and engineering fundamentals including:

    1. Mechanics
    2. Strength of materials
    3. Reliability
    4. Electrical/electronic packaging design
    5. Kinematics

6. Machine design elements
7. Maintainability
8. Printed circuit design principles

Good working knowledge of manufacturing processes. General knowledge of computer systems. Good knowledge of configuration control procedures.

D. Other: Must be willing to work second and/or third shifts.

REFERENCES

The material presented in this chapter was sanitized from material available from both Westinghouse and non-Westinghouse organizations in the public domain. As such, the presented material is a combination of many sources and represents the actual practice in no single company or division.

12 Training

The phasing in of an interactive graphics system, even with extensive planning and preparation, is always a major undertaking. Your success, in terms of increased productivity and job satisfaction, will require a commitment from top to bottom to learning a whole new approach to design and drafting as quickly and thoroughly as possible.

PLANNING FOR TRAINING

Our experience in training computer-aided design/computer-aided manufacturing (CAD/CAM) users, supervisors, and managers has reinforced our belief in the value of taking time to plan a thorough training program with an eye toward the future. Given the normal organizational variables of employee turnover, absence, and tight production schedules, it is in your best interest to plan training with the goal of establishing both broad and deep expertise within your organization.

The planning section of this chapter will help you focus on the following areas to plan your training needs:

Step I Take inventory of your organization to alert yourself to unique needs which will shape your training plans.

Step II Given the alternatives available to you, define a training strategy and select a particular matrix or sequence of courses, for each of your personnel.

Step III Generate a training calendar to meet a workable time-frame for you and your staff.

STEP I TAKING INVENTORY

Graphic system users vary widely in training needs and in circumstances which favor certain training options. Listed below are those factors which will be of importance to you in planning training.

Your Experience with CAD/CAM

As a new user of a graphics system, your training plan should be worked out according to the steps outlined in this chapter. The course sequence should begin with a manager's seminar and continue through advanced application courses.

As an experienced user who meets vendor course prerequisites, you can select courses to meet your projected needs. You may wish to train personnel in anticipation of employee turnover, or anticipated expansion. Advanced courses can assist you in using your present software more productively, or prepare you for the arrival of newly purchased software.

Resources Committed to Training

The resources available to you to put your training plan into effect may include: (1) training credits awarded to you with the system purchase and additional dollars available in your training budget; (2) graphic system work stations available at your site for training; and (3) company personnel who can be assigned training responsibility.

The number of training credits available to you may be determined by consulting your purchase contract or your local sales representative. If your are an experienced user, your system vendor should maintain an up-to-date account of training credit activity and be able to inform you of the number of credits remaining in your account.

Practice is an essential ingredient in becoming proficient in the use of a CAD/CAM system. The greater the amount of system time which can be committed to practice after basic training, the sooner work station users reach high levels of productivity. Many users have been able to designate one or two work stations, or an entire system, for training and practice during start-up operations.

If you have experienced personnel using the graphics system you may have someone to assume the training planning functions. If your company is new to this technology, it is essential that someone be assigned such responsibility following delivery and installation of the system. Assigning training responsibility as a chief duty is a most important element in integrating interactive graphics into your firm's daily business.

Describe Your General Training Requirements

Identify who in your organization requires training. For most businesses, regardless of application, training is needed for four broad categories of personnel:

Work station users. Designers, drafters, and others who will use the system on a daily basis. Consider training one person per work station per shift, plus one or two additional personnel for backup in case of absence.

A manager, supervisor, or lead operator responsible for maintaining work throughput and handling the day-to-day operation of the system as a whole. This requirement may have been counted in the above paragraph.

A department manager responsible for managing the role of the system in the company environment. At some locations a system manager may be responsible for a number of systems, each led by a supervisor.

Other levels of company management for whom familiarity with interactive graphics technology is important or of general interest.

Most vendors offer training to meet requirements of all company personnel involved with interactive graphics.

Describe Your Specific Training Requirements

Which of the following job titles most nearly describe the personnel in your organization who you wish to train? How many people fit into each category?

Mechanical designer or detailer
Printed circuit designer
Electrical drafter or designer
Architect/illustrator
Numerical control programmer who creates geometry and tool paths
Integrated circuit designer
Piping designer/drafter
Programmers who (1) have general responsibilities, (2) write NC postprocessors, or (3) assist designers
Company executive
Department manager

STEP II DEFINING A TRAINING STRATEGY

Once you have clearly specified your training resources, and the number and job functions of the people that must be trained, take time to review the alternatives your vendor offers to allow you to maximize the impact of your training budget.

Each of the training sequences, which follows in Figure 1, recommends a series of courses or programs through which managers, operators, and others should progress to make training and system implementation in general, most effective.

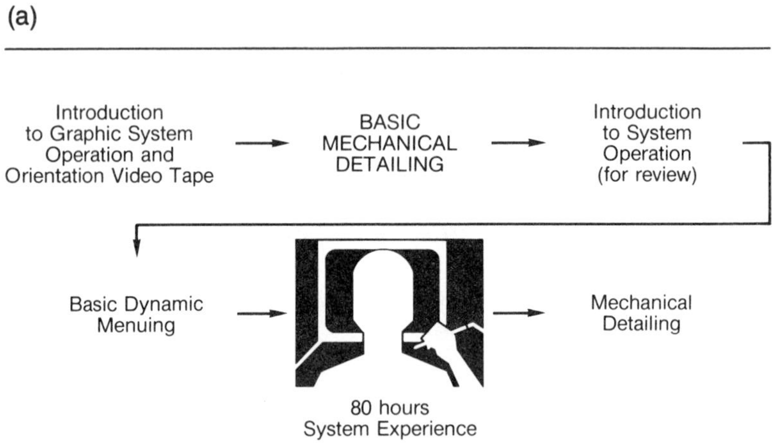

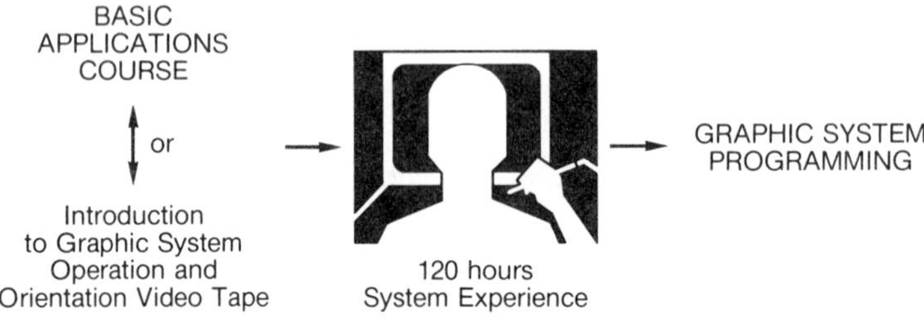

Figure 1 Possible training sequences. (a) Basic mechanical design operator, (b) system programmer.

(c)

- Programmer with responsibility to assist designers.

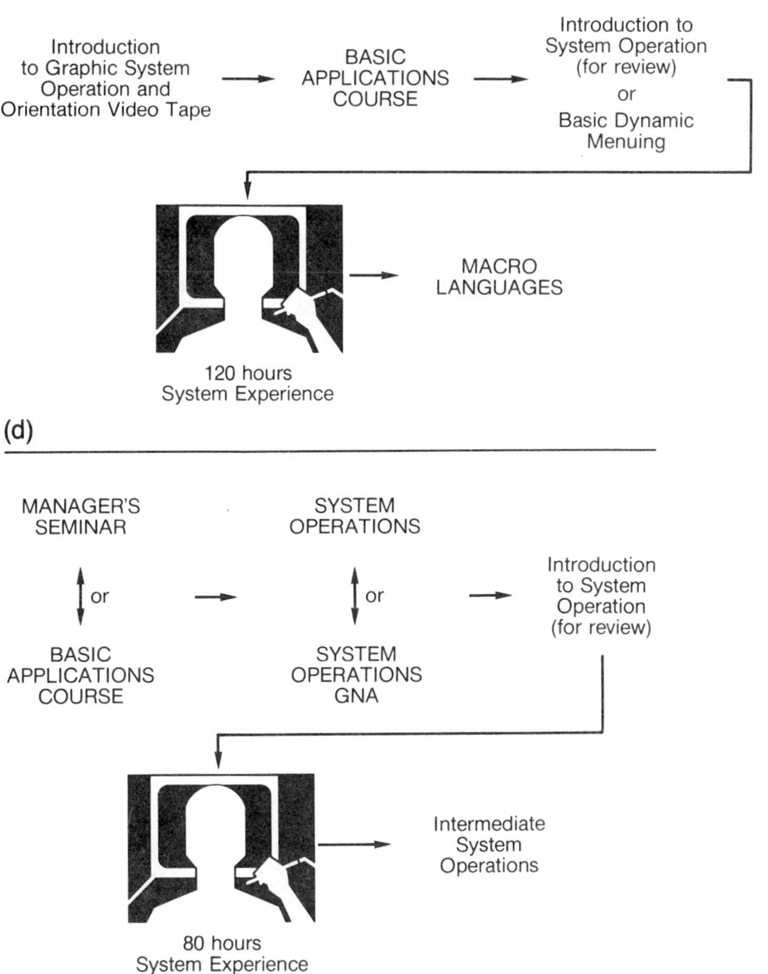

(e)

- Responsible for introduction and implementation of the graphics system

MANAGERS SEMINAR

Figure 1 (c) Advanced sysem programmer, (d) advanced design operator, (e) executive or department manager.

Each sequence begins by specifying a job title which should describe closely the functions of people who must be trained. Choose those sequences which apply to your organization and use them to determine where you wish to use the training credit you have available, then, total other courses and education products to which training credit do not apply or for which additional expenditures are required.

STEP III GENERATING A TRAINING CALENDAR

The final step in completing your training plan is to place it within a workable time frame. To do this, you should *focus your training schedule upon your projected system installation date.*

1. As early as possible, system managers should enroll in the Manager's Seminar course to become acquainted with the system and your vendor's services. Supporting documents from the vendor should also be examined for preliminary training.
2. Systems managers should be scheduled for training two weeks prior to installation. They should arrange to be on-site at the scheduled delivery time.
3. Operators should be trained near the date of installation or shortly after in teams of two or three. Should large numbers of operators need to be trained, you may wish to shift your strategy to the creation of in-house training and training your own in-house trainer.
4. Advanced training should be undertaken by those who have excelled at using the system, and who now meet the prerequisites for additional training.
5. Make use of other available services from your vendor at the proper times. For example, vendor video tapes can be used to train all teams except the first, before they progress through formal courses at your vendor's education center.

A last word before putting your training plan in place. One of the most important factors in gaining fast, productive use of your graphic sytem is experience. Within each course sequence chart, a block representing experience on the system is included. Specific minimum intervals of actual system use between courses are recommended as prerequisites for further training. Take these into account as you complete your planning. Should certain courses not be available at the precise date you feel you need them, you will find additional experience prior to returning to training a significant benefit rather than lost time.

VENDOR-BASED EDUCATIONAL OPTIONS

Your vendor provides a number of training alternatives to suit your particular company profile. The following descriptions will take you one step closer in defining a clear training pathway.

Education Center Courses

Customer training courses should be available from your vendor and should be taught by certified, experienced instructors. Please consult the educational course schedule of your vendor for course dates and locations.

Media Services Training

Your vendor should offer video- and audio-tape training courses for your system. These programs are excellent as supplemental training before and after formal classroom instruction.

On-Site Training

Under certain circumstances, a customer training instructor from your vendor can travel to your site to conduct classroom instruction for courses listed in the vendor class catalog.

Train-the-Trainer

For users who have a large start-up training requirement on-site, most vendors offer a "train-the-trainer" program. Its purpose is to train customer personnel to offer basic system instruction on site. If you have 20 or more people to train this may be a cost effective alternative for you.

Applications Engineering

Your vendor's applications engineers are experts at instructing customers in the use of graphics software. A visit from such an engineer should be incorporated into your total training plan whether your needs are for posttraining support, or more formal on-site training.

Typically, customers will require an applications engineer on site shortly after receiving formal training for purposes of review and reinforcement of graphics operating concepts.

Later, when basic concepts have been mastered, an applications engineer can visit your site for over-the-shoulder assistance or to conduct more advanced seminars tailored to your organization's specific requirements.

The price of initial application engineer support is usually included in your system purchase price, and can be continued as part of a full service maintenance contract. Additional applications engineer support may be purchased separately.

Productivity Services

Your vendor should offer a wide range of consulting services prior to installation, during start-up phases, and later on, after you have been using your system in a production environment. These services include visits to your site for a predelivery consultation and productivity review. Issues of CAD/CAM management are discussed, and recommendations to increase productivity are made.

KEY FEATURES

The courses offered by your vendor should give the following important features:

1. Instructors thoroughly experienced in both system operation and specific industry applications.
2. Individual guidance assured by small class size (10 persons maximum), and the availability of instructors for the full 8 hours daily that the lab is open.
3. Two students per terminal assures plenty of hands-on training during basic courses.
4. Comprehensive schedule of training course on every level from basic terminal operation through user programming, higher-level applications, and management strategies for increasing productivity.

Typical course outlines are described below.

BASIC OPERATOR'S COURSES

PC/ES Basic Operator's Course: 5 Days

Prerequisites: Familiarity with printed circuit board design and fabrication techniques are helpful.

Purpose: To equip the student to start his or her own symbol library; create and annotate an electrical schematic, component diagram, and board; route a simple board; and generate a magnetic tape.

Structure: 50% lecture, 50% lab time.

Content: Basic drawing and editing commands. Operation of the various interactive components. System power-up and shut-down procedures. Use of nodal information and properties. Labs focus on solving representative PC/ES problems.

Scheduling: Optimal time, during and/or right after installation, so that the training can be applied as soon as possible.

MD Basic Operator's Course: 5 Days

Prerequisites: Knowledge and experience in drafting techniques in an engineering/design environment.

Purpose: To equip a student to start his or her own symbol library; create, annotate, and dimension simple two- and three-dimensional drawings (i.e., use the system to do just about any basic graphical tasks required of a designer or draftsman). Also to introduce the basic concepts of numerical control machining.

Structure: 60% lecture, 40% lab time.

Content: System interactive operations. System power-up and power-down procedures. Command syntax. Using the basic drawing and editing commands. Job analysis methods. Magnetic tape management. Introduction to three-dimensional concepts, surfaces and use of three-dimensional and associated commands. Layering and dimensioning. General and special applications. Text insertion. Menu design.

Scheduling: Optimal time, during and/or right after installation, so that the training can be continued immediately upon return to job site.

Application Course (Intermediate Level): 5 Days

Prerequisites: Basic Operator's Course, preferably coupled with at least three months experience on the system (for MD students), or 40–60 days for PC/ES students. Knowledge of operations such as log-in, entering graphics, drawing simple geometric figures usng direct digitizing and explicit coordinates, zooming, controlling and listing parameters, saving and restoring parts.

Purpose: To briefly review topics and procedures covered in the basic course, while extending the operator's knowledge. Graduates will be able to perform on the system at a higher (intermediate) level by mastering additional commands, techniques, and operational methods.

Structure: 40% lecture, 60% lab. Seminar orientation allows ample time to discuss any problems and procedures related to a user's particular application.

Content: PC/ES students learn to refine component placement and routing. MD students learn how to use nodal information, data extract procedures for bill of materials, reports, and procedures for obtaining numerical control manufacturing tapes. Other topics: advanced three-dimensional applications, surfaces and associated applications, advanced part editing techniques, mass properties and finite-element modeling.

Scheduling: Optimal time, after the student has had at least three months on the graphics system (MD operators), or 40–60 hours for PC/ES students.

Management Seminar: 5 Days

Entrance criteria: Open to a manager or high-level supervisor of a design or drafting group.

Purpose: To provide management-oriented information and strategies covering optimal installation operation task scheduling, personnel selection and training. The overall objective is to maximize productivity and accelerate payback.

Manager-to-manager dialogue: Seminar course is conducted by the vendor's training manager and key guest speakers who have been graphic system managers and are thoroughly familiar with the programming, operation, and management aspects of such systems.

Structure: Almost entirely seminar format, following brief, intensive hands-on refresher course in system operation.

Content: Geared to, and largely determined by, user's own application, environment, problems, and objectives. Typical subjects: how to cost-justify your system more precisely. How to adapt the command language to your needs, and in general, how to make the system fit your particular application. Criteria for selecting the first people on the system—the key to success. How to hire, train, and motivate them; hiring practices, wage scales, labor-management considerations, upgrading personnel. Philosophy of terminal layout. How to manage an acceptance test. Creating the optimum environment for productive work (the right lighting, ways to minimize distractions).

Scheduling: Optimal time, 2–3 months before system installation.

INCREASING TRAINING EFFECTIVENESS

Training is most effective when individuals go to courses with realistic expectations of what they can learn that will be useful on the job.

You should have at least two interviews with each person you have scheduled to attend a course; one in which you help the individual plan for participation; and one or more later interviews in which you help relate the course material and instruction to the work situation.

You should have your first talk with the person at least one month before the scheduled course. In this first meeting, ask the person to set learning objectives, and to list what the individual expects and wants from the learning experience. This will help develop some key result areas important to individual functional objectives.

Within one week after the course, meet with each participant for a debriefing. Some questions you might consider are: Will the course content be valuable improving performance? What was the most relevant? What does the participant plan to apply? Were the participant's learning objectives met? Is there anything, as a result of the experience, the participant would like to do differently? Is any support needed from you to do it?

Ask the participant to set some measurable objectives for improving performance in the work situation. Finally, set a time when you both review the progress in relation to accomplishing the objectives.

REFERENCES

Adapted from available Computervision and Westinghouse training materials.

13
System Planning and Organization

Important issues relative to the interactive graphics system can easily be overlooked in the installation process. Issues of data storage, library organization, data base development and so on. If proper attention is not given these issues before and during the installation process, you might find it very expensive to reorganize your system after one or two years of operation.

DATA STORAGE

Several techniques can be used in the storage of data files. Some are more applicable to storing engineering design files by the user uncontrolled by the operating procedures of the facility. Others are more appropriate for storing production design files under control of the procedures adopted by the graphics facility management. See Chapter 14 for details on storage procedures.

Engineering design data files stored by graphics system users on magnetic tape are normally considered short-term storage of personal data bases and libraries. If any control exists on what is stored on the magnetic tape, its purpose is to prevent writing over existing data files. In an open shop, the graphics user is responsible for the transfer of data to and from magnetic tape and disc. The physical storage of the magnetic tape can be informal; the facility may provide cabinets for tape storage, or the user may store the tape at the work station or desk. Retaining engineering historical files is a user-controlled option that requires minimal controls for version identification and possibly for location. Because of the extra effort involved, as well as minimal need for archival recall, engineering historical files are seldom retained for long periods of time in the graphics system.

The storage of engineering design data in a closed shop is normally done under control of formal procedures for use of the magnetic tape facility. With several system users reading and writing data to tape from repetitive workflows, daily controls must be installed. This in turn gives users the ability and freedom to access any job within the tape storage, but prevents interference with other users.

One method of writing engineering data files to magnetic tape is by dumping or copying the disc on a daily basis. Depending on the daily work volume, the techniques may require multiple tape drives to provide sufficient read/write capacity. If a particular day's dump involves 30 data files and a need for the 27th file develops, the read-time to find the requested file is much longer than accessing the first file on the tape. Another technique for data storage is to use small magnetic tapes and store singular data files on individual tapes. This minimizes tape-drive activity as well as wait time for the system user. Although it expands the tape storage facility and requires a system for selecting the right tape, it provides a convenient, usable library for many users to share.

Production data files need a control system for identification of each file version beginning with its release for production. The control system must accurately support the location and version identification of each file, and any other information required for internal interface. Volume of business and data-storage tenure are major factors in deciding which method to use for data storage.

If production data storage is done locally within the facility, the immediate question facing the facility manager is whether or not he or she needs a secure, controlled (for humidity, temperature, and dust) clean room. Long-term tape storage in a normal room environment is risky and perhaps costly if stored files are unreadable. Another important factor is whether enough hardware (central processor unit ports, terminals, and tape drives) is available. Creating single copies of engineering files is acceptable, but redundancy through duplication of production files is a must. The second copy should also be stored remotely in case of a local disaster. The only advantage of local storage is immediate access.

File storage within a centralized graphics facility is another alternative. Most centralized facilities have controlled areas for data storage, as well as the additional capacity and personnel to support additional file storage activity. The data can be transmitted from the local facility to the centralized facility via a communication line or magnetic tape.

If the transmittal activity is basically one way with minimal recall, the magnetic tape method of transmission is a logical alternative. While this method eliminates the need for capital investment and the installation of a communication line, it does take advantage of the centralized storage facility.

On-line communication lines are convenient and easy to use. From the local facility's standpoint, the only effort involved is to direct the terminal to either send or receive data files from the centralized facility. All other procedural requirements such as file storage, generating redundancy, and maintenance of archived files are performed by the centralized facility. If the data storage is to be responsive and allow the user to request any version on file, the centralized facility must also provide an on-line index to allow visibility in retrieving, and visual inquiry before requesting transmittal. Although past experience has convinced many users that the cost and usability of such a centralized facility makes it questionable for storage, it should certainly be evaluated for cost-effectiveness.

LIBRARY ORGANIZATION

The graphics facility library is a collection of frequently used user-defined and implemented blocks of design data. Its organization and definition are probably one of the most difficult and complex tasks associated with the development of the data base.

A number of problems make it difficult to develop a new graphics library:

1. New users are unfamiliar with the new system. Using other facility libraries can certainly save development effort, but usually requires some overhaul for the user's specific needs.
2. The facility cannot become operational until the library is conceptually and functionally defined. New facilities are frequently developed with optimistic start-up schedules that are difficult to achieve, and result in libraries that are defined hurriedly, with only short-term needs addressed.
3. An established facility may add a new work effort with library requirements that do not exist in the present library. If a future computer-aided manufacture (CAM) activity is contemplated, a significant change to the existing library concept might be necessary.
4. After a library has been established and many design files developed from library information, it is extremely difficult to alter the library definition and not affect the existing design files. To correct the problem, a new library must be created for new designs, and the existing library maintained for the old designs. The additional library definition uses valuable disc capacity.

These problems usually require redefinition of the library. It is common for a new facility to redefine its library several times before satisfying a majority of its users' needs. To reduce the impact of this effort, communication with well-established facilities is recommended. In addition, the users or potential users should be surveyed to obtain a better understanding of their library requirements.

DATA BASE DEVELOPMENT

Data base organization and development is normally the responsibility of your graphics vendor. Contact him for manuals describing the details of the data base.

The remainder of this discussion is included for completeness of the data base discussion.

A graphics data base is usually constructed in one of two ways: (1) nodal, where the system contains software intelligence needed to relate different parts of the design data generating outputs reflecting that association; and (2) non-nodal, where the data base is constructed as a graphics file and does not have internal association of nongraphical information within the data base.

The selection of either data base structure is usually related to work application and the need for data associativity in performing that work. Consideration is also given before writing the graphics system to the cost-effectiveness of both present and future work effort without the need for a major overhaul of the data base.

The facility's strategic plans and their relation to the graphic systems software need careful consideration before committing to the use of nodal techniques since they entail additional CPU processing. If the review indicates the need for nodal data, the user has two options for developing it: (1) to input the design data using nodal system commands and have it created as nodal data immediately upon insertion, or (2) to input the design data using non-nodal system commands and have it created initially as a non-nodal file. Subsequently, the data file can be reprocessed through a "nodalizer" program which machine-converts the non-nodal file to a nodal file.

The selection of a non-nodal data base significantly reduces CPU data generation throughput by requiring continual manning. It also requires subsequent processing, but only requires manning to initialize the job. This ties up one of the system tasks. To take care of this, the system hardware should include an inexpensive alphanumeric terminal for file processing instead of using a graphics terminal.

DESIGN DATA LAYERING

Developing methods for layering digital design data is very important to the versatility of the graphics facility workflow. Separation of information in the data base is necessary to facilitate the internal needs of data processing as well as serve its functional structure.

In many design applications, there is a frequent need to work within the part geometry and not with the associated part dimensions. If these two kinds of design data are stored on the same layer within the data base, excess CPU time is spent generating both kinds of data every time either one must be accessed. With some types of plots, as much as 75% extra terminal time can be spent plotting more data than is required.

If the facility's application requires both CAD and CAM data bases, the separation of design data can be even more complex. As a work unit is entered into the system in an engineering CAD application, the layering structure may be fairly simple. When the design becomes a CAM application, the design data can be subdivided to allow outputs to answer both CAD and CAM requirements. A good example is a printed circuit design application. In the CAD data base, all the component location information is sorted in a specific layer of the data base. This data is primarily used to graphically plot the engineering assembly drawing. When the design requires CAM assembly techniques, such as mechanical assembly or autoinsertion, this data layering will allow separate graphics to be generated for assembly and inspection drawings, as well as data for specific numerical control manufacturing programs. The separated layers can be subsequently software-composited for replots of engineering assembly drawings.

The flexibility of design data separation can create problems for the graphics system user. There must be well-defined rules for user selection of the proper layer for data creation as well as for generating outputs. In addition, special system programs called "execute files" can simplify layer selection. They allow the system to select, from a predefined organization a particular layer for a specific need such as data input, part revision, or plotting.

SOFTWARE SUPPORT

The first installation of a graphics system in a company or division is normally a turnkey system for both hardware and software. This is often due to the user's lack of familiarity with interactive graphics technology as well as the need not to interfere with normal operations. The initial installation is usually justified, purchased, installed, and brought on-line according to a specific timetable which does not allow for software education or development.

Special software needs for the first system are usually written by the system vendor. As facility personnel become experienced in using the system software, there is generally a need to modify some of the standard routines or to tailor the system to the company's specific needs.

Expanding the facility, as well as addressing new projects outside the original scope of work, may also require software development. To respond to the need for special software support, the facility manager has three alternatives: (1) purchase services from the vendor, (2) add programmers to the staff, or (3) purchase the services of outside consultants.

The advantage of purchasing either the vendor's sevices or those of outside consultants is that no additional programmers are required within the company. Proceeding in this fashion saves the user the labor-hours it would probably require to give those additional programmers the necessary vendor software training, as well as a typical learning curve familiarization time. More importantly, since the vendor does the software development, all subsequent software releases automatically update the user's purchased programs if the contract was written correctly.

When purchasing software from the vendor, a detailed program-requirements specification must be written by the facility's staff. The specification needs to be clearly written and precise in detail to guarantee a software program that solves the problem. Adding a programmer to the staff significantly reduces the need for a complete and accurate document. It is extremely difficult to define planned requirements, receive the newly developed software, and expect it to work without some changes. Good functional software is usually the result of repetitive action between the vendor's programmer and the system user. This is difficult if the programmer is not knowledgeable about the specific application or is located many miles away and daily communcation is limited to the telephone.

The other notable advantage of having a staff programmer is the local control of software development priorities and schedules. Typically, software development results from a new time-sensitive commitment within the company to automate a new function for additional cost savings.

A disadvantage of having a staff programmer is the need for continual review of software revisions from the vendor. After receiving each revision release, the staff programmer must review the changes incorporated to determine if they affect any of his developed software. This review requires time and occasional coordination with the vendor software staff to interpret the changes.

Another need that in-house programmers must address is the development of interface software for different vendor hardware and systems. As facilities grow and become innovative and flexible, new hardware may be needed for an unrelated work requirement and the original system vendor may not either provide an interface or market it. The responsibility for the feasibility study, as well as the integration of brand X and Y hardware/software, is typically placed on the facility staff. In these situations, vendors X and Y do not normally communicate with each other, but directly support the facility staff in their interface development.

REFERENCE AND ACKNOWLEDGMENTS

Based on format and ideas presented in "How to Organize and Manage a CAD/CAM Facility," by Donald Earll in *The CAD/CAM Handbook*, published by Computervision.

14

Systems Administration

This chapter presents two different approaches to uniform operation of your graphics facility by all personnel. The first, called Generic Drafting Standards and Procedures, attempts in much detail to place all information for a Computervision graphics system in one document. The second, called Outline Procedures, presents a more general loose-leaf format.

The advantages and disadvantages for each format are obvious. Some form of the two formats, perhaps a combination of the two, will provide uniform system administration at your location.

GENERIC DRAFTING STANDARDS AND PROCEDURES

Preface

This manual documents Alpha Corporation, XYZ Division drafting standards, procedures, and methods for operating the Interactive Graphics System. This manual supplements the Corporate Drafting Manual and any related divisional manuals or procedures.

The section on Operating Procedures and portions of other sections of this manual are based on Computervision's CADDS4 Graphics Operators Manual.

Recommendations for the improvement or expansion of this manual should be addressed to: Alpha Corporation, XYZ Division, CAD/CAM Manager, P.O. Box 111, Anywhere, USA 11111.

Computer Graphics System

DOCUMENTATION LIST

1. Systems manager guide
2. User tips
3. CADDS
    - Documentation summaries
    - Data base maintenance guide
    - Converter guide
    - Tablet menus
    - Extents
    - Autohide reference manual
    - Automatic hidden line removal-hidden part command
    - Automatic mechanical interference checking
    - Associative dimensioning
    - Measure length
4. Introduction to CADDS
5. Wiring diagrams basic guide
6. Printed circuit data extract/data merge user guide
7. Graphics Subroutines Manual
8. PCB Application Software
    - Check schematic command
    - PCB design rule checking
    - Net list extraction
    - Check board command
    - Automatic component insertion
    - IPC translator/GET-PUT
    - Relay contact/coil extract report design rules checking and automatic cross referencing
9. Finite-Element and Mass Properties
    - Finite-element modeling
    - 2-01-A Mass properties user guide
    - Nastran out-creates nastran bulk data card images fr. fem data
10. User Interface Reference
11. Data Base Reference Manual
12. General Graphics Environment Reference
13. Numerical Control (NC) Basic Guide
14. Numerical Control Reference Compact II-Put Compact
15. Introduction to VARPRO and PAREX
16. Parametric Element Processor (PEP) User Manual
17. Programming Languages (Fortran-S/TPL)
18. Operator Manual

19. Programmer Reference
20. Plant Design Reference
    - Piping appearance command
    - Pipeline reporting commands
    - Pipeline preparation commands
    - Pipeline modeling commands
21. Mapping
22. Release Bulletins
23. CV Communications
    - 3270
    - 2780
    - CNVET
    - IGES

Introduction

Since this manual documents XYZ procedures for operating the Interactive Graphics System, the philosophy of the Alpha drawing system, as stated in the Corporate Drafting Manual, is restated here:

> The philosophy of the Alpha product drawing system is three fold. First, drawings are structured to reflect the manufacturing process; i.e., how parts are put together. If during the life of the product, new manufacturing equipment makes it economical to assemble the product in different subassembly packages, the drawings should be revised to reflect this change.
>
> Second, drawings are made not only for the purpose of defining the end product design, but also for specifying information which will reduce the overall cost of producing the product. Engineering product drawings which require the manufacturing organization to prepare additional product drawings before proceeding with production invariably introduce discrepancies between the engineering and manufacturing drawings and increase the cost of the product.
>
> Third, drawings are to be unambiguous while at the same time functional. They are to include only sufficient delineation to reduce the overall cost of producing the product. See the appropriate Corporate Standard for functional drawing techniques.
>
> It is pointed out, however, that since the Interactive Graphics drawings are created as an accurate data base, with the potential for NC machining, the functional drafting techniques for manual drawings may not be desirable for application to a programmed drawing.

1.1 CAD LIBRARY DOCUMENTS

The following documents are kept in the CAD room for use by users. If the document is removed from the CAD room, the user should sign out the document in the log book. When the document is returned, the user should sign in the document in the log book.

2.1 SYSTEM START-UP AND SHUT-DOWN

2.1.1 System Start-Up (After Long Weekend or Plant Shutdown)

Ensure that the main AC circuit breaker is in the OFF position
Ensure that all devices (CGP, CIM, disk, magnetic tape unit, etc.) are turned off
Turn on the main AC circuit breaker
Power up CGP (switches are located on the rear panels)
Power up CIM (color interface module) with the switch on the rear panel
Power up disk, magnetic tape unit, all terminals any other peripheral devices

2.1.2 System Shutdown (End of Work Period)

Enter CTRL-S on Silent 700 (in EXECUTIVE MODE)
Press START/STOP on disk drive

2.1.3 System Shutdown (Before Long Weekend or Plant Shutdown)

Logout all tasks.
Enter CTRL-S on Silent 700 (in EXECUTIVE MODE).
Power down all terminals.
Press START/STOP on disk drive.
Remove disk pack and store properly. (Never place disk on top of disk drive.)
Power down disk drive.
Remove any magnetic tapes from mag tape unit and store properly.
Power down magnetic tape unit and computer.
Power down the CIM (switch on the rear panel).
Power down the CGP (switch is located on the lower part of back panel).
Turn main AC circuit breaker to OFF.

2.1.4 System Shutdown (After Power Failure)

Turn main AC circuit breaker to OFF.
Power down each piece of equipment: CGP, magnetic tape unit, disk, etc.
Power down each terminal.

2.2 BOOT-UP PROCEDURE

Step 0 Before attempting to BOOT-UP the system, check for the following conditions:

1. Disk revolving in the drive—if so, cover *should not* be opened and instead skip to Step 2.
   a. Lights are lit on disk drive
   b. Sound
   c. Empty disk cover close by
2. Air blowing in disk well (if not, turn on power switch on back of disk drive).

Step 1 Place disk in the drive.

Step 2 Press CTRL and keys simultaneously on silent 700. Once in proper mode (EXECUTIVE MODE), you get ICP prompt (*).

Step 3 Push START/STOP button on disk drive (unless disk is already spinning).

Step 4 Enter INIT.

Step 5 Enter APL. APL will boot the system. The following message indicates that OS diagnostics are being performed:

Running Low level Microdiagnostic
Low Level Microdiagnostic Passed
Running High level Microdiagnostic
Allow 30 Seconds for Test

High level Microdiagnostic Passed
Switch Register = 0800
  APL Diagnostic Rev. A 4/29/84
Inst. Pass
CHEKS Pass
DPU Pass
MAP Pass
MSIZE Pass
MEMT Pass
DONE
CGOS 200/10

This message indicates a successful boot on ICP.

Step 6 Press CTRL and L keys simultaneously on silent 700. If you are the first person to log in after the system is booted up, the following message appears:

FMCLEAR

This is run at boot-up time to clear any files left open as a result of a reboot operation where the system was not able to close open files before the system reboot.

Step 7 After FMCLEAR, system will ask to set the system clock (based on 24-hour clock, e.g., 1:00 P.M. = 13:00) by displaying the following message:

TYPE TIME AND DATE (MM-DD-YY, HM:MM)

On silent 700, enter the date and time, e.g.,

11-12-82, 8:15

System's response will be

Type in NAME and NUMBER

You have to enter the name and number assigned to you. Then system will respond with:

TASK 0 INDICATED

Step 8 If this is the first boot up of the day, execute the following program:

0 EXECUTE LIB. PROC. STARTUP

This program will delete all TMP, TVFSCRAT, and recover files still on the system, give a summary of charges, a picture of the disk storage area and a listing of ERRLOG. The ERRLOG listing should be placed in the book titled "CV Field Engineer."

2.3 LOG-IN PROCEDURE: DIALOGUE

To log-in to an inactive system from any keyboard:

CNTL-L to log-in task 0
or
CNTL-Rn to log-in specific task n (0 n 4)

TYPE DATE AND TIME (MM-DD-YY, HH:MM)

11-12-82, 08:25

System prompts: TYPE OK TO RUN FMCLEAR
Always type "OK" to perform FMCLEAR when first task is logged in.

To log-in to a task of an active system from inactive keyboard:

CNTL-Rn (n = task no.) to select task n, OR

CNTL-L to log-in to next available task

n system prompt for task

To log-in to a task from a keyboard active in another task:

CNTL-US-DEL Puts active task in background (at any level)

CNTL-Rn (n = task no.) select task.

2.4 LOG-OUT PROCEDURE

n Logout

System will respond with

TASKn TERMINATED

2.5 CRASH RECOVERY PROCEDURE

2.5.1 System Crash. To successfully recover and store data after system or task crash, *verify that you are following this procedure exactly.*

Reboot the system
Each user must log back on their task using CTRL-Rn
Enter CADDS
System will issue the following prompts:

TYPE OK TO CRASH RECOVER

Type "OK" to recover your part

The system then prompts:

TYPE OK TO REGENERATE GRAPHICS

Type "OK"

The system responds with:

PART WAS SUCCESSFULLY RECOVERED AND ACTIVATED UNDER A TEMPORARY NAME. BE SURE TO FILE PART UNDER NEW NAME.

Exit Par F Filename

You have to be sure to issue the above command. File name can be the name that was originally activated.

2.5.2 Task Crash. A part can be aborted and the task returned to OS level by typing CTRL-CC. The next time CADDS is entered on this task, the system will prompt: TYPE OK TO CRASH RECOVER. Unless you want to recover the aborted part (follow recovery procedure in system crash), just list the carriage return and proceed as usual. When crash occurs, the active part on any task gets filed under RECOVER & TMPON (n being the task number). This is the reason that you have to exit part and file it under another name. In case you forget to do so still RECOVER & TMPON can be activated and filed under new name. For housekeeping purposes, delete RECOVER files.

2.6 HELP INFORMATION

In order to use the on-line documentation of the system, one can use the following:

# LIST COMM	Lists all CADDS level commands
# ?	Lists all verbs
# Verb ?	Lists all nouns for verb specified
# Verb Noun ?	Lists all modifiers for the verb-noun combination specified
# ! Verb Noun	Lists description for command
Note:	Hit escape key to stop display Hit space bar to continue display Hit escape key then Q to quite during the listing and return to CADDS level

3.1 STANDARD PRACTICE: PROCEDURE FOR USE OF STANDARD DRAWING FORMATS

3.1.1 Creation of Formats. The graphics for standard XYZ Division drawing formats have been created in separate data bases so that the appropriate one can be inserted into a new part data base at any desired scale. This enables proper alignment of detail, notes, and bill-of-material information for drawing output on standard XYZ Division formats.

The following characteristics pertain to the data bases of the standard drawing formats (refer to Fig. 1, Chap. 9):

All geometry for the format should be created in layer 31.

The lower left-hand corner of the format is to have the coordinate value of (XOYO).

The test to be plotted as standard part of the format (such as "programmed drawing," "NTS," etc.) should be inserted on layer 21.

The standard data base index should be inserted on layer 0.

3.1.2 Procedure for Inputting Standard Formats. After system initialization of new part data base:

ECH LAY A
Select MODE DRAW
INS PRT FMT.__ SCLn
Where n is the inverse of the drawing scale (needed only if drawings scale = 1; e.g., if drawing scale = .5, n = 1/.5 = 2.

These steps accomplish insertion of the drawing format.

3.2 NAMING PART DATA BASE

3.2.1 General. Each graphics data base resident on disc must be filed under a catalog structure and adhere to specific naming conventions. The general format for the name of a graphic data base is:

1.234.567891011121314.1516.1718.1920212223

W.XXX.9999D99H01. 01. S1 11122

DFTM	Dwg#	Group/	Dwg.	Sheet	Mo.	Day	Digit
Number		Item	Rev.	No.			Year
(3 Ltrs.)							

File Type
T-Training
S-Scratch
W-Work
R-Release
N-Non Part File

Example: W.NAB.3100D11GB01
R.3100D11G01.01S2111122 (See Procedure for Inputting Standard Formats)

If a multidetail drawing is created and does not have a group identified, enter a xxx in the group or item spaces of the data base. When a multigroup drawing is created, enter xxx also. The xxx will indicate a drawing with more than one item detailed and no group identification, or a multigroup drawing. A single-sheet drawing should have XX for sheet number. The XX indicates that no other sheets exist.

3.2.1 Released Document Data Bases. When a drawing is completed, signed, and released, rename the drawing data base by changing the file type to R and omit draftsman's initials.

(EXAMPLE: R.999C999H01.01S107102)

All released drawings will have a file type of R and will be saved on the tapes labeled REL which are general released tapes and have all released drawing. Back-up tapes will be labeled REL BU.

3.2.3 Library Parts. Parts which are going to be used frequently should be stored as a library part, the format of library part names should adhere to the following rule.

LIB.MECH.XXX
or
LIB.ELEC.XXXX

Where XXXX is a universal name for the part.

Library parts should be created on layer 0 only and in a very special case when other layers are required, a note in the part should indicate the layers which are in use. After creation of the library part, a hardcopy of the part with indicators to where ORG is and also the name should be placed in the book designatd for library parts.

LIB.PROC.XXXX

Should be used for programs being used by the system and/or operators. A hardcopy of the program should be placed in the book titled "LIB PROC."

3.2.4 Restore Parts from Released Tape. A part restored from a released tape must not be retained on disk with the same part name as the released name. Rename the part by using your initials and other required information and delete the original part from disk.

3.2.5 Drawing Naming Convention. Each part on the data base can have a number of drawing associated with it.

CADDS system entries can be done in one of two different modes: *model* or *draw* mode. Any changes in model mode will reflect on all drawing associated with that part, and any changes in draw mode will be reflected *only* on the activated drawing.

All geometry should be created under drawing M using model mode and for dimensioning, drawing format, and text another drawing using 1, 2, 3, etc. and draw mode should be used.

The ACTIVATE DRAWING command is used to file the currently active drawing and to activate a different one, which may be either old or new. If old, it is displayed zoomed to the extents of the screen. If new, its size parameters are established either explicitly by command modifiers or from default values. A new or old drawing may be activated in either model or drawing mode.

If drawing mode is in effect prior to part activation, and a part is entered, the system automatically activates a drawing named DEFAULT, using the currently available default parameters. Also, each drawing is activated at the currently defined scale factor. However, drawing scale may be changed each time a drawing is activated.

ACTIVATE DRAWING NAME (modifiers)

For name, use the naming convention stated before. For modifiers you can specify the size (A, B, C, D, or E) of the drawing, if not, the default is size C. Modifiers HGTn WDTn specify explicitly the height and width of the drawing when plotted true size. The drawing size effectively defines a final clipping boundary through which any view pictures and/or drawing graphics which try to extend further will be clipped. Modifier n may be an integer or real number. Use these modifiers to achieve a vertical or horizonal format.

Scale (SCL). For use in DRAW mode only, for current drawing only. Specifies the ratio of the size of drawing entities as displayed to the actual size of the object being drawn.

There are three permissible formats of scale specification: (1) A single numerical value (e.g., SCALE 2.5), (2) a ratio of undimensioned numbers (e.g., SCALE 5 to 2), (3) a ratio of different units (e.g., SCALE 10 IN to 1 KM).

3.3 LAYERING STANDARDS

A part file can have up to 256 layers. A layer is like a page in a book. Layers may be overlayed on each other. A complete drawing may be a composite of many layers. The information on each layer is under the control of the person creating the part. The remainder of this section provides the standards in effect of the use of CADDS system at XYZ Division.

This standard is to provide a common understanding by all users. Any part a user enters has, on layer 0, a layering index and other data that is pertinent to information communication. See the layering description in this section.

Experience has shown that intelligent use of layering can save many hours for every hour added initially.

Layer	Description
0	Index text key on the key file
1–20	Geometry
21	Dimension

Layer	Description
22	Details
33	Graphic text
34	Format text bill of material
50	Partial format
51	Format
60	Dotted and phantom lines
61	Weld symbols
62	Balloons
100–253	SPARES—As required for construction
254	Scratch layer

Taping Procedure—Identifying and Creating Tapes and Back-Up Tapes

4.1 GENERAL TAPE REQUIREMENTS

Tapes and back-up tapes must be maintained to assure proper storage of data bases. There are basically two types of data to be saved on tape:

Complete and released document/program data bases which will never be changed. It may, however, be used/copied again to produce a new revision of the document/program.

In-work document/program data bases which may change many times before being released and require saving only the latest data base.

This section addresses the procedure to be used to effectively save and back-up the above two types of data.*

4.2 TAPE NUMBERING (SERIALIZATION)

Each new tape when put into production use is assigned a serial number. The number is logged in the tape number log book located on the CAD documentation table.

The log requires the following:

Example

TAPE NO	PROD CODE	TAPE STATUS	SOFTWARE REV	DATE
51	REL	RELEASED	2.01	12/15/82

*Only the parts which follow XYZ naming convention will be backed up.

4.2.1 Tape Number. When a new tape is required, assign the next two sequential numbers. The first number is for the production tape and the second is for the backup of the production tape.

Example. A new volume "in-work" is needed. The next available number in the log book is 52. The tape number of the volume "in-work" tape would be #52 and a second tape will be labeled tape #53 and will be the back-up tape for 52.

4.2.2 Product Code. List the product code for which the tape will be used. (See Sec. 3.3.)

4.2.3 Status. List the tape status

REL n	=	Released data based
REL BU to n*	=	Back-up tape for released data bases
IN-WORK n	=	In-work data bases
IN-WORK BU to n*	=	Back-up tape for in-work data bases

*List the Tape Number this tape backs up.

4.2.4 Software Revision. List the present CADDS software revision.

4.2.5 Date. List the present date. The date will record the age of the tape.

4.2.6 Tape Label

PROD CODE DATE
CREATED BY
STATUS
SOFTWARE REV TAPE NO.

Definition of data is the same as tape log.

4.3 GENERAL OPERATING PROCEDURES

4.3.1 General. To effectively manage tape and tape content, the taping coordinator will assure all taping procedures are followed and coordinate all taping efforts.

4.3.2 Daily Procedure. On the last day of each week, a full daily will be produced to save all parts and programs on the system. On the remaining days, a daily tape will be produced to save all parts and programs worked on since the creation of the last full daily. This will provide a four-day backup of all work in progress. Execute programs have been created to make all daily tapes and are on the system.

Full Backup — LIB.BACKUP.BIG
Since Backup — LIB.BACKUP.INC.

Both of these programs are run from system level and all dailies are made at high density.

Tape Marked	Used On	Save	Save Since
Monday	Monday	All Parts and Programs	Monday
Tuesday	Tuesday	All Parts and Programs	Tuesday
Wednesday	Wednesday	All Parts and Programs	Wednesday
Thursday	Thursday	All Parts and Programs	Thursday
Friday	Friday	All Parts and Programs	Full Backup

Caution: Keep all in-work data bases on the in-work tapes.

The disk should not be considered a permanent storage media. You may, however, rely on the disk storage of data bases for four days because the daily tapes back up the disk for a running five-day period.

All in-work data bases include the date as part of the part number and should be saved on tape with the date of the last changes. As the parts are added to the tape under later dates, the tape listing should have the parts with earlier dates marked off.

4.4 PREVENTIVE MAINTENANCE

4.4.1 Tape Head Cleaning. The tape heads need cleaning at least once each week. This will only be done by using the mag-tape-head spray and lens cleaning papers.

4.4.2 Handling Tapes. Tapes must not be handled on the taping surface. Load the tape by touching the first foot of tape only and pulling the first foot through before inserting tape in tape unit read/write heads.

4.4.3 Tape Labeling and Storage. All tapes must be properly labeled and stored. Do not lay tapes on the following: disk drive, CRT, plotting surface, or any electrical or magnetic equipment.

The backup tapes are kept in the security room in the basement.

4.4.4 Tape Error. When an error is encountered while reading or writing a tape, the tape must be identified by number or error condition to key personnel for corrective action.

Implementing New Software

When a major new software revision is provided, the check out and implementation must be in a planned manner to reduce confusion and delays in conversion.

5.1 COMPUTERVISION'S SOFTWARE REVISION NUMBERING SYSTEM

A number, of the format *N.MMMX*, is used to identify software

N.MM_X

revisions were:

N = Major family of software change (increments by 1 for each change).
MM = Level of refinement to that family.
X = Level of changes to last family refinement (alphabetic, beginning with A; absence of this letter indicates no change is integrated).

Example:
2.00 — First release of new family of software change.
2.01 — First refinement of software family.
2.01-A — First change to Rev. 2.01.

5.2 PROCEDURE FOR EVALUATION OF NEW SOFTWARE

A new software family release must be evaluated by working on a separate disk so as not to hamper productive work.

5.2.1 Disk. The cover of each disk in use should be labeled with the following information: (1) Software revision currently on disk; (2) number of users (tasks) for which the disk is configured; and (3) date that the disk was loaded.

5.2.2 Evaluation. Evaluations may have to be scheduled for third shift or weekends to avoid downtime on a multiterminal system.

5.2.2.1 Obtain listings of new features, bug fixes, and system changes.
5.2.2.2 Print out verb-noun correspondence: #LST COM (from CADDS)
5.2.2.3 Test all of the new features.
5.2.2.4 Create new parts, exercising typical mode of operation plus new features.
5.2.2.5 Load parts created on previous revision and perform typical modifications to insure data base integrity under new revision.
5.2.2.6 Document problems and communicate them directly to Computervision or via bug sheet procedure, depending on seriousness of problem. Note. Minor refinement updates may be implemented into the productive systems without evaluation per steps 3 and 4 when authorized by drafting management.

5.3 FINAL RELEASE VERSION

If the fixes of final released software are extensive, it may be necessary to subject it to repeat the evaluation trials.

5.4 CONVERT TO NEW REVISION

The plan for conversion to the new revision software should include:

5.4.1 Conduct a full demonstration of the new features for the user.
5.4.2 Acquire and review all available documentation from Computervision which may help in implementation.
5.4.3 Train operators for any special features.
5.4.4 Incorporate changes in the operators manual.
5.4.5 Implement any conversion operations necessary to permit compatibility with existing data base.

OUTLINE PROCEDURE—REBUILDING A GRAPHICS SYSTEM SOFTWARE DISK

1.0 PURPOSE/SCOPE

To establish the procedures for completely rebuilding the Graphics Computervision System data base and software. This procedure does not apply when it is desired to save the file manager.

2.0 FUNCTIONS AFFECTED

Interactive Graphics Facility.

3.0 REFERENCE DOCUMENTS

1. Graphics Systems Manager Guide
2. Graphic System Operator Manual
3. Graphic Data Base Structure Procedure
4. Release Bulletin for Current Software Revision

4.0 DEFINITIONS

None

5.0 REBUILD SYSTEM PROCEDURES

1. Save User Parts and Libraries on Tape. Load a tape on the tape drive unit and save files for the disk rebuild system procedures of Reference Document: Graphic Data Base Structure Procedure.

2. Preparing the Disk. Insert specific directions here.
3. Formatting the Disk. Insert specific directions here.
4. Coldstarting the System. Insert specific directions here.
5. Initializing the File Manager. Insert specific directions here.
6. Loading and Initializing Application Software. Load the software tapes in order as indicated in Release Bulletin (3.4) for Current Software (Reference Document Section).
7. Loading Saved Parts. Load the tape saved in Save User Parts and Libraries on Tape (5.1) and restore the parts. The disk build is now complete.

6.0 ATTACHMENTS

None

OUTLINE PROCEDURE—GRAPHICS SYSTEM DAILY OPERATIONS

1.0 PURPOSE/SCOPE

To establish procedures for daily operation of the Interactive Graphics system.

2.0 FUNCTIONS AFFECTED

Interactive Graphics Facility.

3.0 REFERENCE DOCUMENTS

1. Graphics System Manager Guide
2. Graphics System Operator Guide
3. Graphics Data Bases Structure Procedure

4.0 DEFINITIONS

None

5.0 PROCEDURES

5.1 Start-up. The following applies to initial daily start-up (if needed) and does not apply to start-up after a system hang.

5.1.1 Insure the air conditioner is on and not iced up. Do not start the system if the ambient temperature in the room exceeds 85 degrees F.

5.1.2 Turn on the main circuit breakers on the central processor and disk drive.

5.1.3 Press the start button on the disk drive, and wait until the ready light stops blinking and stays on. If the ready light does not stop blinking after a minute, or the fault light comes on, contact the systems engineers. *DO NOT PROCEED ANY FUTHER IF THIS HAPPENS.*

5.1.4 (The remainder of this section is specific to the graphics system installed. Insert the recovery directions here.)

5.2 Daily Taping. Parts are to be saved by outlined procedures every day. These are covered in the Data Base Structure procedures.

5.3 Shutdown. If the graphics system is completely powered down after operation, the following applies to a standard shutdown at the end of the day. It does not apply to system shutdown for start-up after a system hang.

5.3.1 Make sure the correct tape storage procedure has been run for the day.
5.3.2 Logout all but the command console.
5.3.3 Execute the normal logout macro from the remaining terminal. The terminal will logout automatically within five minutes. Wait for this to finish before proceeding.
5.3.4 Depress the STOP switch on the front of the computer to the STOP position. Hold momentarily and release. Then press the switch to the RESET position, hold momentarily and release.
5.3.5 Press the start button on the disk drive. The disk will begin slowing down.
5.3.6 Turn off the main circuit breakers on the disk drive and computer.
5.3.7 Before a long weekend shutdown, turn off the power, to printers, tablets, and graphics tubes.
5.3.8 The system is secure.

5.4 Crash Recovery (Basic). This must be followed in order to save as much work as possible. *DO NOT* follow 5.2 or 5.3 except as directed herein. If the system has been repeatedly going down, i.e., more than once an hour, refer to section 5.5.

5.4.1 If any terminals still respond, attempt to file a logout. *File the part under some dummy name.*
5.4.2 *Do not* execute the normal logout macro.
5.4.3 Reset the system per paragraph 5.1.4.
5.4.4 Reboot the system per paragraph 5.1.5 through 5.1.8. If the system asks for a new last catalog name, use "XXX" and a carriage return. Notify the people who were working on those parts. The system is now ready for general use.

5.5 Repetitive Crash Recovery. In the event of the system going down frequently, consult the following system manual for the procedure to provide diagnostic information for field service personnel. *This should be done only* by those experienced with the operating system.

6.0 ATTACHMENTS

None.

OUTLINE PROCEDURE—GRAPHICS SYSTEM TAPING

1.0 PURPOSE

To present general procedures useful for system back-up and archival taping, to insure minimum data loss in case of a system failure or accidental part deletion.

2.0 FUNCTION AFFECTED

Interactive Graphics Facility.

3.0 REFERENCE DOCUMENTS

3.1 System Manual
3.2 Operator Manual
3.3 Graphics Data Base Structure Procedure

4.0 DEFINITIONS

4.1 Daily Taping. Taping files created or modified that particular day.
4.2 Weekly Taping. Taping files created or modified within the past week.
4.3 Archival Taping. Taping final released parts for permanent storage.
4.4 Disk Taping. Taping all parts from a disk in preparation to load them onto a new disk.
4.5 Standards Taping. Taping of standard parts and associated files for permanent archival.

5.0 PROCEDURES

These procedures cover the entire spectrum of parts developed at this division. All parts are preserved by at least one of the following procedures. Attachment 6.1 shows parts saved by each taping sequence.

5.1 Loading the Tape. Place diagram and instructions for your system here.
5.2 Daily Taping. For daily taping, an executive program, UTIL.TAPE.DAILY has been prepared to be run at systems level. Other

tasks do not have to be logged out but only parts filed up to that time will be saved. Daily tapes are saved for one week.

5.2.1 At the end of the work day, load the tape for that day on the tape drive unit.

5.2.2 At the command console or any of the design stations, at system level, enter the command:

n EXECUTE UTIL.TAPE.DAILY

5.2.3 Follow instructions printed at the terminal until the tape starts. Once taping begins, the execute file can be left to run.

5.2.4 To modify catalogues saved during the daily since-taping, contact the systems engineer.

5.3 Weekly Taping. For weekly taping, run the UTIL.TAPE.WEEK execute file at system level. Weekly tapes are saved for one month (four weeks).

5.3.1 At the end of the working week, load weekly tape for that week on the tape drive unit.

5.3.2 At the command console design station, enter the following command:
n EXECUTE UTIL.TAPE.WEEK

5.3.3 Follow instructions printed at the terminal until the tape starts. Once taping begins, the execute file can be left to run.

5.3.4 The catalogs saved during the weekly taping can be changed only by approval of the systems engineer.

5.4 Monthly Taping. For monthly taping, execute the file UTIL.TAPE.MONTH. Monthly tapes are to be saved for three months.

5.4.1 On the last working day of the month, load the monthly tape on the drive unit.

5.4.2 At a terminal, enter the command: n EXECUTE UTIL.TAPE.MONTH

5.4.3 Follow instructions printed at the terminal until the tape starts. When taping begins, the execute file can be left to run.

5.5 Archiving Part Files

5.5.1 Load the appropriate archival tape on the tape drive unit.

5.5.2 From systems level, type: n EXECUTE UTIL.TAPE.RELEASE

5.5.3 Upon completion, mount the back-up release tape and from systems level, type: n EXECUTE UTIL.TAPE.RELBUP

5.5.4 All archival tapes are duplicated for offsite backup storage, so the above procedure must be duplicated for the duplicate archival tape except the archive option should not be used.

5.5.5 Once the part file has been saved on the archive tape, it should be deleted from the system by using the DELETE command at systems level.

5.5.6 The back-up archive tape is to be stored off-site.

5.6 Disk Taping. Full disk taping is required when all disk parts are to be transferred from one disk to another.

5.6.1 Load a scratch tape on the tape drive.

5.6.2 From systems level, type: n EXECUTE UTIL.TAPE.DISK.

5.6.3 The tape may then be loaded onto another disk using either Replace = NO or Replace = YES depending on the circumstances.

5.6.4 NOTE only catalogs named in accordance with the convention specified in reference 3.3 will be saved.

5.7 Standards Taping. Standard parts will be archived and backed-up separately since they are generally operational in nature. Examples are:

Menus	Library parts
Keyfiles	Utilities
Forms	Programs

5.7.1 Mount the standards tape on the tape drive.

5.7.2 At any terminal, type:
n EXECUTE UTIL.TAPE.STD (for standard parts)
n EXECUTE UTIL.TAPE.LIBRARY (for library parts)

5.7.3 For the standards and library back-up tapes, type:
n EXECUTE UTIL.TAPE.STD #2
or
n EXECUTE TUIL.TAPE.LIB #2

6.0 ATTACHMENTS

6.1 Parts Saving Matrix

(See next page.)

Catalog	Tape						
	Daily (5.2)	Weekly (5.3)	Monthly (5.4)	Disk (5.6)	Library (5.7)	Stnd. (5.7)	Release (5.5)
AE	X	X	X	X			
PL	X	X	X	X			
WD	X	X	X	X			
CH	X	X	X	X			
ARCH				X		X	
FORM						X	
SPT						X	
BUG	X					X	
Keyfile	X					X	
R	X			X			X
LIB	X				X		
L	X				X		
MACRO						X	
UTIL						X	
DEMO							
TL	X					X	
CU	X	X		X			
Initials	X	X		X			

OUTLINE PROCEDURE—GRAPHICS DATA BASE STRUCTURE

1.0 PURPOSE/SCOPE

To provide a *uniform* standard for file naming and structure.

2.0 FUNCTIONS AFFECTED

Interactive Graphics Facility.

3.0 REFERENCE DOCUMENTS

None.

4.0 DEFINITIONS

None.

5.0 PROCEDURE

Cataloging. The general catalogs to be used are:

AE	BUG	DEMO
PL	KEYFILE	TL
WD	P	(Your initials)
CH	R	
ARCH	L	
FORM	APRG	
SPT	UTIL	
LIB	CU	

If parts do not follow this cataloging convention, their integrity cannot be guaranteed. A brief description of each catalog follows:

5.1.1 AE Applications engineering jobs that are currently in work
5.1.2 PL Product line jobs that are currently in work
5.1.3 WD Wiring diagrams and electrical drawings that are currently in work
5.1.4 CH Charts and graphs
5.1.5 ARCH Archival tape listings
5.1.6 FORM Standard forms (i.e., drawing formats)
5.1.7 SPT Standard parts such as menu graphics
5.1.8 BUG Any specific part that has been called in or sent to the vendor as a bug
5.1.9 KEYFILE All keyfiles
5.1.10 R Released parts

5.1.11 L Library parts
5.1.12 LIB Wiring diagram library parts
5.1.13 MACRO All macro programs *that are released* for general use
5.1.14 UTIL Utility execute files that are released for general use
5.1.15 DEMO Demonstration parts
5.1.16 TL Graphics for tool display
5.1.17 CU Casual usages (training)
5.1.18 (Your initials) Established user inwork and personal files

These catalogs are supported by taping procedures shown in Section 6 of the Graphics System Taping Procedure.

5.2 PART NAMING

Using the previously defined catalogs, the part naming procedures follow:

5.2.1 Procedure for AE, PL, WD, and CH Catalogs

5.2.1.1 Using AE as an example, name the part:AE.CHARGE NUM.YOUR INITIALS.IDENTIFYING NAME. DATE.
5.2.1.2 Everyday, change the part name by changing the date (i.e., last catalog) to the current date and work on that part. This will offer a several day backup to your part. Delete any parts over three days old.
5.2.1.3 Upon completion of the part, and drawing signoff, rename the part to: R.AE.CHARGE NUM.IDENTIFYING NAME. Delete all old versions, and notify the technician for archival.

5.2.2 Procedure for L, FORM, SPT, and DEMO Catalogs

5.2.2.1 Using SPT as an example, name your part: YOUR INITIALS.SPT.IDENTIFYING NAME.DATE
5.2.2.2 Rename the file everyday is in work per 5.2.1.2
5.2.2.3 Upon completion of the part, rename it SPT. IDENTIFYING NAME and delete all old versions. Notify the technician to have it archived.

5.2.3 Procedure for MACRO, UTIL, and TL files

5.2.3.1 These are all text files. While they are being written and debugged, they are to be named:

(YOUR INITIALS).MACRO.IDENTIFYING NAME
.UTIL.
.TL.

The identifying name should be consistent with established naming within that particular catalog.

5.2.3.2 When the file is complete, and debugged, it must be verified by another user.

5.2.3.3 After successful verification, rename the file:

MACRO.IDENTIFYING NAME
UTIL.IDENTIFYING NAME
TL.IDENTIFYING NAME

Delete the old version and notify the technician to have it archived.

5.2.4 Procedure for CU (Casual User) Files

5.2.4.1 The CU catalog is not supported for full archival since it is intended for temporary use. The naming configuration is: CU.(YOUR INITIALS).PART NAME.

5.3 DRAWING NAMING

Drawing within the parts are to be named as follows:

5.3.1 Drawing 1 for the basic model. It is to contain only the part geometry and only model entities.

5.3.2 Drawings for special purposes should be identified as such i.e., DRAWING FEM.

5.3.3 The drawing used to make the final part drawing should be: DRAWING NUM.SHEET NUM.REVISION NUM.

5.4 LAYERING

Data base layering will be a function of the part being worked on.

5.4.1 Wiring Diagrams. Reserved.

5.4.2 Detailed Parts

Layer(s)	Usage
0	Do not use or temporary use only
1	Index layer
2-15	Design data
18-19	Bill of material information
20-25, 30-35, . . . , 190-195	Part geometry, different layer groups for different components
26, 36, 46, . . . , 186, 196	Dimensions for geometry on previous five layers
27, 37, 47, . . . , 187, 197	Cross-hatching

Layer(s)	Usage
28, 38, 48 . . . , 188, 198	Minimum material condition
29, 39, 49 . . . , 189, 199	Maximum material condition
200-254	Reserved

5.4.3 Design Layout Guidelines. The product design layout contains all geometry and data to define the total part, assembly, manufacturability, and quality requirements for a given product. This data is obtained from the Design Engineering, Design Drafting, Analytical Engineering, Manufacturing Engineering, and Q.A. Engineering groups. The design layout, after completion, will be used to produce Engineering and Manufacturing drawings and data to manufacture and test the product.

Test requirements make it necessary to use the following guidelines when the graphics system is used for design layout.

5.4.3.1 Naming and drawing scale

5.4.3.1.1 All design layouts will use a multi-digit part/drawing number. The system name will follow the same convention as previously described.

5.4.3.1.2 The drawing scale should be determined in the same manner as a manual layout.

5.4.3.2 Multiple data base requirements. The design layout for a small or limited part design can usually be input by use of one data base. A large design layout (large number of detail parts) is best handled with multiple data bases. The following are guidelines to be used when multiple data bases are required.

5.4.3.3 Data base 1 description. Data Base 1 will contain the overall design layout geometry and the envelope geometry for the detail parts. The geometry of data base 1 is used primarily to check fits/clearance of final-part assembly.

5.4.3.4 Data Base 2 through data base n. The remaining data bases follow the same naming convention. The second data base through the last data base will contain major subassembly detail. The envelope geometry will be created on a separate layer so it can easily be input (copied) to the overall layout (Data base 1).

5.4.3.5 Generally the following layer assignments should be used.

General	First Major Part	Second Major Parts . . . etc.
0 not used	10 matl min.	20 matl min.
1 index layer	11 matl nom.	21 matl nom.
2 envelope geometry	12 matl max.	20 matl max.
3-9 use as needed	13 mach min.	23 mach min.
	14 mach nom.	24 mach nom.
	15 mach max.	25 mach max.
	16 dim. & notes	26 dim. & notes
	17 dim. & notes	27 dim. & notes

The attempt is made to maintain min. malt. geometry on layers ending in 0 and nom. machined geometry on layers ending in 4 and the same for the remaining material and part conditions.

6.0 ATTACHMENTS

None.

OUTLINE PROCEDURE—GRAPHICS SOFTWARE CONTROL AND MAINTENANCE

1.0 PURPOSE/SCOPE

To establish and control Vendor software, release document software problems, and catalog information pertaining to the software on the Interactive Graphics system.

2.0 FUNCTIONS AFFECTED

Interactive Graphics Facility.

3.0 REFERENCE DOCUMENTS

3.1 Rebuilding the Graphic System Software Disc Procedure.

4.0 DEFINITIONS

None.

5.0 PROCEDURES

5.1 New Software Release

When new software is received from the vendor, do the following:

5.1.1 Verify contents to packing slip. File the packing slip.

5.1.2 Write the calendar date in ink on the cover of any user manuals received with the shipment.

5.1.3 Place the user manuals in labeled binders and put them in the graphics system user library. Superceded manuals should be removed from the library and *filed. Do not throw them away.*

5.1.4 There will be a "Release Bulletin" with the shipment. File it in the Release Bulletin binder maintained by the systems engineer.

5.1.5 Mark the new tapes with a sequence number (any unique name). Do not release them for general use.

5.1.6 Build a disk per reference 1.9.1 but do not use for production. Perform routine operations on the new software disk as available to determine if there are any radical problems with it.

5.1.7 When it is apparent the new software is basically functional, it may be used in production. All bugs should be noted and duplicated prior to calling them in.

5.1.8 When the new software is released, remove the old software tapes from the computer room and package them together. Archive these tapes.

5.2 DOCUMENTATION RELEASE

5.2.1 As documentation is received from the vendor, the receipt date is to be written on the cover in ink. The documentation is then to be logged in and filed in its respective category. The documentation should be kept separate by the following categories:

5.2.1.1 User Manuals*
5.2.1.2 User Guides*
5.2.1.3 Release Bulletins
5.2.1.4 Software Technical Memos
5.2.1.5 Installation Guides

5.2.2 These files should be kept in binders in the graphic system user library. *Remove superceded copies from library and file. Previous revisions of all others remain.

5.3 BUG REPORTING

With new software releases, will be new software bugs. All bugs are to be reported to the systems engineer to be logged prior to calling the vendor. Before reporting the bug, do the following:

5.3.1 Make sure it can be duplicated. Try it again, unless it crashes the system.

5.3.2 Have someone else verify it.

5.3.3 Try to figure out a work-around for yourself and others that may have this problem.

5.3.4 Run a hardcopy of the screen and/or the text as necessary and give to the systems engineer to call in.

6.0 ATTACHMENTS

None.

REFERENCE

The material presented in this chapter was adapted from material gathered from both Westinghouse and non-Westinghouse organizations in the public domain. As such, the developed materials are a combination of many sources and represent the actual practice in no single company or division.

15

Preventive Maintenance

The purpose of this chapter is to make you an "instant expert" on preventive maintenance (PM). When you have finished this chapter you will be able to talk to the person who normally does your system PM and know if he or she knows what to do. In addition, you will be able to look at what he is doing and the equipment he has brought with him and know he is doing a good job. The person that does your PM is normally called a field engineer (FE). One further note, the hardware covered may not exactly match your graphics hardware but the underlying concepts are the same.

OVERVIEW

Preventive maintenance is performed on a regular basis by your vendor for a number of reasons:

1. To prevent future downtime of your graphics system by using system diagnostics
2. To resolve any lingering or intermittent problems that your system is encountering
3. To perform general cleaning, including:
   a. Cleaning all exposed surfaces of dirt and dust build-up
   b. Cleaning or replacing filters
   c. Replacing missing hardware: screws, ty-wraps, cable ends, covers, etc.
   d. Ty-wrapping cables and routing them neatly and out of the way
4. To promote good customer-vendor relations

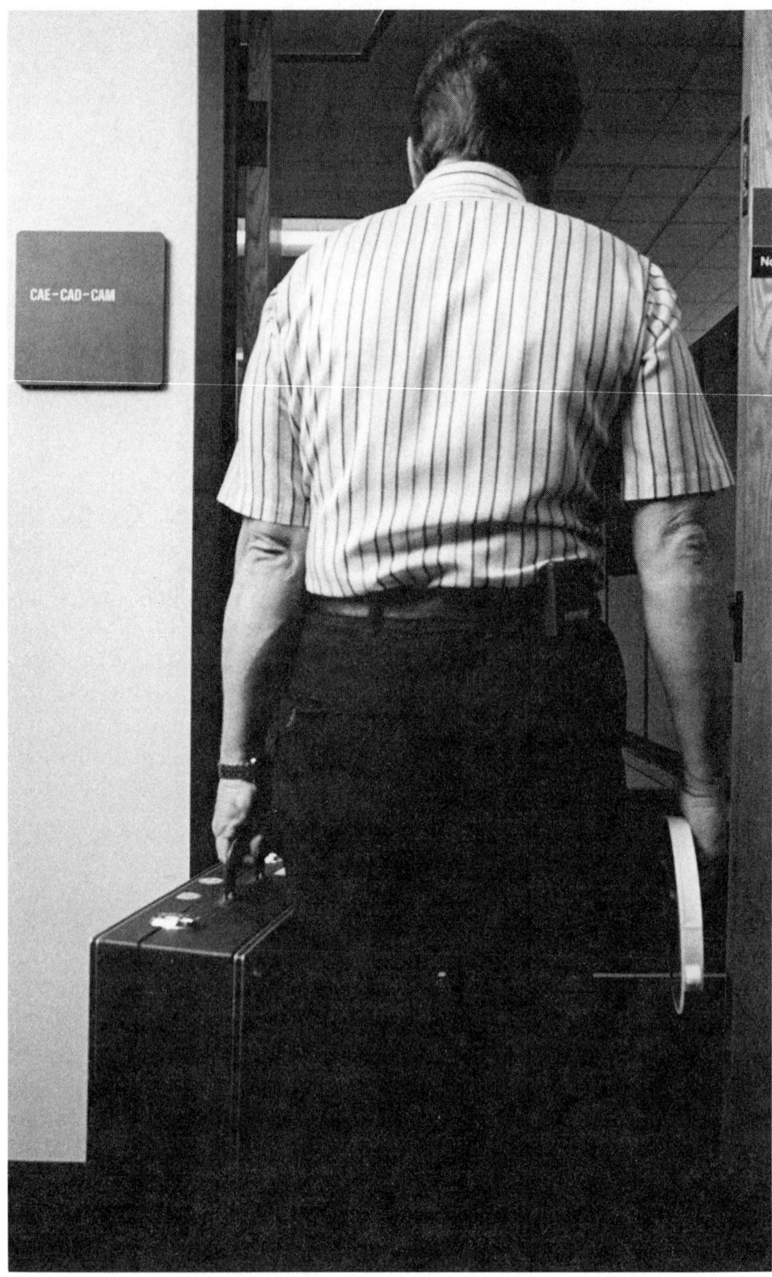

Figure 1 The field engineer.

WHAT IS PREVENTIVE MAINTENANCE?

The whole concept of PM goes back to the early years of computers and vacuum tubes. Originally, computers used thousands of vacuum tubes to accomplish simple tasks that can be done today with one processor chip. Those first devices had to be looked after constantly, just to ensure marginal operation. It was not unusual to perform preventive maintenance on one of those early computers twice or even three times a day. In those days, a PM sometimes lasted through an entire 8-hour shift, and took two or three persons to complete. The bulk of the time was spent hunting for gassy tubes, cleaning out dust accumulations, and reseating every one of those thousands of vacuum tubes. Printers were a mechanical nightmare and display units were a whole different ballgame.

Today, two PMs a year is a good average for the type of computer equipment in use. For systems residing in a below average environment, the time between PMs should be shortened. The field engineer should work with you to ensure that the environment is adjusted to meet the vendor's specifications for your graphics hardware.

Always keep in mind that PM stands for preventive maintenance, and not postmortem. You should feel that a PM is good for your system and the time it takes to complete it is time well spent. Sometimes it is hard to see physical evidence of a PM well done, especially with a system that has no problems. At that point you need to be satisfied with the knowledge that PMs are necessary for your system's continued good operation.

When problems are found during a PM, be sure that the FE and/or yourself log the information for future use and be glad that because of the preventive maintenance procedure you just avoided a service call.

The remainder of this guide presents a list of reminders for your FE. Most FEs who will work on your system have their own way of doing PMs, but if you don't have something in writing about PM, you will never know if your FE forgot to check all the right things. Hopefully, this guide will provide basic routines that can be followed during PM if you ever need to do it yourself, and also will help you to get a better grasp of all the things that should be accomplished during a PM.

Recommended PM Material List in the system engineers tool kit:

- Digital voltmeter
- Vacuum cleaner
- Alcohol (91% isopropyl)
- Ty-wraps: a good assortment
- Rags or paper towels
- Diagnostic magnetic tape
- Screws, nuts, washers, etc.
- Assorted hardware for repair of damaged connectors
- Assorted fuses
- Window cleaner or all-purpose spray cleaner
- Disk air pressure gauge to check output of absolute filters
- Small brush
- Stock of basic replacement parts, filters, fans, belts, etc.

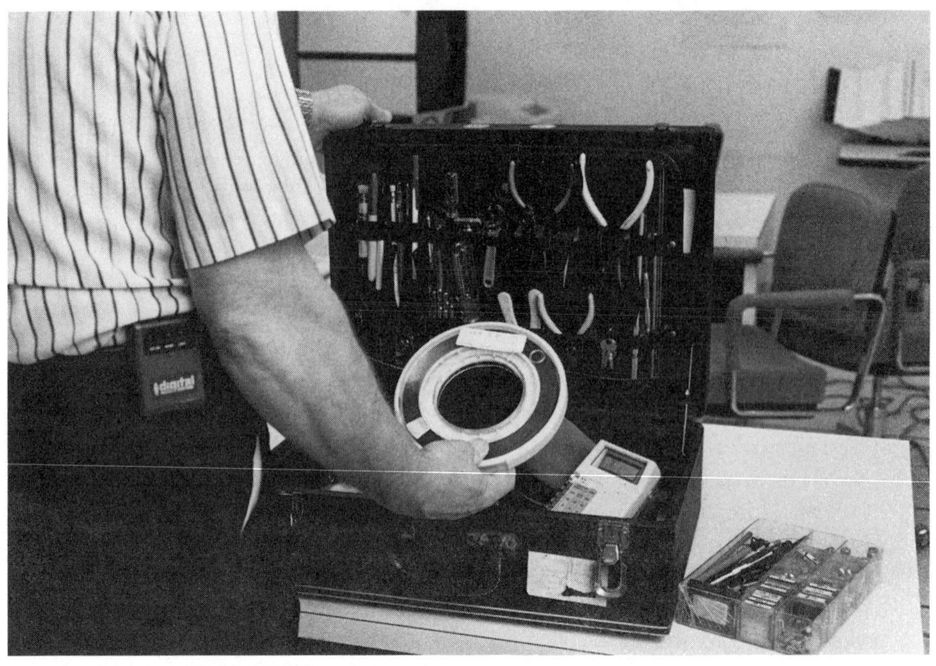

Figure 2 Field engineer tool kit.

Figure 3 Field engineer working on a graphics terminal.

COMPUTER OR CENTRAL PROCESSOR UNIT

Visual Inspection: Completion Time 15 to 90 Minutes

The FE should inspect all plugs and connectors to ensure proper seating and reseat if necessary. Verify the functionality of all front panel switches and indicators. Inspect all fans to insure that they run freely without bearing noises or excessive heat. Remove any dirt or dust buildup on or around the fans. Make sure that all cabinet covers and doors, front and back, are installed and fit properly. Check the primary air filter in the chassis and clean if necessary. Ty-wrap and route all cables so that they cannot be kicked or stepped on. Check the backplane area for loose or hanging wires that may cause shorting of backplane pins. Verify that all connectors are not missing strain-relief hardware and replace if necessary.

Diagnostics

The FE should first gather all available information to help make the determination as to which diagnostics to run. Input from you on things you have observed, the site log, and an overall knowledge of the graphics systems should be sufficient to make this decision. Use common sense in selecting diagnostics that will be most beneficial to the continued trouble-free operation of the system. Running diagnostics on a 100% functional system will instill confidence in the correct operation of the system.

Optional

The FE should check all power supply voltages and note the values. Keep them displayed on the inside of the tape-drive door for future use. Label all cables and boards and note the rev level of the hardware. The power supply readings can be used as a starting point to diagnose problems. After the PM, if these voltages are checked periodically and compared to the original readings, the FE may be able to foresee a problem with the power supply.

Computer or CPU Checklist

Connectors are all properly seated
All switches and indicators function properly
Fans are clean and functional
Cabinet doors and covers are all in place
Primary air filter is clean
Cables are all in good condition
Cable routing looks good
Backplane area is neat and free of loose wires
Strain relief is installed and functional on all connectors that require it
Exterior surfaces are fairly clean

DISK DRIVE PM GUIDE AND CHECKLIST

Inspection: Completion Time 15 to 30 Minutes

The FE should be sure to remove the disk pack first. Inspect the area around the pack cover lid for dirt or loose debris. If necessary, use a piece of masking tape or a slightly dampened cloth to remove any dirt. Check underneath the drive for any debris that could get sucked into the primary filter and block airflow. With power still applied to the drive, remove the primary filter and clean or replace if necessary. Check the condition of all data cables. Ensure that there are no cuts or bad kinks present and the cables are routed so that they cannot be stepped on or rolled over by the drive. Check the copper spindle ground and clean or realign it if necessary. Check the DC power supply voltages, any excessive AC ripple should be noted. Remove power from the drive. Remove the access cover to expose the activator coil and heads. Carefully load the heads manually (with the pack removed) and move the carriage back and forth. The carriage should literally float, once the heads are free, with very little pressure. If any resistance or rough spots are felt, the rails should be cleaned with a lint-free cloth. Visually inspect all switches and indicators to ensure proper functioning. Since vibration is present in disk drives, ensure that all printed circuit boards and connectors are properly seated. Replace the absolute filter. This filter should be replaced every 6-12 months depending on the environment. The best method of checking the status of an absolute filter is by testing the air flow with an air pressure gauge. If the filter fails the test, replace it. After replacing the absolute filter, be sure that the FE lets the disk run by itself for at least 15 minutes to purge the system of debris. Most FEs complete the disk drive PM first, then let it purge for the remainder of the PM routine.

Disk Drive PM Checklist

Disk pack area is clean and free of debris
Area under the drive is free of debris and obstruction
Primary filter is clean
A and B data cables are in good condition
Spindle ground is clean and functions properly
DC voltages checked and are within tolerance
AC ripple is within given limits
Carriage is in good condition
All switches and indicators function properly
All PC boards and connectors are seated properly
Absolute filter has been replaced (if necessary)
Drive has been purged for at least 15 minutes

VACUUM COLUMN MAGNETIC TAPE DRIVE—PM GUIDE AND CHECKLIST

Inspection: Completion Time 10–20 Minutes

The FE should clean the interior surfaces of the vacuum column if necessary. Inspect the tape path. All rollers should spin freely and should be smooth in spots that come in contact with the mag-tape. The grommets used to seal the vacuum column door should be functioning properly and the hex-head screws used to hold the vacuum column down should all be snug. Tape positioning in the vacuum column should be checked and adjusted if necessary. As the capacitive tape position transducer in the vacuum column gets old and dirty, the positioning adjustments may change enough to cause a poor vacuum and make a service call necessary. Refer to the tape drive manual for this procedure. Check that all connectors are properly seated and all switches and indicators are functioning normally. The magnetic tape should fit snugly on the hub and should not wobble or rub the tape. Adjust if necessary.

Tape Drive PM Checklist

Vacuum column is clean
Tape path is clean and free of obstructions
All rollers run freely
Grommets are in good condition
Tape positioning looks good
Connectors are properly seated
Tape fits firmly on the reel and does not slop
Tape reels do not wobble excessively or rub the tape

DIRECT DRIVE MAGNETIC TAPE DRIVE—PM GUIDE AND CHECKLIST

Inspection: Completion Time 5–15 Minutes

The FE should inspect the tape path for dirt deposits and scratches which may damage the magnetic tape. Make sure all rollers are free-spinning and secure on their shafts. Check the tape reel hubs to insure a good fit and no wobble. Adjust or tighten hub set screws if necessary. Inspect all connectors for proper seating. Fuses should be checked to make sure they are the proper rating. All switches and indicators should be checked for proper operation and replaced if necessary. Check the tension arm positioning to insure that they are within given tolerances. Adjust if necessary. If the tape drive cabinet has a cooling fan installed, make sure it is clean and functioning properly.

Direct Drive Tape Drives PM Checklist

Tape path looks good
All rollers are functional
Reel hubs look good
Magnetic tape fits securely on hub
Magnetic tape does not wobble or slip
Connectors seated properly
Fuse ratings checked
All switches and indicators function properly
Tension arm positioning is within tolerance
Fan is clean and functional

SILENT 700 PM GUIDE AND CHECKLIST

Inspection: Completion Time 5–15 Minutes

The FE should check that the print quality is clear and readable. Clean the printhead and rollers if necessary. If print quality is too poor, replace the head. Make sure the cooling fan is functional. Wipe off the case of the unit and also clean the keys if necessary. Inspect the switches and indicators to insure proper operation. Adjust the print contrast control only after verifying a clean printhead and then only if absolutely necessary.

Silent 700 Checklist

Good print quality
Switches and indicators function properly
Cooling fan is working
Unit is clean and free of dirt or paper dust build-up
Alphanumeric keys are clean and functional

GRAPHICS TERMINAL—PM GUIDE AND CHECKLIST

Inspection: Completion Time 5–15 Minutes

The FE should check all cables for proper seating and be sure they are in good condition. Make sure that all tablet surface reference pins are in place. Inspect the plastic tablet surface for cracks or large chips and replace if necessary. Check the quality of the graphics hardcopy printer and adjust the darkness control if necessary. Inspect the printhead for dirt deposits and clean or replace if necessary. Check the digitized pen tip for excessive wear and install a new one if need be. The keyboard should be checked for sticky keys and inspected for debris that may have become lodged between the keys. Check the functionality of all switches and indicators. Inspect the picture quality of the monitor. If quality is reasonably good, there should not be any need for adjustment. If adjustments are absolutely necessary, keep in mind that the picture is used only as a graphic representation to reflect what is actually contained in your graphics data base. When a color monitor is involved, convergence and color purity should be observed and adjusted only when necessary. Tablet tests may be beneficial to the completion of the PM.

Graphics Terminal PM Checklist

All cables are properly seated
All cables are in good working condition
Printer quality is good
Digitized pen is in good condition
The keyboard and all keys have been inspected
All switches and indicators are functional
Picture quality is reasonably good

STORAGE TERMINALS—PM GUIDE AND CHECKLIST

Inspection: Completion Time 5–25 Minutes

The FE should check that all cables are in good condition. Any cable with strain relief should be inspected and replaced if necessary. Check the input device for keys that repeat and repair if necessary. Check all switches and indicators to ensure proper operation. Observe the quality of all output screens and adjust if necessary, keeping in mind that the storage display is a graphic representation of your data base. If the storage scope has a very foggy appearance toward the bottom of the screen, the green glass face of the tube should be removed and the dirt build-up should be cleaned off with a good cleaner. Check the operation of the cursor and the tablet by moving the pen back and forth across the tablet. It should move smoothly in all areas and not leave large traces. Overall picture quality should be fairly good. Cables should be checked for proper seating. Use ty-wraps to route internal cables.

Storage Terminal PM Checklist

Cables in good condition
Input device is functioning properly
All switches and indicators function properly
All CRTs have fairly good picture quality
Storage scope green glass filter is clean
Pen and tablet function normally
Cables seated properly
Cables are routed neatly and ty-wrapped out of the way

CALCOMP PLOTTER—PM GUIDE AND CHECKLIST

Inspection: Completion Time 10–30 Minutes

The FE should inspect all belts for any tears, cracks, or folds that could catch the pen and cause larger problems later. Make sure the belt tracking holes are not overly enlarged or torn and that the belt does not skew on the drum as it is run forward and reverse. Align the belt tracking support roller assembly if necessary to get rid of belt skew. Check both X and Y drive gears for missing teeth or flat spots by "feeling" and listening to them as you move the pen carriage and platen belt back and forth manually. While doing this, check the backlash adjustment on both gears. Replace any gear that has missing teeth or flat spots. Installing a new gear at PM time will probably avoid a future service call. Ensure that all switches, sensors, buttons, and indicators function properly. Replace any bad ones. Check the operation of all bearings to ensure that they roll smoothly. Check the pen block assembly for dried ink deposits and loose debris and clean if necessary. Inspect the logic chassis for dust build-up on the boards and mother board. If necessary, brush off the dirt and vacuum it up. Verify the proper operation of the muffin fan located in the rear of the logic cage. Also check the air output vents behind the chassis. Vacuum if necessary.

Calcomp Plotter PM Checklist

Platen belt is in good condition
Platen belt skew is correct
X and Y gears are in good shape
Backlash adjustment is correct
All switches, sensors, and indicators function properly
Carriage drive band is in good condition
All bearings operate smoothly
Pen block assembly is in good condition
Logic cage is clean and free of dust deposits
Fan functions properly
Air output vents are clear of dust and debris

VERSATEC PLOTTER—PM GUIDE AND CHECKLIST

Inspection: Completion Time 10–30 Minutes

The FE should inspect the writing head for toner or paper residue and clean if necessary. Insure that the backplate is clean and free of any pitting or rough edges. Inspect the muffin fans located in the logic card cage, nib card cage, and servo chassis. Make sure they are all running smoothly at full speed and replace any bad ones. Inspect the air filters inside the rear cover panels. Remove and wash in a warm water and mild detergent solution when dirty. After all cleaning and adjustments are complete, examine the plot quality to insure that the plotter is functioning normally. Refer to the Versatec Printer/Plotter manual for a more detailed description of the PM procedure.

Versatec Plotter PM Checklist

Writing head is free of toner and debris
Backplate is free of debris and pitting
All muffin fans function properly
All air filters are clean
Plot quality is good
All cables are properly seated
All PC boards are firmly seated
All switches and indicators function properly

TEKTRONIX HARDCOPY UNIT—PM GUIDE AND CHECKLIST

Inspection: Completion Time 5–15 Minutes

The FE should vacuum the unit because the hardcopy unit tends to collect an enormous amount of paper dust. Remove any loose pieces of paper in the transport area. Check copy quality remembering that the copy should be acceptable as a graphic representation of the drawing and not of the blueprint quality. All switches and indicators should be functional and the light/dark control should vary the plot output accordingly.

Hardcopy Unit PM Checklist

HCU has been vacuumed inside and out
The transport area is clear of any loose pieces of paper
Copy quality is acceptable to the customer
All switches, controls, and indicators function properly

REFERENCE AND ACKNOWLEDGMENT

This chapter owes its form to a rough draft procedure by Guiseppe Policani, Computervision Eastern Regional Manager of Customer Support, for his FEs that never quite made the light of day, but surfaced briefly one day at a Westinghouse Computervision Users Group Meeting. My file system rescued it from total obscurity.

AFTERWORD

Lastly, because you will need help from your graphics vendor at some point in time—have him fill out the form that follows. Do this before you sign the acceptance for the hardware/software—the vendor will still be in the ''answer all questions'' mode of operation.

CALL FOR HELP LIST

	Telephone number	Person's name
To report hardware problems		
To report software problems		
To get software information		
To register for a course		
To purchase any services/products		
Audio/visual media		
Documentation		
Productivity services		
Remote diagnostic services		
To purchase additional products		
Hardware		
Software		
Product information		
To discuss material contracts		
To contact		
Salesmen		
District Managers		
Application Engineer Managers		
Regional Manager		
National Account Manager		
To request/schedule appointments		
Engineering support		
For general installation information		

PRODUCTIVITY MEASUREMENT

16
Evaluation

The subject of evaluation of computer-aided design/computer-aided manufacturing (CAD/CAM) systems and the productivity associated with this technology has been elusive. Productivity measurement is of great concern to many users of CAD/CAM. It is not uncommon to hear such questions as "How do we evaluate the performance of these systems?" "What impact have these systems made on our company or corporation?" "How do we measure productivity or CAD/CAM systems?"

This section will present several approaches, methodologies, and techniques that have been identified in ongoing studies by vendors and users of this technology.

PRODUCTIVITY REPORT

The contents of a typical productivity report are as follows:

Overview
Organization
Personnel
Standards
PC/ES library and layering
Training
Equipment
Environment
PC/ES work flow chart
Attachments

It can be seen from the following hypothetical example that there are many factors that affect the productivity of a CAD/CAM system. This topic will be discussed in the section on Framework for Analysis.

OVERVIEW

The CAD facility at ABC Company, Charleston, has been in a push-and-pull-atmosphere since its conception. The idea of a CAD design group has not been fully realized. The system has been in place 4 years. There has been a significant turnover of management with no real leadership or enthusiasm for interactive graphics until recently.

The Engineering Support Manager who has control over CAD has been in this position for a relatively short time. This person and individuals from CAD/CAM group, have had a major impact on generating a new awareness and enthusiasm for CAD/CAM development.

There has been relatively little education, training, or formal library standards set for operators to follow to run an effective CAD/CAM facility. Until this is done it will be very difficult for the turnaround in attitude of manual versus automated design to be noticed.

ABC Company, Charleston, has the potential to become one of the most recognized CAD areas in ABC Company.

ORGANIZATION

In the present organization, the Automated Drafting Department is under the control of the Engineering Operations Department. This department also controls the manual design group.

Manufacturing and quality assurance, along with engineering, all have a strong influence in setting direction of the CAD group.

ORGANIZATION RECOMMENDATIONS

To maximize productivity, CAD must be recognized as a separate entity from the traditional design and drafting function. Although there are numerous alternatives, we have attempted to propose one method which will serve as an illustration of the integration of CAD, with proper responsibility alignment. In order to maintain the required documentation standards, configuration control, and engineering change control, a dotted line responsibility should be maintained to engineering documentation.

PERSONNEL

Management

Observations

The management positions have been in place for a relatively short time.

Engineering Support Manager, 6 months
Engineering Operations Manager, 15 months
CAD/CAM Development Engineer, 18 months

These vital positions were filled with individuals possessing minimal background in interactive graphic systems.

Recommendations

1. (See Training Recommendations.)
2. Mandate the implementation of dedicated projects to CAD.
3. Run two like projects; one manual, one CAD for analysis of time savings.
4. Set up slush funds in budget for seminars and user meetings.
5. Actively communicate with other CAD/CAM groups within ABC Company.

CAD Supervisor

Observations

Within the last six months a CAD supervisor has been put in place. He seems to have a good hold on a lot of the problems which surround the organization of a CAD department. There have been a number of basic standards put in place and are now being instituted (i.e., naming convention of parts, savfiles, and archiving procedures, etc.).

Recommendations

1. Set standards and oversee their implementation. (See standards.)
2. Help generate enthusiasm for CAD and personal recognition within the group (i.e., write-ups in ABC Company CAD Newsletter on a job well done, entry level positions with promotions and more responsibility).
3. With management, set time frame for new CAD work and updates of manual designs to Graphic System Data Base.
4. Designate one person to control all library parts. This position may be an entry level CAD position with basic PC/ES background, does not have to be a designer.

CAD Operators/Designers

Observations

In most cases there is a minimum knowledge of what the CAD system will do for them. Designers are working in basic CAD syntex with no strong desire to learn what the system will do. Attitudes toward the use of the system at a higher level of productivity are low. They feel that an increase output which will reduce the backlog of work will result in reducing overtime and finally the job itself.

Recommendations

To counter this inhibiting attitude, an advancement/compensation plan must be established to increase utilization. The increase value of an operator resultant of dual capability should be evident to a company.

STANDARDS

Observation

There are a number of work disciplines submitted to the CAD area:

PC/ES
MD
Instrument installation
Liquid crystal displays (LCD)
Name plates
Thermocoupling layouts
Numerical control (NC)
Test fixtures
Tool paths
Instrument proposal drawing

Recommendation

For each of these to be input and tracked in an orderly manner, it is mandatory that an input package be standardized for each. This package should be reviewed by the CAD supervisor and accepted or rejected based on its contents. The CAD supervisor should also evaluate and schedule the work to be put into the system.

PC/ES LIBRARY AND LAYERING

Observation

Library development has been one of the major inhibiting factors in the CAD group. Over the past few years, parts have been built with a black box approach with little or no use of nodal information. There have been three different libraries used with no standards set in any of their parts.

Without a library standard, to be used by all designers, work is generated using manual drafting techniques rather than the automated design capabilities of the CV System (i.e., Autoplace, Autoroute, Data Extract, etc.).

Recommendations

Management and designers must be made aware of the importance of a standard library with nodal information and layering, and that the CAD system is not a drafting aid/tool. See attachment:

1. Vendor recommended layering for parts, schematic, and PC boards.
2. Creation of a schematic drawing from a basic guide to production.
3. Creating a printed circuit board part library from a basic guide to production.

TRAINING

Observation

From interviews with designers and observations of their use of the system, training levels are below average (i.e., basic knowledge of syntax, lack of understanding of system capabilities, constant use of RPNT instead of SAV DIS and RST DIS, use of ZOM ALL and ZOM WIN instead of establishing displays, use of DIS GRD instead of GRD WIN, etc.).

Some designers have been to advanced training courses, but are not able to experiment with new commands or what was learned in general because of little or no time available during shifts to explore the workings of new commands or software due to schedules in production work.

There is no formal in-house training. All new CAD operators spend one to two weeks with a CAD/CAM specialist to become familiar with the system before training with the vendor.

Recommendations

1. *Systems Manager Seminar.* A three-day highly interactive learning session to optimize system management. This course may be obtained under full service contract as a substitute for a three-day in-house A.E. training course.

2. *A.E. In-House Training*. A.E. in-house training should be set up through your vendor regional office. Training areas are needed in: (1) building and use of nodal library; (2) autoplace (when software is released); (3) autoroute; (4) data extract for PC/ES.
3. *Full Service Contract*. Training. It has been determined that you are entitled under your full service contract to four man-weeks of on-site applications support. This support is limited to one-week blocks to be scheduled at mutually agreed upn times, through the vendor regional office.
4. *Management Awareness of CAD/CAM Education Media*. A representative from your CAD area should attend CAD/CAM seminars or user group meetings. These meetings are invaluable for learning new techniques and gaining insight to what other CAD/CAM groups are doing.

It is strongly recommended that if at all possible the CAD/CAM specialist attend the vendor's Annual Users Conference in Atlanta in September, many areas of concern will be covered in paper presentations and in the workshop session on PC/ES.

Additional tutorial or applications-oriented seminars are vital aids to continue and stimulate interest in computer aid design. Without interest, it is difficult to become a state-of-the-art design group.

EQUIPMENT

Equipment installed in CAD areas at present consists of:

1 — CGP 100
1 — NOVA
1 — 40 Mega word disc
1 — 16 Mega Work Mohawk
5 — 19 in. Design terminals
2 — Mag tape drives (9 channel)
1 — CALCOMP Plotter 960
1 — Interact 4
1 — Teletype with paper tape punch
1 — Hardcopy unit
1 — TN 200 with cassette

Equipment scheduled:

1 — 19 in. Design terminal
1 — CGP 200 (1984)

The CAD area has sufficient equipment to produce in a productive manner under present and any future CAD/CAM involvements.

ENVIRONMENT

Observations

CAD room layout: adequate but congested
Disk and CGP area: poor
Partitions: almost none
Lighting: improper, tremendous amount of glare on screens
Noise: level of noise is high
Temperature: good

Recommendations

See attachment: Site preparation guide

1. Room layout. The vendor recommends that all noise-generating equipment (i.e., CPU, disk, and plotters) be partitioned off from the design terminals. Several advantages are gained by this:

   a. Control of computer system environment without discomfort to the operators.
   b. A higher level of concentration by operators, due to relatively quiet atmosphere.
   c. No distractions occur due to mechanical noise from equipment, especially important during training.

2. Terminals. It is recommended that terminals be located close enough to allow normal communications between operators, without discomfort.
3. Lighting in the area of the plotters and digitizers can be the same as used in a typical drafting area. However, the area where the design consoles are situated is more critical. Since the design console uses a storage cathode ray tube (CRT), direct or backlighting will cause an annoying glare on the CRT. This glare can cause the operators to develop eye fatigue, which can be considered a safety hazard. Therefore, we have the following recommendations in this area:

   a. Provide a lighting scheme that allows lighting directly above or behind the user work station to be extinguished without affecting the illumination in the rest of the room. (Note user work stations should be indirectly lighted, however, work tables should be directly lighted.)
   b. Provide dimmer switches for all overhead lighting in the user work station area.
   c. Avoid white or light colored walls and floors, particularly in the area facing the terminals. Darker colors can sharply reduce reflective glare.
   d. Fluorescent ceiling lights should be equipped with light-diffusing baffles.

4. Room Partitions. Floor-to-ceiling partitions should be used to isolate the system from the passageways of normal traffic flow. They should be used in the system areas to separate the noise-generating equipment from the design consoles. The most frequently used partitions are the movable steel type, which are approximately 90% reusable. They also provide a one-hour fire rating and a much broader range of color and effective acoustical muting than do the plasterboard-type partitions.

Because of operator communications, we do not recommend installing partitions between individual stations.

ATTACHMENTS

1. Site preparation guide
2. CAD text nodes
3. CAD nodal text
4. CAD connect nodes
5. CAD printed circuit board auto placement: extract working component library file
6. Printed circuit board autoplacement place board

(Note: Attachment items 5 and 6 are preliminary and subject to change.)

ACKNOWLEDGMENTS

The material in this section was sanitized from material available from Computervision. As such, the presented material is a combination of many sources and represents the actual practice in no single company or corporation.

FRAMEWORK FOR ANALYSIS

Productivity measures seem to be easier to apply at higher levels of organizations (i.e., company, corporation, etc.). For example, the U.S. Bureau of Labor Statistics typically measures national productivity in terms of gross domestic product (GDP) per labor-hour. Gross domestic product is the total market value of goods and services produced within the United States. The GDP figures used in productivity calculations are indexed to express them in 1972 constant dollars.

Gross domestic product is highly analogous to a typical corporate productivity measure: value-added. Therefore, national productivity trends can be compared with corporate internal numbers. The value-added measure is easy to apply since value-added per employee is closely related to operating profit.

Value-added − salaries and benefits − other costs = operating profit

Figure 1 CAD justification.

The definition of value-added per employee is:

$$\text{Value-added per employee} = \frac{\text{revenues} - \text{direct material costs}}{\text{employee head count}}$$

One can see how this measure is easily applied since the variables in the ratio are readily accessible.

The value-added per employee may work as a measure of productivity in some CAD/CAM organizations, but engineering and system managers need tools and indicators (that compose a comprehensive set) to evaluate performance and identify areas of operation which can be improved.

Many organizations justify and then attempt to measure their CAD/CAM organization by comparing CAD to manual operation (Fig. 1).

If we simply apply this comparison we may find that the operation is either more or less productive as a result of automation. But this approach does not give any indication as to *why*. Therefore, the necessity to develop indicators that comprise a comprehensive set at the lowest possible level.

In order to develop a comprehensive set it is necessary to divide a CAD/CAM operation into areas or components (Fig. 2). By analyzing the composition of each component, decisions as to what is measurable can be made. It should be stressed that it is extremely important to identify the tangibles and intangibles. These must be identified and made clear to any user of a measurement system.

Framework Components

The first component of the framework is the system itself. In order to identify measures of system performance, one must look at the important attributes associated with the system. For example, hardware, software, application packages, revision levels, etc. Once the attributes are identified, a decision as to which of the attributes are tangible should be made. Then one can develop indicators for the tangible components of system operation.

The system has many tangible attributes and can be measured. For example, mean time between failures or up-time, downtime, response statistics, ease of use, and many more.

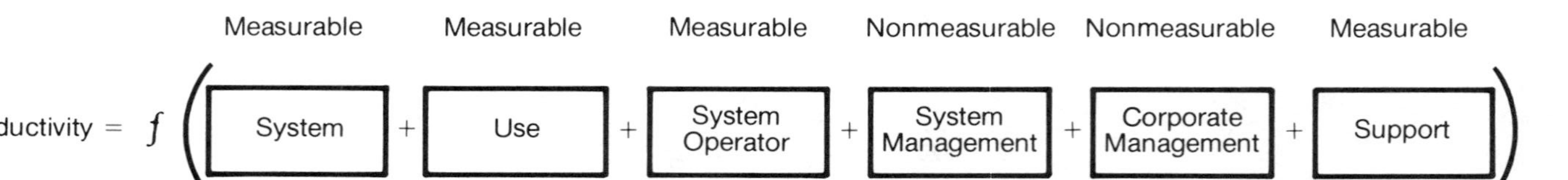

Figure 2 Productivity components.

Another important component is system utilization. Its attributes include the number of terminals, number of shifts, type of work (development/production), and so on. This component is also measurable by utilizing various job accounting packages.

The system operator component has many attributes which include:

Experience
Proficiency
Efficiency
Personal attributes
Attitude
Morale
Enthusiasm
Quality of work life
Money
Career path

One of the keys to a productive CAD/CAM operator is the type and extent of training. The level of training is an important attribute (see Figs. 3 and 4). The system operator is a measurable component in the framework. For example, some companies have established "baselines" for various applications and complexities of work. These "baselines" are established by "time-trailing" work and thus identifying "automated create times." Then by applying the Shah and Yan equation, one can obtain an efficiency factor E for an individual operator:

$$E = (I_i \times S_{s_i}) \div Sm_i$$

where

S_{m_i} = average labor-hours to manually produce a category i drawing (including revisions)

S_{s_i} = average labor-hours utilizing CAD/CAD to produce a category i drawing

E = efficiency with which a designer operates CAD/CAM

The following summarizes this methodology:

1. Select a representative cross-section of engineering work by application and complexity and categorize.
2. Establish manual create times (this may have to be estimated based on historical information).

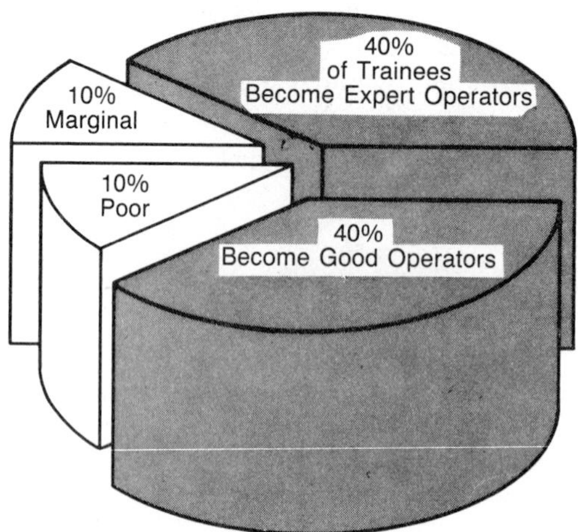

Figure 3 CAD operators. (Source: Daratech Inc., Cambridge, MA.)

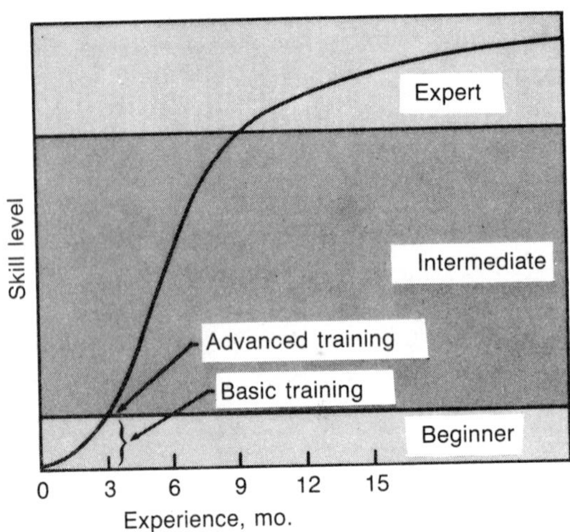

Figure 4 CAD learning curve. (Source: Daratech Inc., Cambridge, MA.)

3. Establish automated create times by "time trailing" the engineering work (utilize an experienced operator).
4. Develop productivity ratios for each category by dividing the automated create time by the manual create time. Therefore, one now has a realistic productivity ratio based on specific organization work.
5. Apply the Shah and Yan equation to develop efficiency factors for each category of work (these efficiency factors are for the operator who conducted the "time-trailing").
6. Apply the Shah and Yan equation to other system operators' work.

This is one suggested approach to the measurement of the system operator component.

The fourth component in the framework is system management. This is a nonmeasurable component, but the system management attributes can be evaluated through review processes. The attributes of this component include:

Knowledge of the system
Proper expectations concerning the system
Utilization of system tools
Back-up practices
System accounting procedures
File management practices
Procedures established
Training of operators
Scheduling/loading practices
Data control for security

The next component in the framework for anlaysis is senior management (senior management includes all managers above the system manager level). This component is also considered to be nonmeasurable, but is an essential part of the success of any CAD/CAM system. The most important attribute is the understanding of the system limitations and capabilities. Other attributes include:

The state-of-the-art of CAD/CAM technology
Resources necessary for success
CAD/CAM's role in the product cycle

The final component is vendor support. This component is measurable based upon mean time to respond (MTR) to a service call.

CONCLUSION

By viewing a CAD/CAM operation in terms of this framework, one can put productivity issues into perspective. The following section will cover productivitity basics. What is productivity?

ACKNOWLEDGMENTS

A complete derivation and discussion of the Shah and Yan equation is presented in the technical paper, "A Practical Technique for Benefit-Cost Analysis of Computer-Aided Design and Drafting Systems," authored by R. R. Shah and G. Yan, Atomic Energy of Canada Limited.

PRODUCTIVITY BASICS

Over the years, productivity has had many common misunderstandings associated with it. It is not a measure of production; it is not a measure of costs; it does not measure the cost of a resource; and it is not precisely a measure of efficiency. Productivity is a measure of the relationship between quantity of resources used and quantity of output. Simply, it is a ratio of some measure of output to some measure of input.

Some basic concepts of productivity:

Output is *any* product or service and input is *all* the resources used to produce it. The focus can be at any level, depending on organization and mission. For example:

$$P = \frac{O}{I} = \frac{\text{No. of drawings produced}}{\text{Total labor (direct, indirect, mgt., etc.) + materials + capital (machinery, facilities, ec.) + energy}}$$

$$P = \frac{O}{I} = \frac{\text{No. of wiring diagram drawings produced}}{\text{Associated labor + materials + capital + energy}}$$

The first example is from the point of view of a complete engineering department; the second is a subset covering one important function within the department. Productivity is improved whenever the ratio increases. More output with constant input, constant output with less input, and output increasing more than input are some of many ways. Pure productivity measures are ideal, sometimes hard to come by in nonmanufacturing areas. Other types of productivity measures include partials, correlated partials, and surrogates. For example:

Partials: output divided by only *one* of the inputs

$$P = \frac{O}{I} = \frac{O}{I} = \frac{\text{No. of drawings produced}}{\text{Hr of drafting time}}$$

$$P = \frac{O}{I} = \frac{O}{I} = \frac{\text{No. of drawings produced}}{\text{Cost of support equipment}}$$

The first example is a *labor* partial, the second is a *capital* partial.

Correlated partials are used when they provide "good enough" answers and when obtaining the actual data would be difficult or not cost-effective to obtain.

Surrogates. These are not true productivity measures but they are usually easy to get and they can be very useful indicators of productivity. The main consideration is that a connection can be shown between the surrogate measure and either input or output.

For example:

1. Quality level. As the number of defects decrease, the net output increases and/or the input decreases.
2. Rework. When the amount of rework decreases, input decreases. Also, net output can increase if the system was being operated at maximum capacity.
3. Timeliness. When projects are completed quickly, there tends to be less overall use of resources. The same reasoning applies when schedules are met rather than slipped.
4. Effectiveness. This is a measure of the correctness of what is being done. If correct, then resources are not being wasted.
5. Efficiency. This is a measure of the correctness of what is being done compared to a standard. If correct by the standard, resources are being well utilized.

Good productivity measures have the following characteristics:

Significance. The measurement covers a meaningful (nontrivial) part of the total output and input under consideration.

Understandability. The meaning of the measure is nonambiguous.

Interpretability. The results are easy to interpret and they show where action is required.

Practicality. The measurement is reasonably easy to implement, is able to accommodate change (organization, technical, etc.) and has a positive benefit-cost ratio.

Good productivity measures should have at least three key attributes:

The measure should emphasize that people are the most important resource.

There is a strong link between productivity and profitability.

The measure should be easy to understand and represent a common denominator yardstick that can be used by both corporate and divisional management when they plan for the future.

Table 1 Productivity Indicators in Industrial Companies

Function	Partial productivity indicators		Total-factor productivity indicators		Total productivity indicators		Other nonstandard productivity indicators	
	No. of times reported	%	No. of times reported	%	No. of times reported	%	No. of times reported	%
Manufacturing	30	41.1	1	1.4	2	2.7	40	54.8
Sales	16	39.0	0	0.0	0	0.0	25	61.0
Marketing	6	22.2	0	0.0	0	0.0	21	77.8
Purchasing	4	15.4	0	0.0	0	0.0	22	84.6
Personnel	3	11.5	0	0.0	0	0.0	23	88.5
Finance/accounting	5	23.8	0	0.0	0	0.0	16	76.2
Legal	1	14.3	0	0.0	0	0.0	6	85.7
Engineering	2	8.3	0	0.0	0	0.0	22	91.7
Research and development	0	0.0	0	0.0	0	0.0	16	100.0
Quality assurance	7	18.9	0	0.0	0	0.0	30	81.1
Maintenance	5	16.1	0	0.0	0	0.0	26	83.9
Industrial engineering	0	0.0	0	0.0	0	0.0	18	100.0
Data processing	2	7.7	0	0.0	0	0.0	24	92.3
Administration	4	18.2	0	0.0	0	0.0	18	81.8
Word processing	10	55.6	0	0.0	0	0.0	8	44.4
Distribution/warehousing	7	24.1	0	0.0	0	0.0	22	75.9
Planning	1	12.5	0	0.0	0	0.0	7	87.5
Average (%)		19.3		0.1		0.2		80.4

Table 2 Productivity Indicators in Nonindustrial Companies

Function	Partial productivity indicators		Total-factor productivity indicators		Total productivity indicators		Other nonstandard productivity indicators	
	No. of times reported	%	No. of times reported	%	No. of times reported	%	No. of times reported	%
Manufacturing (operations)	9	36.0	1	4.0	0	0.0	15	60.0
Sales	12	42.9	1	3.6	0	0.0	15	53.5
Marketing	1	9.1	1	9.1	0	0.0	9	81.8
Purchasing	0	0.0	0	0.0	0	0.0	11	100.0
Personnel	1	8.3	0	0.0	0	0.0	11	91.7
Finance/accounting	5	31.3	0	0.0	0	0.0	11	68.7
Legal	0	0.0	0	0.0	0	0.0	4	100.0
Engineering	3	30.0	0	0.0	0	0.0	7	70.0
Research and development	0	0.0	0	0.0	0	0.0	4	100.0
Quality assurance	0	0.0	0	0.0	0	0.0	5	100.0
Maintenance	2	18.2	0	0.0	0	0.0	9	81.8
Industrial engineering	1	10.0	0	0.0	0	0.0	9	90.0
Data processing	1	6.7	0	0.0	0	0.0	14	93.3
Administration	2	20.0	0	0.0	0	0.0	8	80.0
Word processing	8	53.3	0	0.0	0	0.0	7	46.7
Distribution/warehousing	7	53.8	0	0.0	0	0.0	6	46.2
Planning	1	12.5	0	0.0	0	0.0	7	87.5
Average (%)		19.5		1.0		0.0		79.5

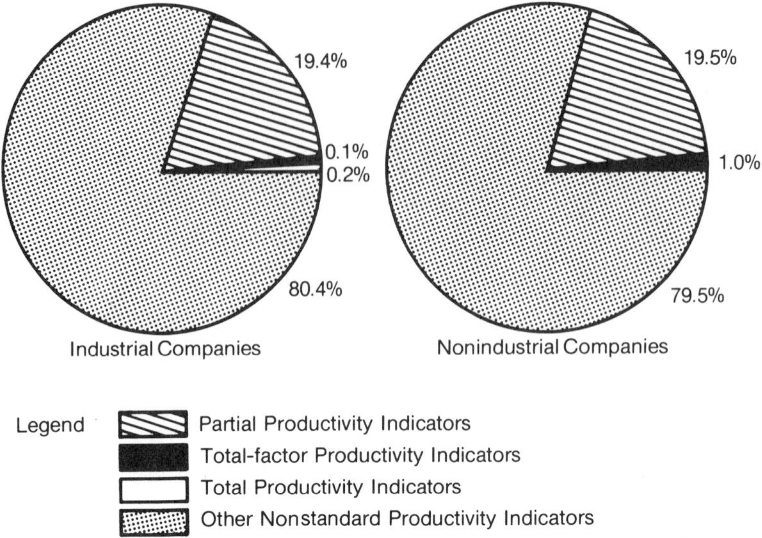

Figure 5 Productivity indicators.

It should be noted that measures must be developed within an organization/department. Useful measures can be developed by looking at organizational objectives and major problems that exist in the operation. Nonstandard productivity indicators, such as surrogates, are the types of measures typically used in engineering organizations. A survey indicated that 91.7% of engineering organizations in industrial companies use nonstandard productivity indicators, and 70% in nonindustrial companies (see Tables 1 and 2; Fig. 5).

ACKNOWLEDGMENTS

Most of this section was directly influenced by A. M. Healy, IBM Corporation. Tables 1 and 2, were reprinted from David J. Sumanth, "Productivity Indicators Used by Major U.S. Manufacturing Companies: The Results of Survey," *Industrial Engineering*, May 1981, p. 73; and David J. Sumanth, "Survey Results: How Major Non-Industrial Corporations Measure their Productivity," *Industrial Engineering*, September 1981, p. 32.

HOW TO DEVELOP MEASURES

Productivity measures must be developed within the organization to be evaluated. Useful measures can be developed by looking at organizational objectives and major problems that exist in the operation. There exist many techniques for measuring productivity of CAD operations. Several methodologies will be presented in this sector. The first being a case study of an IBM/Westinghouse joint effort.

IBM-Westinghouse Joint Effort: CAD Productivity Measures Case Study

Introduction

Two companies, International Business Machines (IBM) and Westinghouse, joined forces under the auspices of the American Productivity Center (APC) to define useful measures of productivity for their computer-aided design (CAD) operations.

Their motivation was straightforward; a problem existed with no solution in sight. They both needed better measures of productivity for their CAD operations, to help them manage their ongoing operations and explosive growth, yet good measures did not exist. When it was proposed that they might both gain from a "two heads are better than one" approach, they agreed to a joint effort centered around a group problem-solving process called Nominal Group Technique (NGT). The two companies were also led to expect another benefit: personal and professional development for their employees who participated in the group process.

The APC had its own set of motivations: first, to provide a model of cooperative effort between companies. Such cooperation is one of the factors that distinguishes Japanese industries and accounts for their success. It was felt that some of the obstacles barring similar cooperation among U.S. companies are more perceived than real, and that a demonstration would help break down the barriers. Secondly, the APC stood to gain useful information on one way to develop productivity measures.

It is the purpose of this paper to report what was done, to some degree how it was done, and the results, in three principal sections: (1) planning and preparation; (2) group processes; and (3) follow-up and implementation, followed by a summary and conclusions.

PLANNING AND PREPARATION

Overview

Two planning sessions were held, about one month apart. The first was to clearly establish objectives, to identify major elements of the action plan, and to complete a potential problem analysis. The second was to work out the fine details of the plan and to establish schedules and responsibilities. The major topics covered are shown in Figure 6.

- Feasibility Check
- Approval — Mgt and Legal
- Overall Schedule
- Key Roles
- Task Statement
- Participant Selection
- Confirmation Letter
- Travel and Food
- Security Clearances
- Joint Meetings
  - —Physical
  - —Supplies
  - —Process Aids
  - —Schedule
  - —Aux. Activities
- Assessment of Results
- Follow-On Activity

Figure 6 Major planning items.

In the final plan, two all-day meetings were scheduled; the first at Westinghouse's Baltimore location, and the next day, at the IBM facility near Burlington, Vermont. The two meetings were to be identical in terms of objectives and structure; with the only difference being the host location and the individual participants. That particular meeting schedule was chosen to satisfy four objectives:

1. Gain as much useful information as possible.
2. Provide additional value to the participants (e.g., a chance to see how others do similar work).
3. Equalize the expense between the two companies.
4. Gather data on process variables such as "host or visitor."

The following sections describe some of the important aspects of planning and preparation.

Essential First Steps

Two questions needed to be answered before serious planning could begin: (1) Is the proposed joint effort feasible from a technical point of view? (2) Are there any overwhelming problems of legality or management approval?

To answer the first question, a feasibility study was done to determine whether there was enough similarity in the functions performed by the two CAD organizations to warrant the joint effort. This is an important point because the synergism expected from the joint effort depended on the two companies having similar tasks to perform but different traditions of problems and solutions related to those tasks. First, a terminology comparison established that key words such as "graphics," "application," and "user" had the same meaning in both companies. Then, with the jargon under control, a CAD application common to both companies was identified—with the idea that the effect of synergism would be most pronounced if the participants were all associated with the same CAD application.

The second question was expected to be more difficult; possibly a "show stopper." At this point, of course, the idea was defined only at a conceptual level: representatives of both companies would meet together, under the auspices of the APC, for one or two days, to define productivity measures for CAD operations. The idea, presented that way to upper management in a "what do you think?" fashion, was received with enthusiasm. The lawyers were equally supportive; one said "Great idea! Large companies tend to be too ingrown . . . it's good to see how others are doing things—and I don't foresee any consuming legal problems." An important object lesson can be seen here, namely, that perceived obstacles may have no substance at all when tested! The consensus was that the APC's role of coordinating and facilitating helped to alleviate the concerns and objections that otherwise might have been raised.

Potential Problem Analysis

Potential problems were identified early in the planning phase and were separated into three categories; problems that would be likely to occur before, during, or after the joint meetings. Within each category, the problems were ranked according to seriousness and each was given an estimated probability of occurrence. The product of those two factors showed where preventive action was most needed. For example, the possibility of management alienation was a high scorer in the "before" category. This led to two separate preventive actions: first, the decision-making managers (those who would decide whether or not to accept the recommendations of the joint effort) were brought into the process quite early by being told what to expect (useful measures of productivity) and by being asked to define evaluation criteria for the ideas that would be generated during the joint meetings. Second, the resource managers (the managers of the areas from which participants would come) were given an early briefing on what was proposed, with emphasis on the anticipated benefits and on the "breaking new ground" aspects.

Another example: a potential problem, in the "during the joint meetings" category, was that some of the participants might have to back out at the last minute, as sometimes happens in the business world. The solution, to minimize the serious consequence of skill gaps in the joint meetings, was to find alternates; volunteers in each skill category who agreed to fill in on short notice if necessary.

Approval Process

There were two kinds of approval needed, management and legal, and two levels of planning, conceptual and detailed. And, to make it more interesting, three organizations, IBM, Westinghouse, and the APC involved in the approval process.

The approach taken was to get tentative approval based on a conceptual plan, then to return for final approval of the detailed plan.

The final agreement contained two parts:

1. Legal, which covered confidentiality, inventions and copyrights, publication, and duration of the agreement.
2. Operational, which described the joint effort in outline form.

Key Roles

The NGT process involves two group leadership roles; the facilitator and the scribe. The facilitator should be skilled in dealing with groups and in using NGT; the scribe should be knowledgeable in the area being discussed, and should be able to record information quickly and legibly. One person can fill both roles, but the process moves more quickly, more smoothly, if one person is the facilitator and another the scribe.

The plan identified a facilitator and a scribe; and two site coordinators, one for each company. In addition, two APC representatives were named as advisors and observers.

Site Coordinators

An individual was recruited at each of the two sites to coordinate all the activities related to preparing for and conducting the joint meetings. The site coordinators assisted in the selection of participants, they made the arrangement for meeting rooms, supplies, food, transportation, security clearances, etc. In addition, they provided for a diversion at midday; presentations and guided tours to let the visitors see how their hosts handled CAD operations.

The Task Statement

Wording of the statement, which is the basic instruction given to participants at the beginning of an NGT meeting, was viewed as a critical item. Several versions were considered and discussed with others familiar with CAD or NGT. The final wording was intended to provide a good balance between ambiguity and specificity, so as to encourage creative thinking while establishing necessary boundaries.

Participant Selection

The selection of participants was identified as critical, and was considered from several points of view:

What skills need to be represented
How many participants and at what level in the organization

Technical and personal characteristics of the participants
Characteristics of the participating organizations.

The CAD world is clearly divided into two parts; users and providers; with a further but less clear subdivision of providers into (1) those who provide the terminals or work stations, (2) those who write applications programs, and (3) those who provide the comptuer system and output devices such as plotters and printers. Since the users were most directly associated with the output of the overall CAD operation, it was decided to make them the focal point of the joint effort. Accordingly, horizontal and vertical cross-sections were defined as follows for each company (Fig. 7):

Horizontal cross section. Three users plus one person (manager or engineer) from each of the provider areas (terminals, programming, computer system)
Vertical cross section. The three users; one manager, one engineer or technician, and one designer or operator.

The resulting total of 12 participants, six from each company, is within the recommended range for NGT groups. Group composition was the same for each of the two days, but with different individuals.

At the individual participant level, the desired technical characteristics were experience and knowledge, several years experience and one of the most expert persons in the job. Personal characteristics included natural leadership ability, innovative skills (not afraid to try new things), dependability, highly motivated to "do better."

Over and above the technical and personal characteristics was an essential requirement—that participation be strictly voluntary. Ideally, the participants should not only be willing but eager to be involved.

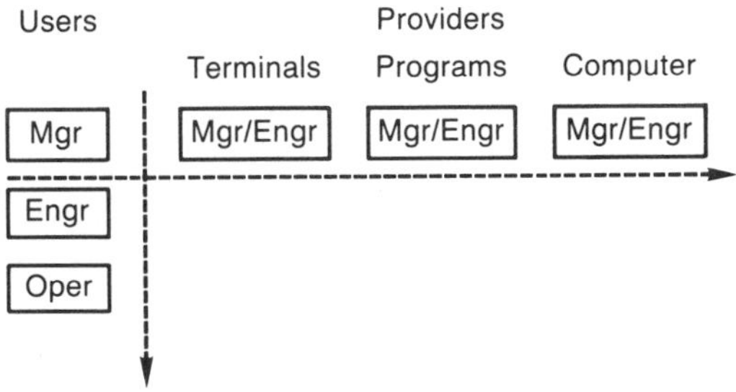

Figure 7 NGT group composition.

Finally the desired characteristics of the participating organizations (the immediate organization of the participant) were identified as: (1) healthy attitude toward change and (2) in need of help.

Confirmation Letter

A personalized letter was sent to each participant; to confirm participation in the joint meeting, and to satisfy the following objectives:

1. Explain the purpose of the meeting
2. Reinforce motivation
3. Identify leaders and coordinators
4. Define participants' responsibilities
5. Convey the basic concepts of productivity measurement

GROUP PROCESSES

NGT Sessions

The standard NGT process (Fig. 8) was employed, starting with silent generation response to the task statement: "Please list below, measures or indicators of productivity of your CAD operation." Before silent generation, the task statement was discussed and three instructions were given:

1. For "productivity," think of performance, effectiveness, or efficiency—if that helps
2. For "your CAD operation," think of it from your point of view as a user or provider
3. Good sources of productivity measurement ideas are:
   a. The objectives of your organization
   b. Problem areas in the CAD operation

1 Silent Generation

2 Round-Robin

3 Clarification

4 Voting

Figure 8 The NGT process.

	Round-Robin	Clarification
Day 1	69	44
Day 2	51	46

Figure 9 Number of ideas.

A comparison of the number of ideas generated during each of the two meetings (Fig. 9) suggests the following: on the first day, there was a freer flow of ideas followed by a rather severe pruning during the clarification step; on the second day, the listing of ideas was done more cautiously, more precisely, so relatively little editing was necessary. Both approaches produced the same net number of ideas.

The voting and ranking results (Fig. 10) show a steep exponential fall-off of total vote versus idea rank number, with close similarity between the two days. The voting indicated a high degree of discrimination among the competing ideas. For reference, the "ideal" curve represents perfect discrimination (i.e., this would be the result if all participants voted identically) and the "unranked" curve represents no discrimination (all ideas considered equal).

A retrospective examination of the ideas revealed a few more than perhaps should have been linked together and their respective votes combined. With that modification, the vote versus rank curves move even closer to the "ideal" (Fig. 11); suggesting that additional effort during the clarification step would be worthwhile whenever the NGT process is used.

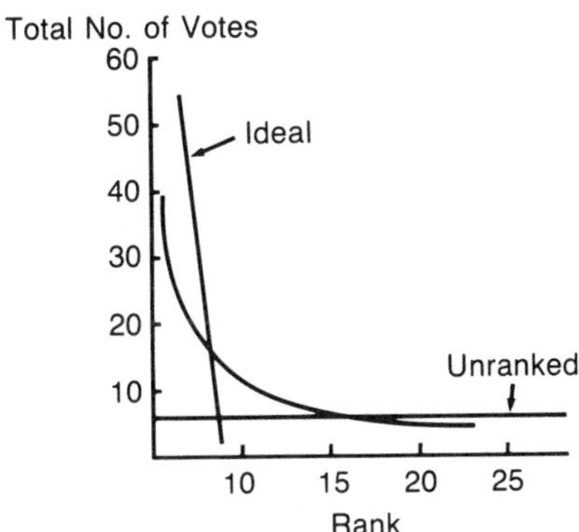

Figure 10 Voting and ranking.

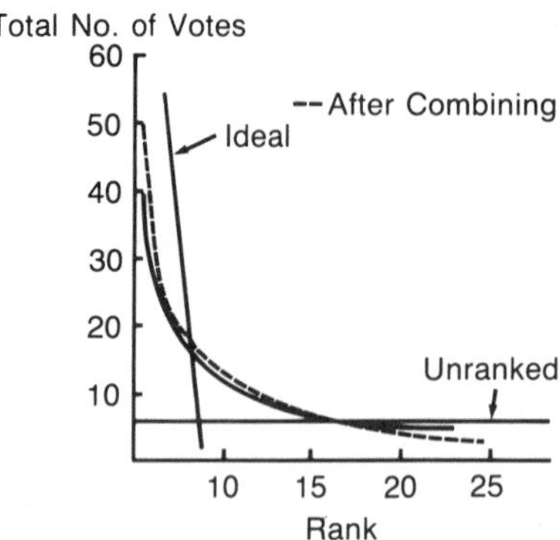

Figure 11 Voting and ranking after combining.

There is a belief that idea generation follows this pattern; a flurry of ideas based on things that are uppermost in the mind, then a gradual drying-up followed by a second wind which produces ideas that come from synergism (thinking about what others have said and synthesizing, hitchhiking, etc.). Figure 12 supports the belief. It shows that about half of the "top 10" ideas come from the first 25% of the list but about 20% of the best ideas come from the *end* of the list. This result argues in favor of finding ways to optimize the round-robin step—to take it far enough to get that last burst of good ideas, but stopping short of damaging levels of participant discomfort.

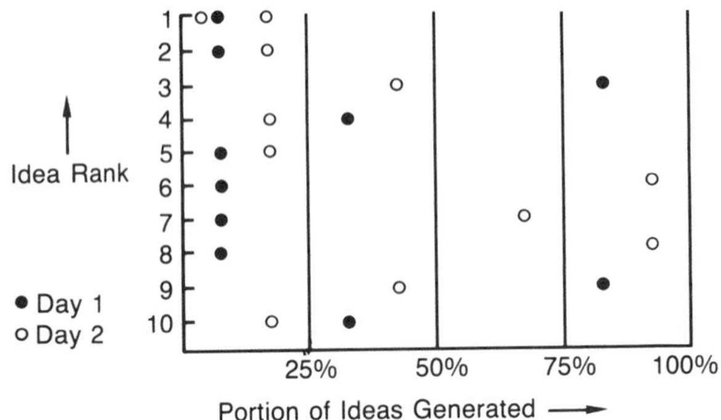

Figure 12 Idea generation.

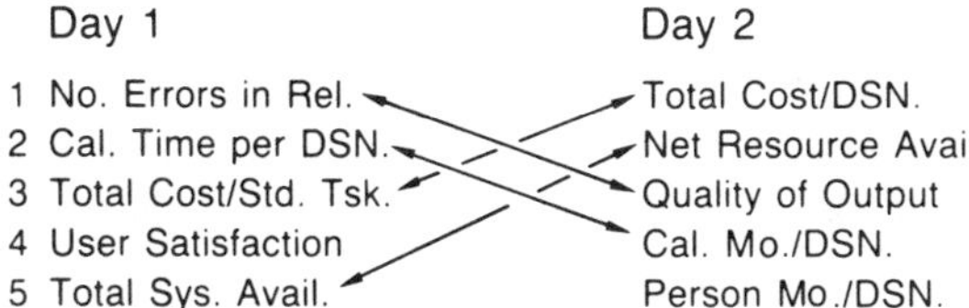

Figure 13 Top five measures.

In Figure 13, the top five ideas of each day are compared and connections are shown where the same basic ideas are expressed with different words. The correspondence is very high and, considering the fact that the day one and day two participants had absolutely no opportunity to interact, the ideas are likely to represent highly useful measures of productivity.

Prior to the joint meetings, there was some speculation about differences that might be seen in certain comparisons; for example, an interesting hypothesis was that there would be a "home team" effect such that team members representing the host location would be more vigorous participants. In fact there was very little difference between the locals and the visitors but if anything, the visitors were slightly more active!

Breakout Sessions

Following the NGT sessions, the top-ranked ideas were further discussed and evaluated with the objective of progressing another notch along the path to implementation. Because there were some differences in the two companies' CAD operations, it was decided that the participants could better deal with the "local realities" of implementation by separating into two groups, each representing one company.

The work session was structured, with the following process steps:

1. Silent generation
2. Free form discussion and recording
3. Voting and ranking
4. Sanity check

and the process was facilitated by use of the worksheet shown in Figure 14. The worksheets were customized for each company by having numbers written in for "low," "medium," and "high" against each of the four evaluation criteria. This was done in advance, with numbers obtained from the implementation decision makers in each company.

Idea no. ____________ Key words ____________

Voting and ranking ____________

- Evaluation

	Low	Medium	High
Effort (total NM to implement)			
Time (calendar time to implement)			
Investment (cost, other than MP)			
Coordination (how many depts. involved)			

What data are needed for this measure? ____________

Where and how can the data be obtained? ____________

Who would use this measure. And how? ____________

- Resources
  I will volunteer to work on this project ____________
  I nominate the following person(s) to work on this project?
  ____________ ____________ ____________
  ____________ ____________ ____________

- Action plan
  The FIRST STEP in the implementation of this ideas is to ____________
  And I envision the following sequence of events AFTER the first step:
  ____

- Obstacles
  The most significant roadblock or obstacle to successful implementation of this idea is:
  ____

- Productivity improvement
  This measure would lead to better understanding of the following productivity barriers or problem areas: ____________

Name (optional) ____________

Figure 14 Worksheet.

Before the session started, the objectives and overall structure of the meeting were explained; followed by instructions on how to use the worksheet:

1. Evaluation. Circle the numbers that most closely agree with your estimates of the amount of effort, time, etc. The numbers entered in the boxes come

from the key decision makers so your estimates will be helpful to them in the decison process. Then record your thoughts regarding data and how the measure would be used.

2. Resources. The idea here is to help implementation by identifying people who could contribute. Volunteer if: (a) you are interested in helping and (b) you have relevant expertise. Nominate others (by name, not title) whom you believe have expertise.
3. Action plan. Often, the hardest part of any plan is figuring out how to get *started*, so focus *just* on that at first. Then, list the major events that would follow—all the way to implementation.
4. Obstacles. Identify the biggest obstacle, it could be a financial constraint, an individual, a legal issue, etc. Be specific, it helps if you say why or how the item is an obstacle.
5. Productivity improvement. With the idea that better understanding of problems leads to improvement, your answers will show the decision makers where they can expect to see productivity improvements as a result of implementing this measure.
6. Name. The forms will be collected and your name will be helpful in case the implementation team wants to discuss some of your ideas with you. However, if putting your name on the form would inhibit you in any way, then omit it. The rule is "getting the truth is more important than getting your name."

The process was employed as shown in Figure 15, with silent generation followed by discussion and recording, two of the measurement ideas at a time, until all the top ideas had been covered. After that the last two steps of the process were completed.

For the silent generation step, participants were asked to fill out a separate worksheet for each of two measurement ideas and they were allowed a total of eight minutes (four minutes per measure)!

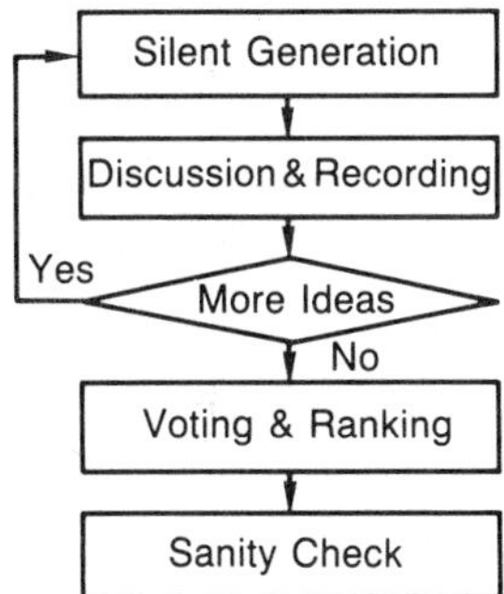

Figure 15 Breakout session.

During the discussion step, key information was recorded for one measurement at a time, on flip-chart-size copies of the worksheet. For example, show-of-hands votes for the estimates of low, medium, and high; and some of the responses to the other questions were written on the flip charts. The main idea of this step was to get a healthy information exchange; participants were encouraged to hitchhike on each others' ideas and to add information to their worksheets as new thoughts come to mind. Discussion was limited to about five minutes per measurement.

For the voting step, participants were asked to take into account:

1. The information that came out during the work session.
2. Their own assessment, for each proposed measure of:
   a. Significance. Does the measure cover a nontrivial portion of the overall CAD operation?
   b. Understandability. As a measure, would its meaning be clear?
   c. Interpretability. Would the measure help decision makers know what actions were needed?
   d. Practicality. Would the measure be fairly easy to implement; could it accommodate change (organizational, technical, etc.) and would it have a positive benefit-cost-ratio?

Voting and ranking followed the NGT conventions.

The sanity check step consisted of a free-form discussion based on the question "Do the results of this meeting—the voting and ranking—make sense; are we missing any important information that would help the decision makers and that would help get the best measures implemented?"

The end results of the breakout sessions are summarized in Figure 16. The fact that 80% of the proposed measures changed rank, compared to their original order, shows the significance of the implementation-oriented work session.

3	Maintained Original Rank	20%
4	Changed Rank ± 1	22%
3	Changed Rank ± 2	20%
4	Changed Rank ± 3	22%
1	Changed Rank ± 4	6%
1	Significant Change (Words)	6%

Figure 16 15 Measures evaluated.

Feedback Questionnaire Results

A questionnaire (Fig. 17) was used to:

1. Assess the value of structured joint efforts (1,4).
2. Determine the degree of individual commitment to the group decisions (2).
3. Get a feeling for the likelihood of closure (implementation) (3).
4. Estimate the amount of experiential learning that occurred (5).

The results were interpreted as follows:

The structured joint meeting was an excellent way to meet the objectives of identifying useful measures of productivity and of revealing productivity improvement opportunities. The opportunity to interact with others, and the exposure to group decision processes, were both considered to be of high personal value.

There was a very high level of personal support for the group decisions, indicating both agreement and commitment.

FEEDBACK QUESTIONNAIRE	1	2	3	4	5
1. Do you feel that the following objectives were met?					
• Identify useful measures of productivity	1	3	5	● 14	
• Identify opportunities for productivity improvement		9	● 7	7	
2. Do you PERSONALLY support the group decisions on					
• Productivity measures		3	3	● 16	1
• Productivity opportunities		4	2	● 14	
3. Will the ideas be implemented?		10	● 11	2	
4. How much value was there to you, personally, in today's meeting?					
• Interaction with others		2	3	● 16	2
• Exposure to NGT process		1	3	● 13	1
5. Do you foresee using NGT, or other group processes, yourself?			11	● 7	5

● = Median value

6. Comments (Typical)

"Best aspect was sharing with a similar group from another company"
"Fantastic opportunity to work with others"
"Extremely useful to me personally; other areas could benefit also"
"Program should be expanded to other areas"
"Useful and interesting interactions"
"Excellent idea to use groups from different companies"
"I find the NGT process very interesting and useful"

Figure 17 IBM-Westinghouse joint effort CAD productivity measurement and improvement.

A degree of conservatism showed up regarding participants' estimates of whether or not the ideas would be implemented. This probably comes from their past experience and is very useful input to the decision makers! For example, news of actual implementations, fed back to the participants, would tend to improve their confidence in the acceptance of ideas.

Experiential learning was judged to be high, based on: (1) the assumption that people tend to use things they understand, and (2) the response indicating that many of the participants plan to use group processes in their own work.

The results of the questionnaire were fed back to the participants, who were all extremely interested, as well as to their managers and the decision makers.

Follow-up and Implementation

After the joint meeting, each company dealt with the ideas independently.

In IBM, the site coordinator continued on with the follow-up and presentation to the decision maker. He convened two meetings of all the IBM participants for the purpose of combining their two lists and then discussing, clarifying, evaluating, and revoting. The result was six proposed CAD productivity measures (Fig. 18a) that were strongly endorsed by the participants.

Presentation to the decision-making manager led to the following actions:

1. Two of the proposals were accepted for implementation and four were assigned to investigation.
2. Tentative plans were made to expand the use of group problem-solving processes within the organization.

At Westinghouse, the ideas (Fig. 18b) were presented to the decision maker just as they came from the breakout sessions. As a result of that presentation the following took place:

1. A decision was made to implement three of the measures and to investigate seven others.
2. Plans were made to use NGT at several Westinghouse divisions and locations to help meet an established corporate goal of increasing productivity by 6.1% a year.

By the model pictured in Figure 19 it can be seen that the proposed measures are at the "tentative yes" position in the implementation sequence. Good progress so far, but there's still a lot of work ahead and continued attention will be necessary.

Total system/net resources useability
Compute resource to complete a task
Quality of CAD output
User satisfaction
Calendar time to complete a task
Total cost of the design

a) IBM

No. of errors in release
Calendar time to complete a task
Toal cost per standard task
Drawing calendar time vs. standard
Response statistics
User satisfaction with CAD
Weighted % of each task process which can be automated
Total cost for the design
Quality of CAD output
Cost savings as a function of investment
Person months per design cycle
Ease of engineering changes
Net resource availability
Calendar months per product design cycle

b) Westinghouse

Figure 18 Proposed productivity measures.

For example, most of the measures are still expressed in high-level form such as "quality of CAD output," and will need to be broken down into several lower level measures such as "number of engineering changes to correct CAD errors," "amount of rework or scrap attributed to CAD errors," and so on. Many of the lower level measures were discussed during the NGT meetings and the breakout sessions, so use of those who volunteered to help with implementation will maintain continuity of focus and interpretation.

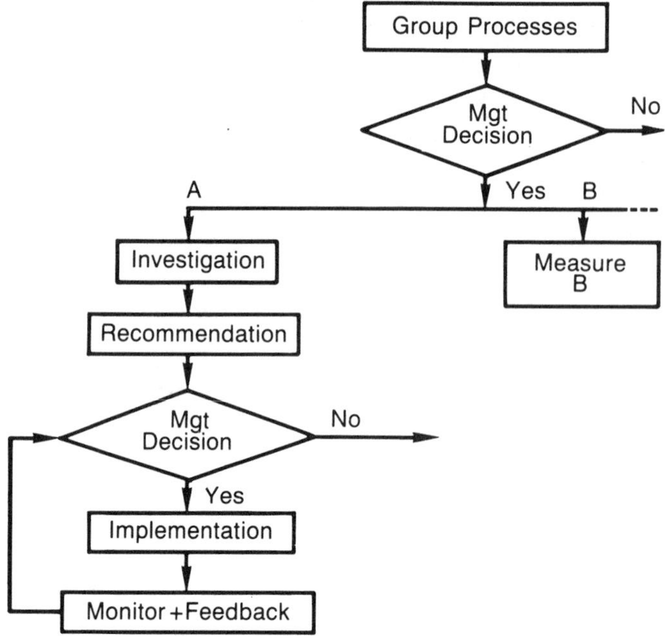

Figure 19 Implementation sequence.

Summary

A comparison of the results to the reasons for having the joint effort shows that:

1. The primary objectives were met; useful measures of CAD productivity were identified and will almost certainly be implemented. The measures in turn will lead to productivity improvement.
2. A model for intercompany cooperation, facilitated by a neutral party, has been demonstrated.
3. All participating individuals and organizations received something of value from their participation.

The group process activities were not set up as a controlled experiment, so the observations and results are not presented as proof of anything; but these same observations and results strongly support the contentions of those who advocate such group processes for situations where no one person has all the answers and where a high level of personal commitment is needed. These were exactly the conditions pertaining in the search for CAD productivity measures. The process

Rank	Idea No.	Idea	Vote	Total
1	2.	Number of errors in release	4777666	43
2	7.	Measured drawing time (calendar) against established norm (new CAD vs. old CAD vs. manual)	765557	35
3	65.	Total cost per standard task	5712572	29
4	18.	User satisfaction with CAD system	31767	24
5	3.	Calendar time to complete a task	23474	20
6	6.	Total system availability	7613	17
7	5.	Weighted percentage of each task process which can be automated	654	15
8	1.	Response statistics	5622	15
9	51.	Percentage of total number of tasks which can be affected downstream	427	13
10	22.	Number of pre-release design iterations to a finished product	525	12
11	30.	Percent of system utilization	433	10
12	19.	Number of units produced per day (std. or weighted)	36	9
13	27.	User CAD session hours per fixed number of interactions (Measure *system*)	135	9
14	15.	Number of CAD interactions to complete a task	62	8
15	48.	Number of proposals accepted (win ratio)	44	8
16	4.	Drawings checked vs. drawing accepted	15	6
17	8.	Plan vs. actual output at several management levels (group output, not individual)	6	6
18	55.	Ability to maintain increased workload with same number of people	6	6
19	13.	Work station working conditions (opinion survey)	23	5
20	40.	Ratio of change incorporation time per change	14	5
21	62.	Number of interactions/day	5	5
22	9.	Hours, and the variables that make up those hours	4	4
23	24.	Tool knowledge (amount of time to learn)	4	4
24	32.	Number of CAD software bugs found (per release)	31	4
25	44.	User session time to complete a task	31	4
26	49.	Work time vs. waiting time per job	4	4
27	23.	Ratio of labor hours (cost vs. material cost, per design)	3	4
28	68.	Ratio of standard design building blocks to total number of blocks	3	3
29	16.	Ratio of standard parts to total parts used	2	2
30	28.	Documentation cost per product	2	2
31	43.	Number of different part numbers vs. total number of parts	2	2
32	17.	New user capabilities added/calendar time	1	1
33	31.	Weighted scale for system downtime (service contract)	1	1
34	52.	Reduced manufacturing errors	1	1
35	11.	Number of N/C tool paths (N/C tape)	0	0
36	20.	Plan vs. actual output at *individual* level	0	0
37	39.	Normalized CAD CPU (minutes per session hour)	0	0
38	42.	Number of design steps from beginning to end	0	0
39	45.	Ratio of microfilm acceptability per total number of drawings	0	0
40	57.	Ratio of designs to assets	0	0
41	60.	Number of entities in the data base per hour of system time	0	0
42	66.	Percentage of recommendations implemented effectively	0	0
43	67.	Absenteeism	0	0
44	69.	Number of entities vs. number of interactions	0	0

Figure 20 CAD productivity measurement and improvement, September 21, 1981.

yielded good solutions and a high level of commitment. A significant factor, according to the participants, was the synergism generated by exposure to others' thinking.

The breakout sessions produced better definition of the proposed measures and some adjustments in ranking, a result of considering the local realities. Equally important, the major elements of a proposal to management were developed; and the participants' level of agreement and commitment was increased.

The productivity measures that were recommended for implementation do not constitute a comprehensive set. Yet, they represent a substantial beginning and it is reasonable to assume that the group process approach will be used to identify additional measures as needed; especially once the first few are successfully implemented.

Rank	Idea No.	Idea	Vote	Total
45	10.	Cost per circuit	Deleted During Clarification Phase of N.G.T.	
46	12.	Productively influencing others who provide hardware/software		
47	14.	Improved quality of design data		
48	21.	Benefits derived downstream from initial outputs		
49	25.	Actual availability of hardware		
50	26.	Improved effectiveness and efficiency of individual design time		
51	29.	Morale/attitude of users		
52	33.	Proper utilization of all equipment for efficient thru-put		
53	34.	Ratio of design time to CAD session hours		
54	35.	Number of design changes, post release		
55	36.	Freedom of design		
56	37.	Adequate support tools		
57	38.	More output per person		
58	41.	User perceived response time		
59	46.	Capacity of entire environment		
60	47.	Compare CAD time to manual for a given job		
61	50.	Improved profitability due to reduced cycle time		
62	53.	Reduced field changes		
63	54.	Worker/job satisfaction		
64	56.	Application familiarity		
65	58.	Automation of tasks relative to leverage gain by automation		
66	59.	Weighted user queue		
67	61.	Stock dividend/price earnings ratio		
68	63.	Number of manufacturing tool reworks		
69	64.	Complexity of the environment		

Figure 21 IBM-Westinghouse joint effort CAD productivity measurement and improvement, September 21, 1981.

1. Number of errors in release
2. Calendar time to complete a task
3. Total cost per standard task
4. Measured drawing time (calendar) against established norm (new CAD vs. old CAD vs. manual)
5. Total system availability
6. Response statistics
7. User satisfaction with CAD system
8. Weighted percentage of each task process which can be automated

Figure 22 Westinghouse breakout session, September 21, 1983.

CONCLUSIONS

Given the appropriate conditions, such as existed in the effort to define useful measures of CAD productivity, a group process like NGT can be expected to give excellent results in terms of problem solution and individual commitment to the solution.

The synergism produced by exposing participants to others' way of thinking is probably at a maximum when two or more companies get together. Still, some of the same effect could reasonably be expected within a company if different locations or departments, etc. joined forces.

Figures 20 through 25 illustrate total ideas generated and ideas deleted during the clarification phase. Also included are the results of the Westinghouse breakout sessions.

ACKNOWLEDGMENTS

The "IBM-Westinghouse Joint Effort: CAD Productivity Measures Case Study" was reprinted with permission from the American Producivity Center. The case study was conducted by A. M. Healy and M. E. Coticchia. The nominal group technique was developed by Andre L. Belbecq and Andrew H. Van de Ben in 1968.

Rank	Idea No.	Idea	Vote	Total
1	1.	Total cost for the design	357775	34
2	2.	Net resource available	456644	29
3	22.	Quality of CAD output	76276	28
4	5.	Calendar months per product design cycle	64456	25
5	7.	Person months/design cycle	7453	19
6	45.	Profit change as f (investment)	2671	16
7	28.	Ease of engineering changes	564	15
8	46.	User friendly system	634	13
9	20.	Reduction in turnaround time	5161	13
10	6.	Number of corrective revisions/product	3315	12
11	15.	Person machine time vs. person drafting time	174	12
12	41.	Rise of profits per manhour	75	12
13	8.	Quality of accuracy of input data	74	11
14	27.	Cost value machine vs. drafting	37	10
15	24.	Product density	162	9
16	18.	Hardware utilization	35	8
17	51.	Number of transactions per unit output	242	8
18	33.	Total cost of documentation	7	7
19	9.	Design thru-put	6	6
20	4.	Number of documents produced per unit time	312	6
21	3.	System responsiveness	5	5
22	14.	Number of loops in design cycle	32	5
23	25.	Rework labor and scrap cost	5	5
24	38.	Program capabilities	23	5
25	50.	User acceptance	41	5
26	40.	Number of separate steps in design process	13	4
27	26.	Amount of waiting time per design	21	3
28	30.	Training cycle (length)	3	3
29	35.	Human/environmental factos (QWL)	2	2
30	19.	Number of user inputs to design system	2	2
31	21.	Machine uptime	2	2
32	16.	Devices analyzed per CPU min	11	2
33	10.	Accuracy of engineering analysis	0	0
34	11.	Reduction of processing time	0	0
35	12.	Number of design stations per CPU	0	0
36	13.	Customer acceptance	0	0
37	23.	Flexibility of conceptual design	0	0
38	29.	Experience level of operators	0	0
39	31.	Opportunity loss	0	0
40	34.	Tool availability per employee request	0	0
41	39.	Data loss hours	0	0
42	42.	Amount of rework due to process changes in the design cycle	0	0
43	43.	Absenteeism of users	0	0
44	44.	User attrition (turnover)	0	0
45	47.	Customer incentive bonus points	0	0
46	49.	Baseline measurement		

Figure 23 IBM-Westinghouse joint effort CAD productivity measurement and improvement, September 22, 1981.

IBM-WESTINGHOUSE JOINT EFFORT
CAD PRODUCTIVITY MEASUREMENT AND IMPROVEMENT
SEPTEMBER 22, 1981

Rank	Idea No.	Idea	Vote	Total
47	17	Ease of use	Deleted During Clarification Phase of N.G.T.	
48	32	Frustration level of users		
49	36	Number of user interactions per unit task		
50	37	Total design cycle		
51	48	System configuration		

Figure 24 Deleted during clarification phase of NGT.

1. Total cost for the design
2. Quality of CAD output
3. Profit change as (investment)
4. Ease of engineering changes
5. Person months/design cycle
6. Net resource available
7. Calendar months per product design cycle

Figure 25 Westinghouse breakout session, September 22, 1981.

PUTTING THE NGT RESULTS TO WORK

As seen in the case study, the NGT offers a structured approach to developing productivity measures. This technique can be applied to any organization and offer significant benefits:

Management insight into the operation of an organization
Visibility of the information assists in the implementation of actions which can improve the organization activities
A yardstick to measure organizational performance relative to broader organizational goals and objectives.

The next step is to develop a productivity measurement system, and in order to do so, one must establish detailed performance ratios for all activities of the organization.

	Indices	Year '75	'76	'77	'78	'79
1.	$ Value of Total Cost improvement / Salary/Benefits of Engr. Personnel Spent on Cost Improvements and Model Experiments	3.55	1.46	1.83	3.64	3.98
2.	Cost of Engineering Errors / Inventory Cost at Standard (ICS) in 000	0.619	0.610	0.644	0.618	1.063
3.	Operating Managed Cost (Engr) / Gross Sales Billed	0.040	0.054	0.047	0.039	0.034
4.	No. Drawings Handled / No. Draftsmen	678.8	604.2	606.9	662.0	705.5
5.	Warranty Costs in $ / Gross Sales Billed (in 000)	1.563	1.011	1.344	0.692	0.670
6.	No. Days Orders Late / No. Days Orders are in Engineering	0.17	0.23	0.19	0.15	0.12

7. $\dfrac{\text{Strategic Managed Cost (Engr)}}{\text{Gross Sales Billed}}$		0.0011	0.0008	0.0010	0.0010	0.0013
8. $\dfrac{\text{Value Added (Constant \$)}}{\text{No. Employees (Engr)}}$	(in 000)	462.9	506.1	486.3	489.0	510.7
Composite Department Index (CDI)		0.780	0.682	0.688	0.863	0.082

*Statistics are for illustrative purposes only.

$$\text{CDI} = 0.1\,(0.25)\left[\frac{\text{\$ Value of Cost Improvement}}{\text{Salary and Benefit of Engr. Personnel}}\right] + 0.1\,(0.6)\left[\frac{\text{Cost of Engr. Errors}}{\text{ICS (in 000's)}}\right]^{-1}$$

$$+\ 0.4\,(0.03)\left[\frac{\text{OMC (Engr.)}}{\text{GSB}}\right]^{-1} = 0.1\,(1.3 \times 10^{-1})\left[\frac{\text{No. Drawings Handled}}{\text{No. Draftsman}}\right]$$

$$+\ 0.1\,(0.7)\left[\frac{\text{Warranty Costs}}{\text{GSB}}\right]^{-1} + 0.1\,(0.12)\left[\frac{\text{No. Days: Orders Late}}{\text{No. Days: Orders in Engr.}}\right]^{-1}$$

$$+\ 0.1\,(0.001)\left[\frac{\text{SMC}}{\text{GSB}}\right]^{-1}$$

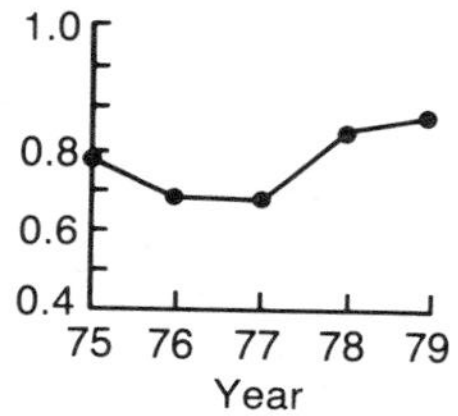

Figure 26 Productivity measurements: engineering department.

The ratios to be utilized should be identified by the manager who is responsible for overall organizational performance. He is in the best position to know the mission, goals, and responsibilities.

Once the performance ratios are chosen, one can start creating a composite index. The index is simply assembled from a weighted combination of selected performance ratios.

For illustrative purposes, an example of productive measurements developed by a typical engineering department is shown in Figure 26. The methodology includes the following five steps:

1. Selection of performance ratios
2. Assignment of weights
3. Establishment of arithmetic base factors
4. Creation of arithmetic base factors
5. Utilization of composite indices

Selection of Performance Ratios

Eight performance ratios were developed to indicate how effectively the engineering department was performing its activities. These eight performance ratios were developed from NGT results shown in Figure 27.

Assignment of Weights

Weights, based on a 100% scale, were assigned to the seven selected ratios which would comprise the composite index. In this example, the first ratio ($ value of cost improvement/salary and benefit of engineering personnel) had an assigned weight of 10%. This weight should be assigned by appropriate management personnel.

Establishment of Arithmetic Base Factors

The numbers which appear in parentheses for each of the ratios of the composite index equation can be called arithmetic base factors. These base factors are used to adjust the ratios so that they could be compared on the same arithmetic base scale.

An examination of the indices for the engineering department will demonstrate the necessity for these base factors. The fourth ratio has a normal range of values which is 225 times that of the first ratio. Therefore, in order to assign weights to these two ratios which would accurately reflect management's view of the relationships between them, each had to be multiplied by an arithmetic base factor. Now each ratio has a normal range of values that is directly comparable to other ratios.

Ideas	Votes	Total
1. $ of cost improvement reported/value improvement orders completed on time	6-6-5-4-3-2	26
2. No. of overdue shop orders	8-7-5-2-1	23
3. Cost of engineering errors (830 acct.)	8-6-4-2-1	21
4. $ COD/GSB	7-6-4-3	20
5. Total engineering cost/GSB	8-6-5	19
6. No. of drawing transmittals	5-4-3-3-2	17
7. No. of orders completed	8-8	16
8. Turn-around time for production work testing	7-7	14
9. Product cost/sales billed $	7-6-1	14
10. Warranty and field problem $ due to engineering/engineering field trouble/GSB/ field failure cost/GSB	8-3-1	12
11. Absenteeism %	7-3-1	11
12. No. of drawings processed	4-2	6
13. Average days to complete customer order	5	5
14. $ of sales due to new/improved products	5	5
15. Competitive cost comparison	4	4
16. $ outside funded project vs. total engineering budget	2	2
17. GSB (premium)/total GSB	1	1
18. Pounds blueprint paper	0	0
19. Internal vs. external failure rate	0	0
20. % time on projects vs. O/H time/amount of 24 time	0	0
21. No. of product development veritifications per year	0	0
22. O/T hours worked	0	0
23. No. of communications with marketing	0	0
24. Engineering equipment availability and adequacy (subjective)	0	0
25. Delays in assigning work (backlog)	0	0
26. Shipments missed due to engineering errors	0	0
27. No. of BOM	0	0
28. % Completed-on-time engineering projects	0	0

Figure 27 Productivity measurement ideas generated through the nominal group technique (for the Engineering Department).

Creation of the Arithmetic Base Factor

The arithmetic base factor for each ratio is calculated as the reciprocal of a number which falls within the ratio's normal range of values. This can be illustrated by the first ratio in Figure 26. The number 3.98 is a number which will fall towards the upper end of this ratio's normal range of values. The reciprocal of 3.98 is .25, which is the arithmetic base factor for the first ratio.

An alternate method for the creation of the arithmetic base factor is to look at the range of numbers and throw out the one which deviates significantly from that range.

Then take the reciprocal of the average from the range of numbers. For example, in the first ratio in Figure 26, throw out 1.46 and the average for the range from 1.83 to 3.98 is 3.25. The reciprocal of 3.25 is .31. Therefore, .31 is the arithmetic base factor.

Utilization of Composite Indices

The choice of base factors will determine the raw overall numerical value for each composite index. The purpose served by this index is the ability to measure the effectiveness of an organization over time.

THE COMPOSITE INDEX

The preceding example suggests some possible indicators which could be applicable in many engineering organizations. A word of caution: since the goals and responsibilities of any organization will be specific to that organization, it is important to recognize that the figures are examples only; measures must be developed within an organization based upon its specific mission, responsibilities, and objectives.

ACKNOWLEDGMENTS

Most of this section was adapted from "Productivity Measurement at the Department Level," produced by the Operations Analysis Department and David L. Rowe, Westinghouse Electric Corporation.

OTHER PRODUCTIVITY MEASUREMENT METHODS

There exist many other methods to measure productivity associated with CAD/CAM systems. The NGT/composite index method discussed in the preceding text is one recommended method. Many other methods can also be used to achieve the same results. This section will present several other techniques currently used in industry.

Shah and Yan Technique

The Shah and Yan technique is based on the analyses of the benefits and costs associated with the operation of CAD/CAM systems. This technique considers economic analysis of CAD in the drawing office environment and assumes that the increase in productivity of existing manpower is the only benefit. The reasoning is that many of the benefits associated with CAD are intangibles (i.e., cannot be translated into monetary terms).

This technique is based on the principles that benefits minus costs equals net gain, and net gain is a measure of the economic viability of a particular installation.

The derivation of the following equations will not be discussed in this part. Rather, it is intended to be a "cookbook" of formulas for the user's ease of use.

Specifically, this technique can be applied to:

1. Derive the cost justification for acquiring a new CAD facility,
2. Determine the number of CAD work stations necessary for a given organization.
3. Determine the operating strategy for new or existing installations, and
4. Monitor the utilization of existing installations.

The following is an excerpt from "A Practical Technique for Benefit-Cost Analysis of Computer-Aided Design and Drafting Systems."

The benefit B_i dollars per given period in producing N_i category i drawings on CAD versus producing manually is given by:

$$B_i = C_D\,(nwH)f_iA(I_i - 1)$$

where

C_D = the average man-hour cost of a designer
n = the number of work stations on CAD
w = the number of working shifts per day
H = the number of single shift working hours in the period
f_i = the fraction of CAD system time allotted to category i drawings ($0 \leq f_i \leq 1$)
A = the average system availability factory, and
I_i = the ratio $S_{M_i}/(S_{S_i}/E)$
S_{M_i} = the average man-hours needed for drafting a category i drawing (including revisions) and, where applicable, extracting data for wiring lists from the drawing manually
S_{S_i} = the average man-hours needed using CAD for drafting a category i drawing (including revisions) and, where applicable, extracting data for wiring lists from the drawing
E = the efficiency with which a designer operates CAD

Overall benefit B dollars per period is thus:

$$B = \sum_i B_i$$

Overall cost C dollars per period is made up of a number of specific cost factors:

$$C = C_T + C_{AP} + C_E + C_I + C_M + C_{SP}$$

where

C_T = the cost of training designers to operate CAD
C_{AP} = the cost of generating application packages
C_E = the amortized cost of the CAD equipment
C_I = the amortized cost of CAD installation
C_M = the cost of the equipment maintenance
C_{SP} = the cost of user support

All the above cost factors are in dollars per period.

If C' is the cost per terminal-hour of a CAD, where

$$C' = \frac{C}{nwH}$$

then, the overall net gain G_i dollars per period if N_i category i drawings are produced on CAD versus manually is:

$$G_i = C_D(nwH)f_i \quad A(I_i - 1) - \frac{1}{U}\frac{C'}{C_D}$$

where U is the system utilization factor given by

$$U = \sum_i f_i$$

Thus, net gain G_i is positive only if

$$I_i > \frac{1}{UA} \frac{C'}{C_D} + 1 \approx \frac{C'}{C_D} + 1$$

since both U and A have values close to one.

Since the terminal-hour cost C' for a CAD can be estimated, the above expression can be used to determine which application, if implemented on CAD, will yield a positive net gain G_i.

Overall net gain G dollars per period is:

$$G = \sum_i G_i$$

The value of overall net gain G at each stage of the CAD implementation phase will vary and will depend on the activities at that stage.

The average number of N_i of category i drawing produced in the period is given by:

$$N_i - (nwH)f_iA(E/S_{S_i})$$

Also, the number of designers P_i needed to produce N_i drawings is given by:

$$P_i = nw\frac{H}{H'}\ f_iA\left[\frac{\frac{M_{S_i}}{S_{S_i}}}{E} + 1\right]$$

where

H' = the average number of hours worked per designer in the period, after taking into account vacation and sick leave and

M_{S_i} = the average man-hours needed for planning, preparation, approval, issue, and distribution of category i drawing produced on CAD.

Computer Impact Value

The computer impact value (CIV) is the ratio of the current cost savings per week using computers to the total cost savings per week going from *all manual* to *optimum* computer use. Thus, it is a measure of progress, numerically less than one. It is calculated using the following expression:

$$CIV = \frac{G\ D_{max}}{D}\left[\frac{H(D - 1) - 40\frac{I}{FE}}{\frac{H(D_{max} - 1) - I}{3}}\right]$$

where

G = fraction of work for which computers are used compared with potential uses $(0 \leq G \leq 1)$

D_{max} = maximum attainable productivity ratio (work output rate using computers, compared to manual)

D = current productivity ratio

H = labor rate, dollars/people-week

I = computer cost, dollars/people-week

F = average planned equipment utilization, hours/week $(0 \leq F \leq 120)$

E = equipment uptime fraction $(0 \leq E \leq 1)$

The computer impact value can also be defined as:

$$CIV = \frac{R_1 - R_2}{R_1 - R_3}$$

where

R_1 = cost of doing all current work manually
R_2 = cost of doing all current work in the present manner
R_3 = cost of doing all current work with optimum computer utilization

The computer impact value coefficient gives an easily comprehended understanding of how much progress has been made in computer utilization. Also, cost reduction potential can be examined as a quantitative result of changing various operational parameters, such as productivity (increase training and incentives), uptime/downtime (improve system reliability), hours worked (expand multishift usage), etc.

The computer impact value is a useful tool to answer typical management questions, such as:

1. Develop a least-cost plan.
2. Recommend the number of people who should be using computers.
3. Recommend the percent uptime improvement.
4. What are the average weekly hours of computer utilization?
5. What is the percent of work for which computers are used?

Pray Technique

This technique is simple to apply and a very useful method of measuring engineering productivity associated with computer-aided design.

The following assumptions are made:

1. The principle outputs to be measured are engineering drawings released.
2. The basic inputs in terms of effort are engineering hours.
3. The availability of equipment is measured in terms of the fraction of total scheduled hours available for productive use. Downtime and training time should be deducted as not available time. One hundred percent availability should be all scheduled hours on-line for productive use.
4. Yield should be considered in terms of drawings that require no changes after release. Exclude category of change which is beyond control, such as prime equipment changes.

Realizing that an absolute value cannot be derived, the following simple relationship can be applied to measure progress over time:

$$P = RAY$$

where

P = productivity
R = rate of drawings released (drawings released per hours of engineering and drafting)
A = availability of CAD (ratio of uptime for productive use to total schedule time)
Y = yield of acceptable drawings (ratio of acceptable drawings with no revisions to total released drawings)

Charts 1–4, drawings/man-hour available, drawing yield and productivity, respectively, can then be constructed. The user can then plot productivity versus time (Fig. 28).

Chart 1 CAD Productivity-Ratio-Drawings/Labor-hour

		JAN	FEB	MAR	APR	MAY	JUN	JUL	AUG	SEPT	OCT	NOV	DEC
1 CAD Dwg Released	#	24	11	18	31	30	46	53					
2 CUM Dwgs Rel	#		35	53	84	114	160	213					
3 Drafting	Hr	7047	12803	11020	9453	10432	13091	12370					
4 CUM Dftg.	Hr		19850	30870	40323	50755	63846	77216					
5 Engineering	Hr	17015	28171	32441	21162	24648	30310	30702					
6 CUM Engrg.	Hr		45186	67627	88989	113637	143947	174649					
7 Engrg. & Dftg.	Hr	24062	40974	33461	30815	35080	43401	43072					
8 CUM Eng. & Dftg.	Hr		61036	98497	129312	164392	207793	250865					
Drafting													
9 Ratio Mthly.	1 : 3	.0034	.00086	.0016	.0033	.0029	.0035	.0042					
10 Ratio CUM	2 : 4		.00176	.0017	.0021	.0022	.0025	.0027					
11 Ratio Qtrly.				.0017			.0032						
Engrg. & Dftg.	RATIO												
12 Monthly	1 : 7	.001	.00027	.00054	.0010	.0009	.0010	.0012					
13 CUM	2 : 8		.00057	.00054	.00065	.00069	.0007	.0008					
14 Quarterly							.0010						
Drafting Hr /Dwg	Based on Terminal Hr /Dwg.												
15 Monthly		24.8	106.	76.3	61	62.2	42.3	54.7					
16 CUM						60.5	55.3	55.9					
17 Quarterly				59.2			53.3						

*Statistics are for Illustrative Purposes Only

Chart 2 CAD Productivity Available

		JAN	FEB	MAR	APR	MAY	JUN	JUL	AUG	SEPT	OCT	NOV	DEC
1 Tot. Avail.	Hr	2304	2584	3128	2856	2720	3104	3192					
2 CUM Total	Hr		4884	8012	10868	13588	16692	19884					
3 Terminal Downtime	Hr	96	42.4	37.2	88.8	64.0	112	48					
4 CUM Term. Downtime	Hr		138.4	175.6	264.4	328.4	440.4	488.4					
5 Training	Hr	303	387.8	302.7	129.1	145.9	132.7	142.5					
6 CUM Training	Hr		690.8	993.5	1222.6	1368.5	1501.2	1643.7					
7 Application Dev.	Hr	303	346.9	530.5	507.7	398.7	347.4	433.5					
8 CUM Appl. Dev.	Hr		649.9	1180.4	1688.1	2086.8	2434.2	2867.7					
9 N/C Appl.	Hr	180	151.4	315.0	139.0	77.6	89.8	67.6					
10 CUM N/C Appl.	Hr		331.4	646.4	785.4	863.0	952.8	1020.4					
11 Unapplied	Hr	828	488.1	491.8	184.1	231.5	620.0	·511.9					
12 CUM Unapplied	Hr		1316.1	1807.9	1992.0	2223.5	2843.5	2331.6					
13 Productive	Hr	595	1167.4	1373.4	1896.1	1866.3	1946.1	3060.3					
14 CUM Productive	Hr		1762.4	3135.8	5031.9	6898.2	8844.3	11904.6					
15 Prod. Utilization	13 : 1	.258	.452	.439	.664	.686	.627	.959					
16 CUM Prod. Util.	14 : 2		.361	.391	.463	.508	.530	.599					
17 CUM Prod. Util. Qtrly				.391			.658						

*Statistics are for Illustrative Purposes Only

Chart 3 CAD Productivity-Drawing Yield

		JAN	FEB	MAR	APR	MAY	JUN	JUL	AUG	SEPT	OCT	NOV	DEC
1 Dwgs. Released	#	24	11	18	31	30	46	53					
2 CUM Dwg. Rel.	#		35	53	84	114	160	213					
3 "A" Type R/N s	#	—	—	—	—		3	6					
4 CUM "A" Type R/N s	#						3	9					
5 No. Dwgs.	1 + 3	24	11	18	31	30	49	59					
6 CUM Dwgs.	2 + 4						163	222					
7 Qtrly. Dwgs.	#						107						
8 Monthly Ratio	1÷5	1	1	1	1	1	.939	.898					
9 CUM Ratio	2÷6						.982	.959					
10 Qtrly. Ratio							.972						

*Statistics are for Illustrative Purposes Only

Chart 4 CAD Productivity-Productivity

	CHART / COL.	JAN	FEB	MAR	APR	MAY	JUN	JUL	AUG	SEPT	OCT	NOV	DEC
R - Monthly	1/12	.001	.00027	.00054	.0010	.0009	.0010	.0012					
R - CUM	1/13		.00057	.00054	.00065	.00069	.0007	.0008					
A - Monthly	2/15	.258	.452	439	.664	.686	.627	.959					
A - CUM	2/16		.361	.391	.463	.508	.530	.599					
Y - Monthly	3/8	1	1	1	1	1	.939	.898					
Y - CUM	3/9						.982	.959					
PRODUCTIVITY													
Monthly	1x3x5	.000258	.000122	.00024	.00066	.00062	.00062	.0010					
PRODUCTIVITY													
CUM	2x4x6		.00021	.00021	.0003	.0004	.0004	.0005					
PRODUCTIVITY													
Quarterly				.00021			.0006						

*Statistics are for Illustrative Purposes Only

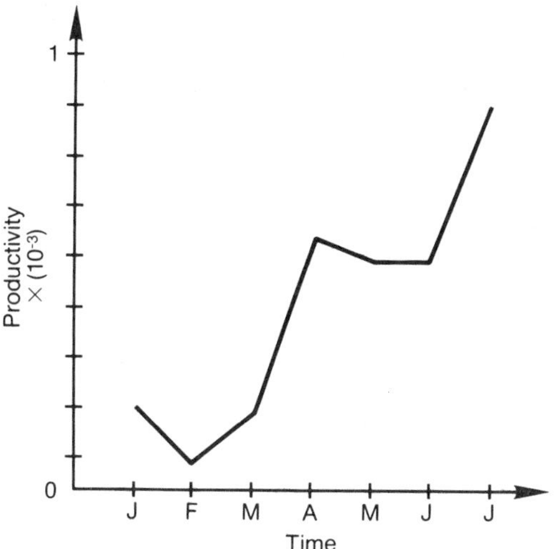

Figure 28 PRAY technique plot.

CONCLUSION

As one can see, these techniques can be applied to measure progress of a CAD/CAM installation. However, most productivity measurement techniques require some degree of record keeping. The next section will examine two software packages that are in use for record keeping purposes.

ACKNOWLEDGMENTS

Much of the Shah and Yan technique was excerpted from "A Practical Technique for Benefit-Cost Analysis of Computer-Aided Design and Drafting Systems," by R. R. Shah and G. Yan, Atomic Energy of Canada Limited. The computer impact values derivation is presented in "Modeling Computer Cost Effectiveness," by Dr. Laird E. Johnston, General Motors. The PRAY technique was developed by E. L. Smith, Westinghouse Electric Corporation.

JOB ACCOUNTING PACKAGES

There are several kinds of job accounting packages available. These packages are usually developed by the vendor, although some are developed by the user. One particular package called WESAVE (Westinghouse Electric System for Analysis Verification and Evaluation) was developed by Computervision and Westinghouse.

WESAVE

WESAVE is a collection of programs for the purpose of reporting system utilization, efficiency, and productivity. Data input is accomplished through the use of the Computervision accounting package and additional prompting PEP programs to track the release of engineering documents and hardware and software maintenance time. WESAVE generates reports and graphs analyzing the activities of each project, department, operator, device, and the total system. The objective of WESAVE is to provide user management with an additional tool for further maximization of productivity.

Drawing Release Report

As drawings are released during the month, the system records each release (see Fig. 29). At the end of each month, a summary is compiled and printed. The information in this report includes:

1. Date of release
2. Author of the document
3. Author's department

DRAWINGS RELEASED IN JANUARY
1981

DATE	DRAWN BY:	DEPT.	PART ID.	REV.	SIZE	# OF SHEETS	TITLE OF DRAWING
1-2-81	JAH	DRAF	Q-12345B	2	187.0	2	BALL AND JOINT ASSEMBLY
	JAH	DRAF	Q-12345C	2	187.0	2	BALL AND JOINT ASSEMBLY
	JAH	DRAF	Q-12345D	2	187.0	2	BALL AND JOINT ASSEMBLY
	JAH	DRAF	Q-12345E	2	187.0	2	BALL AND JOINT ASSEMBLY
	RCG	DRAF	Q-45345C	2	187.0	2	SEALED BEARING ASSEMBLY
	NAY	DRAF	DFK2345B	3	187.0	2	CONICAL JOINT ASSEMBLY
	NAY	DRAF	DFK2345R	2	187.0	3	CONICAL JOINT ASSEMBLY
1-6-81	RKF	DRAF	09907P	3	374.0	2	SEALED CONE DESIGN
	RKF	DRAF	P9907P	3	374.0	2	SEALED CONE DESIGN
	RKF	DRAF	Q9907P	3	374.0	2	SEALED CONE DESIGN
	RKF	DRAF	R9907P	3	374.0	2	SEALED CONE DESIGN
	RKF	DRAF	S9907P	3	374.0	2	SEALED CONE DESIGN
	RKF	DRAF	T9907P	3	374.0	2	SEALED CONE DESIGN
	RKF	DRAF	U9907P	3	374.0	2	SEALED CONE DESIGN
	RKF	DRAF	V9907P	3	374.0	2	SEALED CONE DESIGN
	TDR	DSGN	M44W88	3	374.0	2	SEALED JOINT DESIGN
	BEB	ENGC	GJJ98L	3	374.0	3	UNSEALED CONE DESIGN
	BEB	ENGC	GJJ98P	3	374.0	2	UNSEALED CONE DESIGN
	RKF	DRAF	FG448Y	3	374.0	2	CONE AND ARM DESIGN
	RKF	DRAF	PG448Y	3	374.0	2	CONE AND ARM DESIGN
	RKF	DRAF	QG448Y	3	374.0	2	CONE AND ARM DESIGN
	RKF	DRAF	TG448Y	3	374.0	2	CONE AND ARM DESIGN
	SKS	DRAF	RG448Y	3	374.0	2	CONE AND ARM DESIGN
	SKS	DRAF	XG448Y	3	374.0	2	CONE AND ARM DESIGN
	SKS	DRAF	ZG448Y	3	374.0	2	CONE AND ARM DESIGN
	WMR	DRAF	VDF100	3	374.0	2	JOINT AND ROD DESIGN
	WMR	DRAF	VDF100	3	374.0	2	JOINT AND ROD DESIGN
	WMR	DRAF	VDF100	3	374.0	2	JOINT AND ROD DESIGN
	WMR	DRAF	VDF100	3	374.0	2	JOINT AND ROD DESIGN
	WMR	DRAF	VDF100	3	374.0	2	JOINT AND ROD DESIGN
	WMR	DRAF	VDF100	3	374.0	2	JOINT AND ROD DESIGN
	WMR	DRAF	VDF100	3	374.0	2	JOINT AND ROD DESIGN
	WMR	DRAF	VDF100	3	374.0	2	JOINT AND ROD DESIGN
1-11-81	CAA	DSGN	Z77669	2	187.0	5	CONE ASSEMBLY
1-13-81	EWE	DEV	F4445YPT	3	748.0	2	FLUTTED BEARING ASSEMBLY
	HMC	DEV	H4445YPT	3	748.0	2	FLUTTED BEARING ASSEMBLY
	ADH	DRAF	F4445YPT	3	748.0	3	FLUTTED BEARING ASSEMBLY
	ADH	DRAF	F4445YPT	3	748.0	3	FLUTTED BEARING ASSEMBLY
	ADH	DRAF	F4445YPT	3	748.0	3	FLUTTED BEARING ASSEMBLY
	ADH	DRAF	F4445YPT	3	748.0	3	FLUTTED BEARING ASSEMBLY
1-15-81	SWZ	DSGN	D67-44F	3	675.0	3	ARM-CONE ASSEMBLY
	SWZ	DSGN	D67-44F	3	675.0	3	ARM-CONE ASSEMBLY
	SWZ	DSGN	D67-44F	3	675.0	3	ARM-CONE ASSEMBLY
1-21-81	GWS	ADMI	A45-7JAH	2	748.0	4	ROTARY DRILL BIT
1-22-81	MRH	DSGN	D44098-S	5	93.5	3	BEARING SEAL
1-25-81	HMC	DEV	XR-44J	2	748.0	2	TOOTH BIT
1-28-81	EWE	DEV	F4445ZPT	1	748.0	2	SEALED BEARING ASSEMBLY

Figure 29 WESAVE sample report-drawing release.

4. Drawing number
5. Drawing revision
6. Drawing size (square inches)
7. Number of sheets
8. Drawing title

System Efficiency Report

At the end of each month, WESAVE summarizes the effects of hardware and software maintenance on system efficiency (see Fig. 30). This report calculates:

1. Average service response
2. Average problem correction time
3. Factored system downtime
4. Summary of individual device problems
5. Software maintenance summary

SYSTEM REPORT

I — 81

HARDWARE REPORT:

AVERAGE TIME FOR ALL DEVICES:

SERVICE RESPONCE TIME: 10.35 HOURS

HARDWARE FIX TIME: 18.73 HOURS

FACTORED SYSTEM DOWNTIME PER DAY: 65. MINUTES

AVERAGE TIMES FOR PARTICULAR DEVICES:

DEVICE CODE	NUMBER OF FAILS	AVERAGE RESPONCE TIME	AVERAGE FIX TIME	AVERAGE MINUTES DOWN/DAY
CRT4	1	1.58 HR.	3.08 HR.	6.0 MIN.
CPU	1	15.75 HR.	17.25 HR.	33.4 MIN.
CRT5	1	4.32 HR.	5.57 HR.	10.8 MIN.
PLTI	1	19.75 HR.	49.00 HR.	94.8 MIN.

SOFTWARE REPORT:

A] 10. = NUMBER OF BOOT-UPS
B] 70.0 = PERCENT DUE TO CRASHING
C] 34.9 = HOURS OF SOFTWARE MAINTAINCE
D] 70.1 = PERCENT DUE TO CRASHING
E] 9.0 = HOURS OF RECOVERY TIME

AVAILABLE TIME	HARDWARE DOWN TIME	SOFTWARE DOWN TIME	USEABLE TIME
994.04	37.00 3.7	34.90 3.5	922.14 HOURS 92.8% OF TOTAL

Figure 30 WESAVE sample report-system report.

Productivity

Each month a productivity overview is generated which summarizes one or all of the following: (1) number of entities per design/drawing (a measure of complexity); (2) number of hours per design/drawing (a measure of time); (3) square feet per design/drawing (a measure of size) released by department and by operator (see Fig. 31). In addition, productivity rates are generated by dividing productivity by utilization. In addition, operator performance can be reported through the ability to capture:

The command sequence an operator uses
A summary of commands used to create a design/drawing
The actual time that commands are issued

This report will point out those departments and operators who work most productively.

System Utilization

WESAVE summarizes hours by task, operator, project, and department (see Fig. 32), then creates graphs for long-term analysis of system utilization, efficiency, and the effects of hardware and software maintenance downtime.

The graphs show:

1. Actual logged time
2. Logged time plus downtime equal total possible time available
3. Logged time − recovery time equal net usable time
4. Absolute hardware downtime
5. Absolute software downtime

Departmental Graphs

WESAVE constructs long-term graphs displaying utilization, productivity, and productivity rates.

Operator Graphs

WESAVE constructs long-term graphs displaying utilization, productivity, and productivity rates. Comparisons of operators can be subdivided by departments such that each supervisor can obtain separate information for his department.

JOBLOG

Viewing system usage from the viewpoint of time spent on a job is based on the notion that what is important is not how much the system is being used, but how

PRODUCTIVITY OVERVIEW

I — 1981

TOTAL PRODUCTIVITY = 348.49 SQ. FT.

AVERAGE HOURLY PRODUCTIVITY = 37. SQ. FT./100 HR.

PRODUCTIVITY PER DEPARTMENT

DEPT.	TOTAL HOURS	PRODUCTIVITY SQ. FT.	PRODUCTIVITY RATE SQ. FT./100 HR.
ADMI	340.29	20.78	6.
DEV	58.94	53.72	91.
DRAF	312.09	199.99	64.
DSGN	183.73	63.61	35.
DT	7.07	0.00	0.
ENGC	9.24	10.39	112.
MIN	19.73	0.00	0.

PRODUCTIVITY PER OPERATOR

USER	TOTAL HOURS	PRODUCTIVITY SQ. FT.	PRODUCTIVITY RATE SQ. FT./100 HR.
ADH	50.85	62.33	123.
BEB	8.99	10.39	116.
CAA	67.31	6.49	10.
CLD	42.09	0.00	0.
EWE	47.00	20.78	44.
GWS	147.96	20.78	14.
HMC	11.94	32.94	276.
HRM	125.05	0.00	0.
JAH	48.43	10.39	21.
JMM	7.07	0.00	0.
MRH	61.81	9.74	16.
NAY	22.79	5.19	23.
RCG	23.93	2.60	11.
RKF	36.31	119.47	329.
RMW	25.19	0.00	0.
SWZ	171.88	42.19	25.
TDR	11.09	5.19	47.
TRG	5.21	0.00	0.
WAJ	16.19	0.00	0.

Figure 31 WESAVE sample report-productivity overview.

it is being used. JOBLOG is a program that gathers this type of data by monitoring and reporting major job time elements or in other words, a time profile for a job flowing through a CAD system (Fig. 33). The total time is subdivided into two general time categories for the purpose of gathering statistics: (1) activity time represents time a job is "activated" and work is being performed on it, and (2) status time represents time a job is inactive (i.e., logged off the system for any reason).

DATE: 1, 1981 — SYSTEM: 1

TOTAL HOURS = 931.09

HOURS PER TASK:

TASK	HOURS	PERCENT
0	165.09	17.7
1	138.68	14.9
2	142.63	15.3
3	114.32	12.3
4	63.84	6.9
5	76.68	8.2
6	71.15	7.6
7	28.61	3.1
8	82.99	8.9
9	47.10	5.1

HOURS PER OPERATOR:

NAME	HOURS	PERCENT
ADH	50.85	5.5
BEB	8.99	1.0
CAA	67.31	7.2
CLD	42.09	4.5
EWE	47.00	5.0
GWS	147.96	15.9
HMC	11.94	1.3
HRM	125.05	13.4
JAH	48.43	5.2
JMM	7.07	0.8
MRH	61.81	6.6
NAY	22.79	2.4
RCG	23.93	2.6
RKF	36.31	3.9
RMW	25.19	2.7
SWZ	171.88	18.5
TDR	11.09	1.2
TRG	5.21	0.6
WAJ	16.19	1.7

HOURS PER PROJECT:

PROJECT	HOURS	PERCENT
APLO	50.85	5.5
BIT3	47.00	5.0
BITK	77.21	8.3
K809	96.29	10.3
PTRK	81.08	8.7
RP76	7.07	0.8
SLSH	16.19	1.7
TCHG	8.99	1.0
TRNG	5.21	0.6
WRR	82.04	8.8
WWR	170.24	18.3
ZURJ	288.92	31.0

HOURS PER DEPARTMENT:

DEPT.	HOURS	PERCENT
ADMI	340.29	36.5
DEV	58.94	6.3
DRAF	312.09	33.5
DSGN	183.73	19.7
DT	7.07	0.8
ENGC	9.24	1.0
MIN	19.73	2.1

SYSTEM EFFICIENCY = 92.8%

Figure 32 WESAVE sample report-time.

For any particular application, the activity time subdivides further into a series of key activities. Taking a mechanical design application, the activities may be model creation, detailing, and NC tool path generation. Likewise, a job will be logged off for a variety of reasons, it's gone into drafting check, or engineering review, or it has been placed on hold pending new funding. A comprehensive time profile would appear as a series of time blocks representing major activities interlaced with time blocks representing key statuses.

Status List
I = In work
W = Waiting approval
C = Complete

Figure 34 illustrates these relationships. These lists are presented to the users during LOGON and LOGOFF so that appropriate selections can be made. Checking routines in the user interface allow only selections from the lists so that correct and consistent data is loaded in the data base.

The statistics generated can be used to identify problem areas and bottlenecks, to monitor trends in productivity, to provide a historical basis for estimating new work, to inform management of current job status and activity, and to justify new system expansion (Figs. 35 and 36).

CONCLUSION

Job accounting packages can offer the CAD/CAM user the following:

Reports system utilization
Automates bookkeeping (eliminates human error)
Provides accurate data
Eliminates time required to generate system reports
Informs management of work status
Identifies problem areas and bottlenecks
Monitors trends in productivity
Provides historical data as a basis for estimating new work
Enables justification for system expansion
Shows how changes in the design phase can effect overall process time of a project
Shows a project's chronological progression
Allows comparison of projects
Locates large process and queue time in job flow
Identifies future scheduling problems
Identifies critical time contents of work
Shows operator performance on the system

ACKNOWLEDGMENTS

WESAVE is the result of a joint effort between Westinghouse Electric Corporation and Computervision. The part of this section on JOBLOG contains excerpts from "JOBLOG — Tracking Work on a CADD System," by W. Rivera, B. K. Salmond, and W. Macleod.

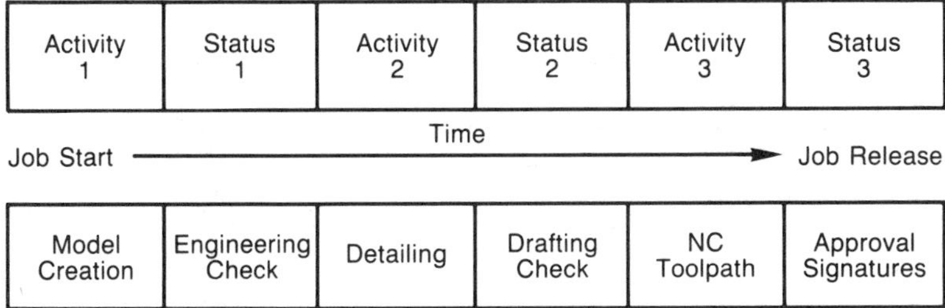

Figure 33 Basic job flow model and example.

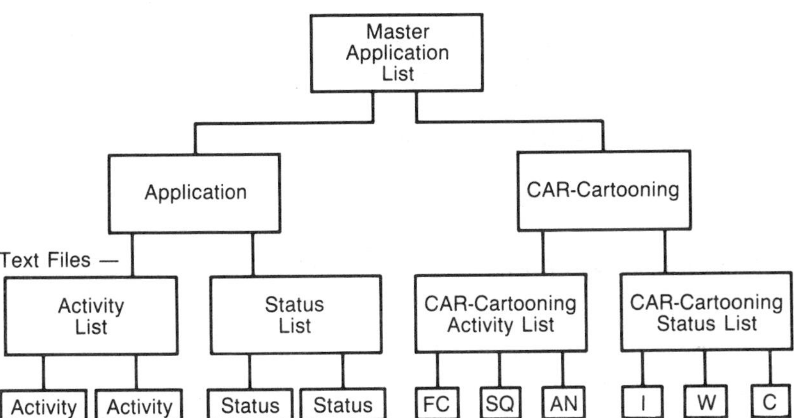

Figure 34 JOBLOG application, activity, and status relationships.

Application - MEC 5-27-82 System Number = 1317

Drawing Number	Dwg Rev	Project	B/C	Start Date	S C	Status Date	A C	Total Days Spent On	Off	Total	C F
SRL0155-00		A	EW9	5- 5-82	I	5-27-82	LM	2.87	19.20	22.07	
SRL0157-00		A	EW9	5-11-82	A	5-26-82	UE	.80	14.12	14.92	
SRL0158-00		A	EW9	5-13-82	I	5-27-82	RE	1.72	12.21	13.94	
SRL0050-00		A	RBF	3-18-82	I	5-20-82	UE	.48	62.16	62.64	
SRL0050-02		A	RBF	3-19-82	I	5- 3-82	UE	1.59	43.65	45.24	
SRL0050-03		A	RBF	3-22-82	I	4-22-82	UE	.99	30.13	31.13	
SRL0050-04		A	RBF	3-31-82	I	5- 3-82	UE	.27	32.47	32.75	
SRL0050-05		B	RBF	4- 6-82	H	4-23-82	UE	.14	16.84	16.99	
SRL0050-06		B	RBF	4-20-82	X	4-20-82	UE	.02	.00	.02	
SRL0050-07		B	RBF	4-20-82	I	4-20-82	UE	.01	.00	.02	
SRL0050-10		B	RBF	3-29-82	I	3-30-82	UE	.00	.00	.00	
SRL0050-99		B	RBF	3-18-82	I	3-18-82	PO	.03	.00	.04	
SRL0051-00		B	RBF	4- 1-82	I	4- 2-82	UE	.12	.79	.91	
SRL0079-00		B	RBF	4-14-82	E	5-13-82	UE	.34	28.10	28.45	
SRL0079-01		C	RBF	5- 5-82	E	5-13-82	UE	.04	7.78	7.83	
SRL0080-00		C	RBF	4-14-82	E	4-15-82	UE	.00	.00	.00	
SRL0080-01		C	RBF	4-15-82	I	4-15-82	UE	.02	.00	.02	
SRL0080-02		C	RBF	4- 7-82	I	5-19-82	UE	2.93	38.79	41.72	
SRL0080-03		C	RBF	4- 7-82	E	4-26-82	RE	.04	19.03	19.07	
SRL0080-04		C	RBF	4-26-82	E	5- 6-82	UE	.14	9.63	9.77	
SRL0080-05		C	RBF	5-10-82	I	5-19-82	UE	.26	8.46	8.73	
SRL0080-06		C	RBF	5- 6-82	I	5-19-82	UE	.48	12.21	12.70	
SRL0080-07		C	RBF	5-11-82	I	5-18-82	UE	.08	6.96	7.04	
SRL0080-11		C	RBF	4- 7-82	I	4- 7-82	UE	.11	.00	.11	

JOB STATUS SUMMARY

I — In Work	52
H — On Hold	6
D — Drafting Check	0
E — Engineering Check	7
A — Artwork Being Generated	11
T — Testing Prototype	0
X — Discontinued	2
S — Signatures for Release	1
R — Released/Archival	6
Total Jobs	85

Weekly Job Status Summary

Figure 35 Partial job status reports.

```
Entry date      = 3-29-82 11:05:40
Application     = MEC
Project         = B
Subassembly     = 000
Budget center   = EL3
Charge number   = A59375BAGAEL3
Status          = I — IN WORK
  Status date   = 3-29-82 11:05:40
  Report date   = 4-14-82 11:59:11
  Status days   = 16
Last activity   = DD — DETAIL DRAWING
  Start date    = 4-13-82 22:59:03
  Stop date     = 4-14-82 1:43:58
Entity count    = 0
Force off ct    = 1
Active time     = 51.183
Long wait t     = 346.200
Short wait t    = .833
```

Activity	Hours	Percent of Total
UE — Update Engrg Model	0.00	0.0%
LM — Layout Model (Creation)	2.17	4.2%
CR — Change/Rework	0.17	0.3%
DD — Detail Drawing	48.85	95.4%
UF — Unfold Flat Pattern	0.00	0.0%
PO — Plot/Output	0.00	0.0%
IA — Into Analysis	0.00	0.0%
RN — Revision Notice	0.00	0.0%
RE — Review	0.00	0.0%
Total	51.18	

Status	Days	Percent of Total
I — In Work	16	100.0%
H — On Hold	0	0.0%
D — Drafting Check	0	0.0%
E — Engineering Check	0	0.0%
X — Discontinued	0	0.0%
S — Signatures for Release	0	0.0%
A — Into Analysis	0	0.0%
R — Released/Archival	0	0.0%
Total	16	

Figure 36 Sample job profile report.

EVALUATION CONCLUSION

Several approaches to productivity measurement of CAD/CAM systems have been presented. Some or all may be applicable to your operation. It cannot be overemphasized that good productivity measures *must* be developed within your organization and tailored to your specific operation.

A final note: the best overall measurement of your system's success can be simply stated:

> How do the actual end results derived from the system compare to your original justification?

REFERENCES

Magazines

Black, W. H. Pitting CAD against manual drafting, *Machine Design*, 1982.

Brayton, G. N. Simplified method of measuring productivity identifies opportunities for increasing it, *Industrial Engineering*, 1983.

Greenberg, L. *A Practical Guide to Productivity Measurement*, the Bureau of National Affairs, Inc., Washington, D.C., 1973.

Gregerman, I. B. *Knowledge Worker Productivity*, American Management Association, New York, N.Y., 1937.

Hines, W. W. Guidelines for implementing productivity measurement, *Industrial Engineering*, 1976.

Jamali, S. Putting a productivity improvement program into action: A six-step plan, *Industrial Engineering*, 1983.

Kristakis, J. Short method makes frequent evaluation of office productivity a realistic objective, *Industrial Engineering*, 1983.

Krouse, J. K. Training CAD/CAM operators, *Machine Design*, 1983.

Mundel, M. Measures of productivity, *Industrial Engineering*, 1976.

Osborn, R. W. Theories of productivity analysis, *Datamation*, 1981.

Rowe, D. L. How Westinghouse measures white collar productivity, *Management Review*, 1981.

Svobodova, L. *Computer Performance Measurement and Evaluation Methods: Analysis and Applications*, Elsevier North-Holland, Inc., New York, N.Y., 1976.

Taylor, B. W. III. Corporate productivity—getting it all together, *Industrial Engineering*, 1977.

Yes, it's possible to rate white collar productivity, *Research Institute Personal Report for the Executive*, 9:7, 1983.

Papers

Cummings, C. J. Productivity and Profitability with CAD/CAM.

Jacobson, H. and Ziegler, B.D. Productivity Risk Analysis and Return on Investment for Intgratd CAD/CAM Projects, 1981.

Pietra Santa, A. M. Measuring the Software Development Process.
Powell, R. E. Justification and Financial Analysis for CAD, 1980.
Snyder, C. A. Printed Circuit Board and Electrical Schematic Productivity Measurement, 1981.
Stewart, W. T. Use of the Nominal Group Technique in Productivity Programs.

Proceedings

Brannon, M. L. Paces: Productivity and Cost Evaluation System, presented to the Applicon Users Group, 1981.
Coticchia, M. E., Crawford, G. W., and Moser, T. D. Evaluation of Computer-Aided Design and Manufacturing (CAD/CAM) Systems: Westinghouse's Approach to Productivity Measurement, Proceedings from NCGA, Anaheim, Calif., 1981.
Coticchia, M. E. and Preston, E. J. Productivity Gained Through CAD/CAM: Can it be Measured? Proceedings of the Computervision Users Conference, Orlando, Fla., 1982.
Feder, A. Test Results on Computer Graphics Productivity for Aircraft Design and Fabrication, Proceedings from the AIAA Systems and Technology Meeting, Los Angeles, Calif., 1975.
Mack, D. D. Productivity Comparisons: The Human and the Machine, Proceedings from the Fifth Annual Applicon Users Group Meeting, Chicago, Ill.
Macleod, W. and Svoboda, L. The Job Tracking System, Proceedings from the Computervision Users Conference, Miami, Fla., 1982.
Packer, M. B. Output Mapping: A Productivity Analysis Technique for Research and Development Organizations, presented at the Second National Conference on Improving the Productivity of Technical Resources, Chicago, Ill., 1981.
Thor, C. G. A Complete Productivity Measurement System, presented at the Symposium on Productivity Measures, Pittsburgh, Pa., 1982.

GLOSSARY

Glossary of Common CAD/CAM Terms and Concepts

FOREWORD

There has long been a need for a glossary of CAD/CAM terms and concepts that would be both comprehensive enough and detailed enough to serve adequately the many diverse groups involved in this technology—first-time and would-be users, academicians, students and suppliers.

In reviewing the many fine glossaries compiled by trade journals, companies, and associations, one discerns a difference in terminology from one application area—and even one source—to another. We hope this glossary will be a step toward much-needed standardization of CAD/CAM technology.

In a technology as broad and fast-changing as CAD/CAM, no glossary can be 100-percent complete and current. Hopefully, future editions of this glossary which are already planned will help close the gap. Meanwhile, we believe this work will prove informative and useful.

EXPLANATORY NOTES

The following terms, widely used in the glossary, have these meanings:

Designer Includes engineers, draftspeople, cartographers, and all who regularly use a CAD or CAD/CAM workstation

---

Operator Used synonymously with designer but implying more the manual aspects of CAD or CAD/CAM workstation operation.

System A CAD or CAD/CAM system (for example, ". . . generated on the system").

User The organization using CAD or CAD/CAM, or the manager or supervisor who determines CAD/CAM procedures (as in "a user-defined format").

Work station Synonymous with terminal.

Acceptance test A test for evaluating a newly purchased system's performance, capabilities, and conformity to predefined specifications prior to acceptance of, and payment for, the system.

Access time (or disk access time) One measure of system response. The time interval between the instant that data is called for from storage and the instant that delivery is completed (i.e., read time). See also Response time.

Accuracy Conformance to a recognized standard. Generally used to denote the number of digits to the right of the decimal point that can be considered significant in a particular value, or that can be supported by a particular algorithm, program, or system. See also Precision.

Addressability The number of positions (pixels) in the X axis and in the Y axis which can be displayed on the CRT. A measure of picture display quality or resolution.

Addressable point Any position on a cathode ray tube (CRT) screen that can be specified by absolute coordinates, which form a grid over the display surface.

ADS See Automated design system (ADS).

AID See Autointeractive design (AID).

Algorithm In CAD/CAM software, a set of well-defined rules or procedures based on mathematical and geometric formulas for solving a problem or accomplishing a given result in a finite number of steps.

Aliasing The occurrence of jagged lines on a raster-scan display image when the detail of a design exceeds the resolution of the CRT.

Alphanumeric (or alphameric) A term which encompasses letters, digits, and special characters which are machine processable.

Alphanumeric display (or alphameric display) A work station device consisting of a CRT on which text can be viewed. An alphanumeric display is capable of showing a fixed set of letters, digits, and special characters. It allows the designer to observe entered commands and to receive messages from the system.

Alphanumeric keyboard (or alphameric keyboard) A work station device consisting of a typewriter-like keyboard which allows the designer to communicate with the system using an English-like command language.

American National Standards Institute See ANSI.

American Standard Code for Information Interchange See ASCII.

Analog Applied to an electrical or computer system, this denotes the capability to represent data in continuously varying physical quantities (as in a voltmeter).

Analog board In printed circuit (PC) board design, it denotes the dominant component type, function(s), or circuit characteristics of a particular PC board. Contrast with digital board which requires a different CAD layout process.

Analysis, engineering (or design analysis) See CAE.

Analytic processing unit See APU® (Analytic Processing Unit).

Annotation Process of inserting text or a special note or identification (such as a flag) on a drawing, map, or diagram constructed on a CAD/CAM system. The text can be generated and positioned on the drawing using the system.

ANSI American National Standards Institute. An association formed by industry and the U.S. government to produce and disseminate drafting and manufacturing standards that are acceptable to and used by a majority of companies and the government.

Application program (or package) A computer program or collection of programs to perform a task or tasks specific to a particular user's need or class of needs.

APT Automatically programmed tools. One of the principal software languages used in computer-aided manufacturing to progam numerically controlled machine tools.

Archival storage Refers to memory (on magnetic tape, disks, printouts, or drums) used to store data on completed designs or elements outside of main memory.

Array (v) To create automatically on a CAD system an arrangement of identical elements or components. The designer defines the element once, then indicates the starting location and spacing for automatic generation of the array.

Array (n) An arrangement created in the above manner. A series of elements or sets of elements arranged in a pattern (i.e., matrix).

Artwork One of the outputs of a CAD system. For example, a photo plot (in PC design), a photo mask (in IC design), a pen plot, an electrostatic copy, or a positive or negative photographic transparency. Transparencies (either on glass or film) and photo masks are forms of CAD artwork which can be used directly in the manufacture of a product (such as an IC, PC board, or mechanical part).

Artwork master A highly accurate photographic representation of a circuit design generated by the system for use in the fabrication process.

ASCII American Standard Code for Information Interchange. An industry standard character code widely used for information interchange among data processing systems, communications systems, and associated equipment.

Assembler A computer program that converts (i.e., translates) programmer-written symbolic instructions, usually in mnemonic form, into machine-executable (computer or binary-coded) instructions. This conversion is typically one-to-one (one symbolic instruction converts to one machine-executable instruction). A software programming aid.

Assembly drawing A drawing which can be created on the CAD system to represent a major subdivision of the product, or the complete product.

Assembly language A low-level (primitive) symbolic programming language directly translatable by an assembler into a machine (computer-executable) language. Enables programmers to write a computer program as a sequence of computer instructions using mnemonic abbreviations for computer operation codes and names and addresses of the instructions and their operands.

Associative dimensioning A CAD capability that links dimension entities to geometric entities being dimensioned. This allows the value of a dimension to be automatically updated as the geometry changes.

Associativity Any logical linking of geometric entities (parts, components, or elements) in a CAD/CAM data base with their nongraphic attributes (dimensions and text) or with other geometric entities. Thus, the designer can retrieve by a single command, not only a specified entity but all data associated with it. Associated data can automatically be updated on the system if the physical design changes.

Attribute A nongraphic characteristic of a part, component, or entity under design on a CAD system. Examples include: dimension entities associated with geometry, text with text nodes, and nodal lines with connect nodes. Changing one entity in an association can produce automatic changes by the system in the associated entity (e.g., moving one entity can cause moving or stretching of the other entity).

Auto-interactive design (AID) A combination of design automation, where the computer executes programs or routines with no operator intervention, and computer-aided design, where the operators interacts with the computer in the design process.

Automated Design System (ADS) Another term for a computer-aided design system.

Automated drafting system A computer-based system designed primarily to automate the process of drafting. Design capabilities are not included.

Automatic dimensioning A CAD capability that computes the dimensions in a displayed design, or in a designated section, and automatically places dimensions, dimensional lines, and arrowheads where required. In the case of mapping, this capability labels the linear feature with length and azimuth.

Automatically programmed tools See APT.

Auxiliary storage Storage which supplements main memory devices such as disk or drum storage. Contrast with archival storage.

Back annotation A CAD process by which data (text) is automatically extracted from a completed PC board design or wiring diagram stored on the system and used to update logic elements on the schematic created earlier in the design process.

Background processing/mode The processing mode for executing lower-priority programs (such as plotter output or extensive calculations) which do not require user interaction. Higher-priority (foreground mode) tasks are predetermined to preempt such tasks, thereby freeing the work station for programs which require direct user interaction. Contrast with foreground processing/mode.

BASIC Beginner's All-Purpose Symbolic Instruction Code. A problem-solving, algebra-like programming language used in CAD/CAM by engineers, scientists, and others who may not have programming experience. BASIC is easy to learn and use.

Batch processing The technique of processing an entire group (batch) of similar or related jobs or input items on a system at one time without operator interaction. Contrast with interactive graphics system.

Baud rate A measure of the speed of signal transmission or serial data flow between the CPU and the work stations it services. The term baud refers to the number of times the line condition changes per second. It can be measured in signal events (bits) per second. See also Bit rate.

Benchmark The program(s) used to test, compare, and evaluate in real time the performance of various CAD/CAM systems prior to selection and purchase. A synthetic benchmark has pre-established parameters designed to exercise a set of system features and resources. A live benchmark is drawn from the prospective user's workload as a model of his entire workload.

Beta site A user's CAD/CAM site or facility selected by mutual agreement between the user and his vendor for testing out a new system, application package, or hardware or software enhancement before its sale to other customers of the vendor.

Bills of material (BOM) A list of all the subassemblies, parts, materials, and quantities required to manufacture one assembled product or part, or to build a plant. A BOM can be generated automatically on a CAD/CAM system.

Bit The smallest unit of information that can be stored and processed by a digital computer. A bit may assume only one of two values: 0 or 1 (i.e., ON/OFF or YES/NO). Bits are organized into larger units called words for access by computer instructions. Computers are often categorized by word size in bits [i.e., the maximum word size that can be processed as a unit during an instruction cycle (e.g., 16-bit computers or 32-bit computers)]. The number of bits in a word is an indication of the processing power of the system, especially for calculations or for high-precision data.

Bit map A grid pattern of bits (i.e., ON and/or OFF) stored in memory and used to generate the image on a raster-scan display. In a CAD-display bit map, each bit corresponds to a dot in a raster display image. Every bit map allows one logical bit of information (such as intensity or color) to be stored per dot (pixel) on the screen. The intensity or color of each point in the image can be represented as a group of bits, for example as a pattern of 0's and 1's. The entire image, being an area of points, can be represented as an array of those groups in computer memory, on magnetic tape or any other storage medium.

Bit rate The speed at which bits are transmitted, usually expressed in bits per second.

Bits per inch (bpi) The number of bits that can be stored per inch of a magnetic tape. A measure of the data storage capacity of a magnetic tape.

Blank A CAD command which causes a predefined entity to go temporarily blank on the CRT. The reversing command is: unblank.

Blinking A CAD design aid that makes a predefined graphic entity blink on the CRT to attract the attention of the designer.

Boolean logic/operation Algebraic or symbolic logic formulas (adapted from George Boole's work) used in computer-aided design to expand design-rules checking programs and to expedite the construction of geometric figures. In a computer-aided mapping environment, Boolean operations are used either singly or in combination to identify features by their nongraphic properties (e.g., by highlighting all parcels with an area greater than 15 square kilometers, etc.).

BOM See Bills of material (BOM).

Boot up Start up (a system).

BPI See bits per inch (bpi).

B-spline A sequence of parametric polynomial curves (typically quadratic or cubic polynomials) forming a smooth fit between a sequence of points in 3-D space. The piecewise defined curve maintains a level of mathematical continuity dependent upon the polynomial degree chosen. It is used extensively in mechanical design applications in the automotive and aerospace industries. B-splines and B-spline surfaces of up to the seventh degree can be generated on a CAD system.

Bug A flaw in the design or implementation of a software program or hardware design which causes erroneous results or malfunctions.

Bulk annotation A CAD feature which enables the designer to automatically enter repetitive text or other annotation at multiple locations on a drawing or design.

Bulk memory A memory device for storing a large amount of data (e.g., disk, drum, or magnetic tape). It is not randomly accessible like main memory.

Bundled feature A hardware or software module sold as part of a package and not available separately. May consist of interrelated software programs, or hardware, or both. Opposite of unbundled.

Bus (1) In electrical design, a ground or wide circuit path, power conductor, or signal transmission line between two or more component pins or devices. (2) In computer hardware, a circuit or group of circuits providing a communications path between two or more devices, such as between a CPU, peripherals, and memory, or between functions on a single PC board.

Byte A sequence of adjacent bits, usually eight, representing a character that is operated on as a unit by elements of a CAD/CAM system and usually shorter than a word. A measure of the memory capacity of a system, or of an individual storage unit (as a 300-million-byte disk).

Cabling diagram A diagram showing connections and physical locations of system or unit cables, and used to facilitate field installation and repair of wiring systems. Can be generated by CAD.

CAD Computer-aided design. A process which uses a computer system to assist in the creation, modification, and display of a design.

CAD/CAM Computer-aided design/computer-aided manufacturing. Refers to the integration of computers into the entire design-to-fabrication cycle of a product or plant.

CAE Computer-aided engineering. Analysis of a design for basic error checking, or to optimize manufacturability, performance, and economy (for example, by comparing various possible materials or designs). Information drawn from the CAD/CAM design data base is used to analyze the functional characteristics of a part, product, or system under design, and to simulate its performance under various conditions. CAE can be used to determine section properties, moments of inertia, shear and bending moments, weight, volume, surface area, and center of gravity. CAE can precisely determine loads, vibration, noise, and service life early in the design cycle so that components can be optimized to meet those criteria. Perhaps the most powerful CAE technique is finite element modelling. See also Kinematics.

CAM Computer-aided manufacturing. The use of computer and digital technology to generate manufacturing-oriented data. Data drawn from a CAD/CAM data base can assist in or control a portion or all of a manufacturing process, including numerically controlled machines, computer-assisted parts programming, computer-assisted process planning, robotics, and programmable logic controllers. CAM can involve: production programming, manufacturing engineering, industrial engineering, facilities engineering, and reliability engineering (quality control). CAM techniques can be used to produce process plans for fabricating a complete assembly; to program robots; and to coordinate plant operation.

Cathode ray tube (CRT) The principal component in a CAD display device. A CRT displays graphic representations of geometric entities and designs and can be of various types: storage tube, raster scan, or refresh. These tubes create images by means of a controllable beam of electrons striking a screen. The term CRT is often used to denote the entire display device. See also Performance, CRT.

Cell (1) A collection of related geometric and/or alphanumeric data on one or more layers of a design on the system. (2) The physical location or the design of a single data bit in memory. (3) A collection of lines, curves, surfaces, lettering, dimension lines, and possibly other cells all of which form a standard symbol or a subassembly in a design or drawing (especially in IC design).

Centerline The center of an NC machine tool path computed on a CAD/CAM system. Centerline data, in the form of a CL file, ultimately controls the NC machine itself. In normal 2-D–3-D drafting, centerline means a representation of the central axis of a part, or the central axes of intersecting parts. See also CL file.

Central processing unit (CPU) The computer brain of a CAD/CAM system which controls the retrieval, decoding, and processing of information, as well as the interpretation and execution of operating instructions, the building blocks of application and other computer programs. A CPU comprises arithmetic, control, and logic elements.

Character An alphabetical, numerical, or special graphic symbol used as part of the organization, control, or representation of CAD/CAM data.

Characters per second (cps) A measure of the speed with which an alphanumeric terminal can process data.

Check plot A pen plot generated automatically by a CAD system for visual verification and editing prior to final output generation.

Chip See Integrated circuit.

CIM (Computer-integrated manufacturing) The concept of a totally automated factory in which all manufacturing processes are integated and controlled by a CAD/CAM system. CIM enables production planners and schedulers, shop-floor foremen, and accountants to use the same data base as product designers and engineers.

CL file (Cutter location file) A file of data generated from a machine tool path created on a CAD/CAM system or on an APT processor. The CL file provides X, Y, and Z coordinates and NC information which can be postprocessed into tapes to direct NC machine(s). See also Centerline.

Clipping Removing parts of a design displayed on the CRT which lie outside predefined bounds. See also Scissoring.

CNC See Computer numerical control (CNC).

Code A set of specific symbols and rules for representing data (usually instructions) so that the data can be understood and executed by a computer. A code can be in binary (machine) language, assembly language, or a high-level language. Frequently refers to an industry-standard code such as ANSI, ASCII, IPC, or Standard Code for Information Exchange. Many application codes for CAD/CAM are written in FORTRAN.

Color display A CAD/CAM display device. Color raster-scan displays offer a variety of user-selectable, contrasting colors to make it easier to discriminate among various groups of design elements on different layers of a large, complex design. Color speeds up the recognition of specific areas and subassemblies, helps the designer interpret complex surfaces, and highlights interference problems. Color displays can be of the penetration type, in which various phosphor layers give off different colors (refresh display), or the TV-type with red, blue, and green electron guns (raster-scan display).

COM See Computer-output microfilm (COM).

Command A control signal or instruction to a CPU or graphics processor, commonly initiated by means of a menu/tablet and electronic pen or by an alphanumeric keyboard.

Command language A language for communicating with a CAD/CAM system in order to perform specific functions or tasks.

Communication link The physical means, such as a telephone line, for connecting one system module or peripheral to another in a different location in order to transmit and receive data. See also Data link.

Compatibility The ability of a particular hardware module or software program, code, or language to be used in a CAD/CAM system without prior modification or special interfaces. Upward compatible denotes the ability of a system to interface with new hardware or software modules or enhancements (i.e., the system vendor provides with each new module a reasonable means of transferring data, programs, and operator skills from the user's present system to the new enhancements).

Compiler A computer program that converts or translates a high-level, user-written language (e.g., PASCAL, COBOL, VARPRO, or FORTRAN), or source, into a language that a computer can understand. The conversion is typically one to many (i.e., one user instruction to many machine-executable instructions). A software programming aid, the compiler allows the designer to write programs in an English-like language with relatively few statements, thus saving program development time.

Completion rate/percentage Applied to computer-aided PC board routing, it is the percentage of routes automatically completed successfully by a CAD program.

Component A physical entity, or a symbol used in CAD to denote such an entity. Depending on the application, a component might refer to an IC or part of a wiring circuit (e.g., a resistor), or a valve, elbow, or vee in a plant layout, or a substation or cable in a utility map. Also applies to a subassembly or part that goes into higher level assemblies.

Composite map A single map created on the system from a mosaic of individual adjacent map sheets. Individual sheets are brought together, and entities that fall on the neat line (geographic border of the map) are merged into a single contiguous entity whereupon the final sheet can be corrected for systematic errors.

Computer-aided design See CAD (Computer-aided design).

Computer-aided design/computer-aided manufacturing See CAD/CAM (Computer-aided design/computer-aided manufacturing).

Computer-aided engineering See CAE (Computer-aided engineering).

Computer-aided manufacturing See CAM (Computer-aided manufacturing).

Computer graphics A general term encompassing any discipline or activity that uses computers to generate, process and display graphic images. The essential technology of CAD/CAM systems. See also CAD.

Computer-integrated manufacturing See CIM (Computer-integrated manufacturing).

Computer network An interconnected complex (arrangement, or configuration) of two or more systems. See also Network.

Computer numerical control (CNC) A technique in which a machine-tool control uses a minicomputer to store NC instructions generated earlier by CAD/CAM for controlling the machine.

Computer-output microfilm (COM) A technology for generating CAD artwork. A COM device turns out a microfilm from data-base information converted to an image on a high-resolution screen which is then photographed.

Computer program A specific set of software commands in a form acceptable to a computer and used to achieve a desired result. Often called a software program or package.

Configuration A particular combination of a computer, software and hardware modules, and peripherals at a single installation and interconnected in such a way as to support certain application(s).

Connect node In computer-aided design, an attachment point for lines or text.

Connection In PC and wiring diagram construction, refers to electrical connections between pins, components, contacts, or circuits.

Connectivity The ability of an electronic design data base to recognize connections by association of data. Connectivity facilitates design automation and CAM processing.

Connector A termination point for a signal entering or leaving a PC board or a cabling system.

Contact and coil cross-reference report A CAD-generated report that identifies on/off page connections in multisheet diagrams and provides respective wire source and destination data. The report gives the locations of all contacts associated with each coil adjacent to the coil symbol, underlining closed-contact references. The system extracts such contact and coil information from each sheet of the job, sorts by component label, and the places the required cross-referencing text into each drawing.

Convention Standardized methodology or accepted procedure for executing a computer program. In CAD, the term denotes a standard rule or mode of execution undertaken to provide consistency. For example, a drafting convention might require all dimensions to be in metric units.

Coordinate dimensioning A system of dimensioning where points are defined as a specified dimension and direction from a reference point measured with respect to defined axes.

Copy (1) To reproduce a design, figure, or other user-selected data in a different location or format than appears on the existing design displayed on the CRT. (2) To duplicate a file and its contents under another name.

Core (core memory) A largely obsolete term for main storage.

cps See Characters per second (cps).

CPU See Central processing unit (CPU).

Cross-hatching A CAD design/drafting/editing aid for automatically filling in an outline (bounded area) with a pattern or series of symbols to highlight particular part of the design. A series of angular parallel lines of definable width and spacing. Also called area shading in mapping applications.

Cross-referencing A CAD capability. If a relay or network signal has to be continued from one sheet to another, cross-referencing ties together the source and destination connections by automatically typing the appropriate text on both sheets.

CRT See Cathode-ray tube (CRT).

Cursor A visual tracking symbol, usually an underline or cross hairs, for indicating a location or entity selection on the CRT display. A text cursor indicates the alphanumeric input; a graphics cursor indicates the next geometric input. A cursor is guided by an electronic or light pen, joystick, keyboard, etc., and follows every movement of the input device.

Cut plane A capability of CAD systems that enables the designer to define and intersect a plane with 2-D entities or 3-D objects in order to derive sectional location points.

Cutter compensation A method by which the programmed tool path is altered to allow for differences between actual and programmed cutter diameters.

Cutter location file See CL file (Cutter location file).

Cutter path The path of a cutting tool through a part. The optimal cutter path can be defined automatically by a CAD/CAM system and formatted into a numerical control (NC) tape to guide the tool. See Tool path.

Cycle A preset sequence of events (hardware or software) initiated by a single command.

DA See Design automation (DA).

Daisy chain A method of propagating signals along a bus whereby devices not requesting service respond by passing the signal on. The first device requesting the signal responds by performing an action and breaks the daisy-chain signal continuity. This permits assignment of device priorities based on the electrical position of the device along the bus.

Data base A comprehensive collection of interrelated information stored on some kind of mass data storage device, usually a disk. Generally consists of information organized into a number of fixed-format record types with logical links between associated records. Typically includes operating system instructions, standard parts libraries, completed designs and documentation, source code, graphic and application programs, as well as current user tasks in progress.

Data base management system A package of software programs to organize and control access to information stored in a multiuser system. It gives users a consistent method of entering, retrieving and updating data in the system, and prevents duplication and unauthorized access to stored information.

Data communication The transmission of data (usually digital) from one point (such as a CAD/CAM work station or CPU) to another point via communication channels such as telephone lines.

Data communications equipment (DCE) The equipment required to establish, maintain, and terminate communications between data terminal equipment and data transmission circuit(s) such as telephone lines.

Data extract A software program that enables the designer to extract from a CAD/CAM data base user-selected, nongraphic information stored in one or more drawing files. The information is then reformatted automatically into user-defined reports or other documentation generated by the system. See Data merge.

Data link The communication line(s), related controls, and interface(s), for the transmission of data between two or more computer systems. Can include modems, telephone lines, or dedicated transmission media such as cable or optical fiber.

Data merge The software program complementary to data extract. It allows text changes, additions, or deletions made to a completed drawing on the system to be made automatically on the part drawing(s) created earlier by CAD. Data merge also automatically combines text files from both CAD/CAM and mainframe computer data bases to create special reports.

Data tablet A CAD/CAM input device that allows the designer to communicate with the system by placing an electronic pen or stylus on the tablet surface. There is a direct correspondence between positions on the tablet and addressable points on the display surface of the CRT. Typically used for indicating positions on the CRT, for digitizing input of drawings, or for menu selection. See also Graphic tablet.

DCE See Data communications equipment (DCE).

Debug To detect, locate, and correct any bugs in a system's software or hardware.

Dedicated Designed or intended for a single function or use. For example, a dedicated work station might be used exclusively for engineering calculations or plotting.

Default The predetermined value of a parameter required in a CAD/CAM task or operation. It is automatically supplied by the system whenever that value (e.g., text, height, or grid size) is not specified.

Default selection A CAD/CAM feature that allows a designer to preselect certain parameters for a product under design. These default parameters are then used each time a command is given. The designer can override them by selecting a different parameter when entering the command.

Degradation, system The slowdown in execution of tasks that can occur when the CPU is given a task requiring a large amount of computation (i.e., a compute-bound task); or when two or more tasks require the same physical device at the same time (i.e., an input/output-bound task).

Density (1) A measure of the complexity of an electronic design. For example, IC density can be measured by the number of gates or transistors per unit area, or by the number of square inches per component. (2) Magnetic tape storage capacity. High capacity might be 1600 bits/inch, and low—800 bits/inch.

Design automation (DA) The technique of using a computer to automate portions of the design process and reduce human intervention.

Design file Collection of information in a CAD data base which relates to a single design project and can be directly accessed as a separate file.

Design-rules checking A CAD software program that automatically examines a displayed PC or IC design or layout for any violations of user-selected design rules and manufacturing tolerances. Usually associated with electrical applications.

Design system A CAD system.

Detail drawing The drawing of a single part design containing all the dimensions, annotations, etc., necessary to give a definition complete enough for manufacturing and inspection.

Detailing The process of adding the necessary information to create a detail drawing.

Device A system hardware module external to the CPU and designed to perform a specific function (i.e., a CRT, plotter, printer, hard-copy unit, etc.). See also Peripheral.

Diagnostics Computer programs designed to test the status of a system or its key components, and to detect and isolate malfunctions.

Diagram Symbolic representation of a circuit or other objects.

Dial up To initiate station-to-station communications with a computer via a dial telephone usually from a work station to a computer.

Digital Applied to an electrical or computer system, this denotes the capability to represent data in the form of digits.

Digital board In printed circuit design, it denotes the dominant component type, function(s), or circuit characteristics of a particular PC board. Contrast with analog board, which requires a different CAD layout process.

Digitize General description: to convert a drawing into digital form (i.e., coordinate locations) so that it can be entered into the data base for later processing. A digitizer, available with many CAD systems, implements the conversion process. This is one of the primary ways of entering existing drawings, crude graphics, lines, and shapes into the system.

Digitizer A CAD input device consisting of a data tablet on which is mounted the drawing or design to be digitized into the system. The designer moves a puck or electronic pen to selected points on the drawing and enters coordinate data for lines and shapes by simply pressing down the digitize button with the puck or pen. See also Large interactive surface.

Dimensioning, automatic A CAD capability that will automatically compute and insert the dimensions of a design or drawing, or a designated section of it.

DIP See Dual-in-line package (DIP).

Direct access (linkage) Retrieval or storage of data in the system by reference to its location on a tape, disk, or cartridge, without the need for processing on a CPU.

Direct memory access (DMA) A method of transferring blocks of data directly between a peripheral device and system memory without the need for CPU intervention. This powerful I/O (input/output) technique significantly increases the data transfer rate, hence system efficiency.

Direct numerical control (DNC) A system in which sets of NC machines are connected to a mainframe computer to establish a direct interface between the DNC computer memory and the machine tools. The machine tools are directly controlled by the computer without the use of tape.

Direct-view storage tube (DVST) One of the most widely used graphics display devices, DVST generates a long-lasting, flicker-free image with high resolution and no refreshing. It handles an almost unlimited amount of data. However, display dynamics are limited since DVSTs do not permit selective erase. The image is not as bright as with refresh or raster. Also called storage tube.

Directory A named space on the disk or other mass storage device in which are stored the names of files and some summary information about them.

Discrete components Components with a single functional capability per package, for example, transistors and diodes.

Disk (storage) A device on which large amounts of information can be stored in the data base. Synonymous with magnetic disk storage or magnetic disk memory.

Display A CAD/CAM workstation device for rapidly presenting a graphic image so that the designer can react to it, making changes interactively in real time. Usually refers to a CRT.

Distributed processing Refers to a computer system that employs a number of different hardware processors, each designed to perform a different subtask on behalf of an overall program or process. Ordinarily, each task would be required to queue up for a single processor to perform all its needed operations. But in a distributed processing system, each task queues up for specific processor required to perform its needs. Since all processors run simultaneously, the queue wait period is often reduced, yielding better overall performance in a multitask environment.

DMA See Direct memory access (DMA).

DNC See Direct numerical control (DNC).

Documentation (1) A generic term for the wide variety of hardcopy or on-line reports, drawings, and lists generated on the system for use by various departments involved in the design-to-manufacturing cycle (or the design-to-construction cycle in plant design). (2) Handbooks, operator and service reference manuals. (3) Technical memoranda describing some aspects of hardware or software.

Dot-matrix plotter A CAD peripheral device for generating graphic plots. Consists of a combination of wire nibs (styli) spaced 100 to 200 styli per inch, which place dots where needed to generate a drawing. Because of its high speed, it is typically used in electronic design applications. Accuracy and resolution are not as great as with pen plotters. Also known as electrostatic plotter.

Double precision A data format used in CAD/CAM systems. Typically refers to a 64-bit floating-point data format, where the high-order bit is used as a sign, the next eight bits for the exponent, and the remaining 55 bits for the mantissa. This provides a precision of approximately 16 significant figures. Single-precision floating-point formats have half the significant figures and constitute 32 bits. See Floating point.

Dragging Moving a user-selected item on the CRT display along a path defined by a graphic input device such as an electronic pen and tablet.

Drawing The traditional graphic hardcopy representation of a design used to communicate the design during all stages from conception through manufacturing.

Drill tape See Paper-tape punch/reader.

Drum plotter An electromechanical pen plotter that draws an image on paper or film mounted on a rotatable drum. In this CAD peripheral device a combination of plotting-head movement and drum rotation provides the motion.

Dual-in-line package (DIP) An IC packaging configuration consisting of two parallel rows of connection pins, usually on 0.100-inch centers. The most common type of IC package.

Dump To transfer all the data accumulated on the system during a given period between temporary (working) storage (disk, and more permanent storage, e.g., magnetic tape, punched cards, listings, etc.).

DVST See Direct-view storage tube (DVST).

Dynamic (motion) Simulation of movement using CAD software, so that the designer can see on the CRT screen 3-D representations of the parts in a piece of machinery as they interact dynamically. Thus, any collision or interference problems are revealed at a glance.

Dynamic allocation A software feature which allows resources (such as CPU time, file storage space, or disk transfer time) to be allocated on a request basis. For example, if a designer on the system needs extra CPU time, and there is unused CPU time available, it will be allocated to that designer. After the resource has been used, it is returned to the pool. Dynamic menuing provides greater flexibility to use resources more efficiently.

Dynamic tool display A CAD/CAM feature for graphically displaying a figure representing an NC cutting tool. The figure is dynamically moved along an NC tool path displayed on the CRT in order to verify and simulate the cutting procedure.

Dynamics The capability of a CAD system to zoom, scroll, and rotate.

Echo To provide visual feedback to the designer during graphic input to the system, for example, by displaying the command or function just completed, or a design entity being worked on.

Edit to modify, refine, or update an emerging design or text on a CAD system. This can be done on-line interactively.

EIA code A coding system for NC perforated tape known as RS-244-A.

Electrical schematic A diagram of the logical arrangement of hardware in an electrical circuit/system using conventional component symbols. Can be constructed interactively by CAD.

Electron-beam pattern generator An off-line device using data postprocessed by a CAD/CAM system to produce a reticle from which the IC mask is later created. It exposes the IC reticle using an electron beam in a raster scan procedure. See Pattern generation and reticle.

Electrostatic plotter See Dot-matrix plotter.

Element The basic design entity in computer-aided design whose logical, positional, electrical, or mechanical function is identifiable.

Elementary diagram A wiring diagram of an electrical system in which all devices are drawn between vertical lines which represent power sources. Contains components, logic elements, wire nets, and text. Can be constructed interactively on a CAD system. Also called a wiring elementary or ladder diagram.

Engineering drawing See Drawing.

Enhancements Software or hardware improvements, additions, or updates to a CAD/CAM system.

Entity A geometric primitive—the fundamental building block used in constructing a design or drawing, e.g., arc, circle, line, text, point, spline, figure, or nodal line. Or a group of primitives processed as an identifiable unit. Thus, a square may be defined as a discrete entity consisting of four primitives (vectors), although each side of the square could be defined as an entity in its own right. See also Primitive.

Execute file A text file containing a sequence of computer commands which can be run repeatedly on the system by issuing a single command. Allows the execution of a complicated process without having to reissue each command.

Family of parts A collection of previously designed parts with similar geometric characteristics (e.g., line, circle, elipse) but differing in physical measurement (e.g., height, width, length, angle). When the designer preselects the desired parameters, a special CAD program creates the new part automatically, with significant time savings.

Family-of-parts programming An efficient means of creating new parts on the system. Instead of starting from scratch, the designer makes slight changes in the design of existing parts, or uses identical parts, subassemblies, or structures designed earlier. Once the desired parameters are specified to a family-of-parts program, the system generates the new part.

FEA See Finite-element analysis (FEA).

Feedback (1) The ability of a system to respond to an operator command in real time either visually or with a message on the alphanumeric display or CRT. This message registers the command, indicates any possible errors, and simultaneously displays the updated design on the CRT. (2) The signal or data fed back to a commanding unit from a controlled machine or process to denote its response to a command. (3) The signal representing the difference between actual response and desired response and used by the commanding unit to improve performance of the controlled machine or process. See also Prompt.

FEM See Finite-element modeling.

Figure A symbol or a part which may contain primitive entities, other figures, nongraphic properties, and associations.

File A collection of related information in the system which may be accessed by a unique name. May be stored on a disk, tape, or other mass storage media.

File protection A technique for preventing access to or accidental erasure of data within a file on the system.

Fillet Rounded corner or arc that blends together two intersecting curves or lines. May be generated automatically by a CAD system.

Fillet surface The transition surface which blends together two surfaces, for example, an airplane wing and the plane's body.

Filtering A computer-aided mapping capability that employs one of numerous selection algorithms to delete selected points used to define a linear entity. Filtering removes unnecessary points from the data base and simplifies maps being converted to a smaller scale.

Finite elements Finite elements represent the simple subdivisions of a complex structure in a finite element model. See also Finite-element modeling and Finite-element analysis.

Finite-element analysis (FEA) A method used in CAD for determining the structural integrity of a mechanical part or physical construction under design by mathematical simulation of the part and its loading conditions. See Finite-element modeling (FEM).

Finite-element mesh generation A CAD/CAM procedure used in finite element modeling (FEM) in which grid points and elements are automatically generated on the system for specific regions of the model used for engineering analysis. See Finite-element modeling (FEM).

Finite-element modeling (FEM) The creation on the system of a mathematical model representing a mechanical part or physical construction under design. The model, used for input to a finite element analysis (FEA) program, is built by first subdividing the design model into smaller and simpler elements such as rectangles, triangles, bricks, or wedges which are interconnected. The finite element model is comprised of all its subdivisions or elements, and its attributes (such as materials and thickness), as well as its boundary conditions and loads (including mechanical loadings, temperature effects, and materials fatigue). See Finite-element analysis (FEA).

Firmware Computer programs, instructions, or functions implemented in user-modifiable hardware (i.e., a microprocessor with read-only memory). Such programs or instructions, stored permanently in programmable read-only memories, constitute a fundamental part of system hardware. The advantage is that a frequently used program or routine can be invoked by a single command instead of multiple commands as in a software program.

Flat-pattern generation A CAD/CAM capability for automatically unfolding a 3-D design of a sheet metal part into its corresponding flat-pattern design. Calculations for material bending and stretching are performed automatically for any specified material. The reverse flat-pattern generation package automatically folds a flat-pattern design into its 3-D version. Flat-pattern generation eliminates major bottlenecks for sheet metal fabricators.

Flatbed plotter A CAD/CAM peripheral device that draws an image on paper, glass, or film mounted on a flat table. The plotting head provides all the motion.

Flicker An undesired visual effect on a CRT when the refresh rate is low.

Floating point A CAD/CAM technique for representing a number without using a fixed-position decimal point. Instead, the location of the decimal point for each number in a calculation is defined as a power of two. Thus, the calculating capability of the CPU or computer is extended beyond the limit of fixed word length and programming for arithmetic operations is facilitated.

Font A user-selectable appearance characteristic assigned to a specific graphic or nongraphic entity displayed on the CRT to help the designer distinguish that entity in the design.

Font, line Repetitive pattern used in CAD to give a displayed line appearance characteristics that make it more easily distinguishable, e.g., a solid, dashed, or dotted line. A line font can be applied to graphic images in order to provide meaning, either graphic (e.g., hidden lines) or functional (e.g., roads, tracks, wires, pipes, etc.). It can help a designer to identify and define specific graphic representations of entities which are view-dependent. For example, a line may be solid when drawn in the top view of an object but, when a line font is used, becomes dotted in the side view here it is not normally visible.

Font, text Sets of type faces of various styles and sizes. In CAD, fonts are used to create text for drawings, special characters such a Greek letters, and mathematical symbols.

Foreground processing/mode The standard processing mode for tasks on an interactive system. The execution of programs in the foreground mode is predetermined to preempt all other tasks on the system. See also Background processing/mode.

Format The specific arrangement of CAD/CAM data for a particular kind of list or report. Computervision's data extract program postprocesses CAD/CAM data into user-definable formats.

FORTRAN FORmula TRANslation, a high-level programming language used primarily for scientific or engineering applications.

Fracturing The division of IC graphics by CAD into simple trapezoidal or rectangular areas for pattern-generation purposes.

From-to A pair of points between which an electrical or piping connection is made. Hardcopy from-to lists can be generated automatically on a CAD/CAM system. In computer-aided piping, from-to reports are generated automatically to describe the origins and destinations of pipelines.

Function key A specific square on a data tablet, or a key on a function key box, used by the designer to enter a particular command or other input. See also Data tablet.

Function keyboard An input device located at a CAD/CAM work station and containing a number of function keys.

Functionality Refers to a set of system capabilities in terms of what functions they provide.

Gap The gap between two entities on a computer-aided design is the length of the shortest line segment which can be drawn from the boundary of one entity to the other without intersecting the boundary of the other. CAD/CAM design rules checking programs can automatically perform gap checks.

Gate (1) A logic circuit with one output and several inputs designed so that the output is energized only when certain input conditions are met. (2) An individual unit of logic such as an OR gate or an AND gate. In PC design, every gate on a printed circuit board must be assigned to a set of pins—a process which has been automated and optimized by current CAD/CAM software programs.

Gate array An integrated circuit characterized by a rectangular array of logic sites. These sites consist of identical collections of diffused or implanted transistors, diodes, and resistors. Surrounding the array are the input-output circuits for off-chip connections. The final process in creating the desired circuit is the custom metalization of the logic sites and their subsequent interconnections. Gate-array design permits a standard set of logic elements to be used for a wide variety of IC applications. The designer can create a customized interconnection and metalization pattern interactively on a CAD system.

Gate-array design A shortcut method of creating an IC simply by customizing the interconnections to a partially fabricated IC having predefined logic sites.

Geometric design rules User-defined design constraints aimed at ensuring a functional, reliable product. Among the checks performed automatically IC and PC design rules programs are: gap check, width check, overlap check, and illegal entity check. See also Design-rules checking.

Graphic tablet A CAD/CAM input device which enables graphic and locational instructions to be entered into the system using an electronic pen on the tablet. See also Data tablet.

Gray scales In CAD systems with a monochromatic display, variations in brightness level (gray scale) are employed to enhance the contast among various design elements. This feature is very useful in helping the designer discriminate among complex entities on different layers displayed concurrently on the CRT.

Grid A network of uniformly spaced points or crosshatch optionally displayed on the CRT and used for exactly locating and digitizing a position, inputting components to assist in the creation of a design layout, or constructing precise angles. For example, the coordinate data supplied by digitizers is automatically calculated by the CPU from the closest grid point. The grid determines the minimum accuracy with which design entities are described or connected. In the mapping environment, a grid is used to describe the distribution network of utility resources.

Group technology A coding and classification system used in CAD for combining similar, often-used parts into families. Group technology facilitates the location of an existing part with specified characteristics, and helps to standardize the fabrication of similar parts. Grouping of similar parts in a family allows them to be retrieved, processed, and finally fabricated in an efficient, economical batch mode. See Family of parts.

Hardcopy A copy on paper of an image displayed on the CRT, e.g., drawings, printed reports, plots, listings, or summaries. Most CAD/CAM systems can automatically generate hardcopy through an on-line printer or plotter.

Hardware The physical components, modules, and peripherals comprising a system (e.g., computer, disk, magnetic tape, CRT terminal(s), and plotter(s)).

Hard-wired link A technique of physically connecting two systems by fixed circuit interconnections using digital signals.

Hidden lines Line segments that would ordinarily be obscured from view in a 3-D display of a solid object because they are behind other items in the display. On a CAD system with 3-D capabilities, hidden lines can be displayed or removed, as the user specifies.

High-level language A problem-oriented programming language using words, symbols, and command statements which closely resemble English-language statements. Each statement typically represents a series of computer instructions. Relatively easy to learn and use, a high-level language permits the execution of a number of subroutines through a simple command. Examples are: BASIC, FORTRAN, PL/I, PASCAL, and COBOL. A high-level language must be translated or compiled into machine language before it can be understood and processed by a computer. See also low-level language and assembler.

Host computer The primary or controlling computer in a multicomputer network. Large-scale host computers typically are equipped with mass memory and a variety of peripheral devices, including magnetic tape, line printers, card readers, and possibly hardcopy devices. Host computers may be used to support, with their own memeory and processing capabilities, not only graphics programs running on a CAD/CAM system, but also related engineering analysis.

Host-satellite system A CAD/CAM system configuration characterized by a graphic work station with its own computer (typically holding the display file) but connected to another, usually larger computer for more extensive computation or data manipulation. The computer local to the display is a satellite to the larger host computer, and the two comprise a host-satellite system.

Hybrid circuit A circuit constructed of several independently fabricated, interconnected ICs and embodying various component-manufacturing technologies, such as monolithic IC, thin films, thick films, and discrete components. Hybrid circuit design has been automated, in several of its stages, through CAD/CAM.

IC See Integrated circuit (IC).

ICG See Interactive graphics system (IGS) or Interactive computer graphics (ICG).

IGES See Initial Graphics Exchange Specification (IGES).

IGS See Interactive graphics system (IGS) or Interactive computer graphics (ICG).

Inches per second (ips) Measure of the speed of a device (i.e., the number of inches of magnetic tape that can be processed per second, or the speed of a pen plotter).

Initial Graphics Exchange Specification (IGES) An interim CAD/CAM data base specification until the American National Standards Institue develops its own specification. IGES attempts to standardize communication of drawing and geometric product information between computer systems.

Initialize To set counters, switches, and addresses on a computer to zero or to other starting values at the beginning of, or at predetermined states in, a program or routine.

Input (data) (1) The data supplied to a computer program for processing by the system. (2) The process of entering such data into the system.

Input devices A variety of devices (such as data tablets or keyboard devices) that allow the user to communicate with the CAD/CAM system, for example, to pick a function from many presented, to enter text and/or numerical data, to modify the picture shown on the CRT, or to construct the desired design.

Input/output See I/O (Input/output).

Insert To create and place entities, figures, or information on a CRT, or into an emerging design on the display.

Instruction set (1) All the commands to which a CAD/CAM computer will respond. (2) The repertoire of functions the computer can perform.

Integrated circuit (IC) A tiny complex of electronic components and interconnections comprising a circuit which may vary in functional complexity from a simple logic gate to a microprocessor. An IC is usually packaged in a single substrate such as a slice of silicon. The complexity of most IC designs and the many repetitive elements have made computer-aided design an economic necessity. Also called a chip.

Integrated system A CAD/CAM system which integrates the entire product development cycle, analysis, design and fabrication, so that all processes flow smoothly from concept to production.

Intelligent work station/terminal A work station in a system which can perform certain data processing functions in a standalone mode, independent of another computer. Contains a built-in computer, usually a microprocessor or minicomputer, and dedicated memory. See also Distributed processing.

Interactive Denotes two-way communications between a CAD/CAM system or work station and its operators. An operator can modify or terminate a program and receive feedback from the system for guidance and verification. See Feedback.

Interactive graphics system (IGS) or interactive computer graphics (ICG) A CAD/CAM system in which the work stations are used interactively for computer-aided design and/or drafting, as well as for CAM, all under full operator control, and possibly also for text-processing, generation of charts and graphs, or computer-aided engineering. The designer (operator) can intervene to enter data and direct the course of any program, receiving immediate visual feedback via the CRT. Bilateral communication is provided between the system and the designer(s). Often used synonymously with CAD.

Interconnection Anything that connects one displayed entity or connection point on a component to another. In PC board design, copper paths and/or insulated wire are typically used to tie together (interconnect) electronically common nodes. In CAD-generated schematic drawings, interconnections consist of lines connecting elements.

Interface (1) A hardware and/or software link which enables two systems, or a system and its peripherals, to operate as a single, integrated system. (2) The input devices and visual feedback capabilities which allow bilateral communication between the designer and the system. The interface to a large computer can be a communications link (hardware), or a combination of software and hard-wired connections. An interface might be a portion of storage accessed by two or more programs, or a link between two subroutines in a program.

Interference checking A CAD/CAM capability that enables plant or mechanical designers to examine automatically a 3-D data model, pinpointing interferences between pipes, equipment, structures, or machinery. A computer analysis produces a summary of interferences within selected tolerances.

I/O (Input/output) A term used to describe a CAD/CAM communications device as well as the process by which communications take place in a CAD/CAM system. An I/O device is one that makes possible communications between a device and a work-station operator, or between devices on the system (such as work stations or controllers). By extension, input/output also denotes the process by which communications takes place. Input refers to the data transmitted to the processor for manipulation, and output refers to the data transmitted from the processor to the workstation operator or to another device (i.e., the results). Contrast with the other major parts of a CAD/CAM system: the CPU or central processing unit, which performs arithmetic and logical operations; and data storage devices (such as memories, disks, or tapes).

ips See Inches per second (ips).

Isometric (view) A drawing in which the horizontal lines of an object are drawn at an angle to the horizontal and all verticals are projected at an angle from the base. In plant design, pipes are drawn in isometric form for fabrication purposes, and to facilitate coding for stress analysis. Such isometrics are normally presented schematically with unsealed pipe lengths and equal-size fittings. Isometrics can be generated automatically by a CAD system. In computer-aided mapping, isometric drawings are frequently used to display digital terrain models, 3-D subsurface models, or other landform representations.

Iterate To repeatedly execute a series of steps in a computer program or routine; for example, in the optimization of a design on the system. When numerous iterations are required, a CAD/CAM system can significantly speed up the search process to find optimal solutions to problems such as component placement on PC boards, automatic dimensioning, and bulk annotation. In numerical analysis, too, CAD/CAM accelerates the process of converging to a solution by making successive approximations.

Iteration A set of repetitive computations done on the system in which the output of each step is the input to the next step.

Jaggies A CAD jargon term used to refer to straight or curved lines that appear on the CRT screen to be jagged or sawtoothed.

Joystick A CAD data-entry device employing a hand-controlled level to manually enter the coordinates of various points on a design being digitized into the system.

Keep-out areas User-specified areas on a PC board layout where components or circuit paths must not be located and which therefore must be avoided by CAD/CAM automatic placement and routing programs.

Key file See Menu.

Kinematics A computer-aided engineering (CAE) process for plotting or animating the motion of parts in a machine or a structure under design on the system. CAE simulation programs allow the motion of mechanisms to be studied for interference, acceleration, and force determinations while still in the design stage.

Ladder diagram A wiring diagram of an electrical system in which all the devices are drawn between vertical lines which represent power sources.

Land-use map A map constructed on the system to depict one (or a number of types of) land area classification(s). These areas or parcels may be subdivided within a specific classification to delineate a range of densities or values (e.g., the percentage of specific vegetation or population per square kilometer).

Large interactive surface See LIS (Large interactive surface).

Large-scale integated circuit See LSI (Circuit).

Layer discrimination The process of selectively assigning colors to a layer, or highlighting entities via gray levels, to graphically distinguish among data on different layers displayed on a CRT.

Layering A method of logically organizing data in a CAD/CAM data base. Functionally different classes of data (e.g., various graphic/geometric entities) are segregated on separate layers, each of which can be displayed individually or in any desired combination. Layering helps the designer distinguish among different kinds of data in creating a complex product such as a multilayered PC board or IC.

Layers User-defined logical subsdivisions of data in a CAD/CAM data base which may be viewed on the CRT individually or overlaid and viewed in groups.

Layout (1) A visual representation of the physical components and mechanical and electrical arrangement of a part, product, or plant. A layout can be constructed, displayed, and plotted in hardcopy on a CAD system. (2) The specific geometric design of an IC chip in terms of regions of diffusion, polysilicon metalization, etc. The IC layout is a specific implementation of the functionality described in a schematic design and can be created interactively on a CAD system.

Leader A line, which can be generated on the system, leading from a displayed note or dimension, and terminated by an arrowhead touching the part to which attention is directed.

Learning curve A concept that projects the expected improvement in operator productivity over a period of time. Usually applied in the first 1 to 1½ years of a new CAD/CAM facility as part of a cost-justification study, or when new operators are introduced. An accepted tool of management for predicting manpower requirements and evaluating training programs.

Library, graphics (or parts library) A collection of standard, often-used symbols, components, shapes, or parts stored in the CAD data base as templates or building blocks to speed up future design work on the system. Generally an organization of files under a common library name.

Light pen A hand-held photosensitive CAD input device used on a refreshed CRT screen for identifying display elements, or for designating a location on the screen where an action is to take place.

Line font See Font, line.

Line printer A CAD/CAM peripheral device used for rapid printing of data.

Line smoothing An automated mapping capability for the interpolation and insertion of additional points along a linear entity yielding a series of shorter linear segments to generate a smooth curved appearance to the original linear component. The additional points or segments are created only for display purposes and are interpolated from a relatively small set of stored representative points. Thus, data storage space in minimized.

Line speed The maximum data rate that can be transmitted over a communications line. The rate at which signals can be transmitted over a channel, usually measured in bauds or bits per second. See also Baud rate.

LIS (Large interactive surface) An automated drafting table used as an input device to digitize large drawings into the system, and as an output device to plot same.

Load (1) To enter a collection of computer programs into memory for later execution on the system. (2) To enter data into storage or working registers.

Logic board See Digital board.

Logic design A design specifying the logical functions and interrelationship of the various parts of an electrical or electronic system using logic symbols. Also called a logic diagram.

Logic element See Logic symbol.

Logic symbol A symbol used in electrical or electronic design to represent a logic element graphically (e.g., a gate, or a flip-flop).

Logical graphic function A CAD capability which applies Boolean operations (AND, OR, AND/NOT, XOR) to areas of graphic entities. This provides the designer with interactive tools to create new figures from existing ones or to expand a design-rules checking program, for example, in IC design.

Look-ahead analysis A CAD/CAM capability that enables the designer to detect and prevent part gouging once the part under design is actually manufactured. This can happen if the NC tool is too large to navigate the part geometry.

Low-level language A programming language in which statements translate on a one-for-one basis. See also Assembly language and Machine language.

LSI (Circuit) Large-scale integrated circuit. See also VLSI (Circuit).

Machine A computer, CPU, or other processor.

Machine instruction An instruction that a machine (computer) can recognize and execute.

Machine language The complete set of command instructions understandable to and used directly by a computer when it performs operations.

Macro A sequence of computer instructions executable as a single command. A frequently used, multistep operation can be organized into a macro, given a new name, and remain in the system for easy use, thus shortening program development time.

Magnetic disk A flat circular plate with a magnetic surface on which information can be stored by selective magnetization of portions of the flat surface. Commonly used for temporary working storage during computer-aided design. See also Disk.

Magnetic tape A tape with a magnetic surface on which information can be stored by selective polarization of portions of the surface. Commonly used in CAD/CAM for off-line storage of completed design files and orther archival material.

Main memory/storage The computer's general-purpose storage from which instructions may be executed and data loaded directly into operating registers.

Mainframe (computer) A large central computer facility.

Management information system A package of software programs that enables management to obtain company, financial or project data from the system.

Map generalization An automatic mapping process for reducing the amount of graphic and nongraphic information displayed on a map. Often employed in the creation of composite maps from a series of large-scale maps. The process may employ line filtering, symbol revision, reclassification, and other generalizing techniques.

Mask In IC development, the full size photographic representation of a circuit designed on the system for use in the production process.

Mask design The final phase of IC design by which the circuit design is realized through multiple masks corresponding to multiple layers on the IC. The mask layout must observe all process-related constraints, and minimize the area the circuit will occupy.

Mass-properties calculation This CAD/CAM capability automatically calculates physical/engineering information (such as the perimeter, area, center of gravity, weight, and moments of inertia) of any 3-D part under design.

Mass storage Auxiliary large-capacity memory for storing large amounts of data readily accessible by the computer. Commonly a disk or magnetic tape.

Matrix A 2-D or 3-D rectangular array (arrangement) of identical geometric or symbolic entities. A matrix can be generated automatically on a CAD system by specifying the building block entity and the desired locations. This process is used extensively in computer-aided electrical/electronic design.

Memory Any form of data storage where information can be read and written. Standard memories include: RAM, ROM, and PROM. See also Storage.

Memory map A list of addresses or symbolic representations of addresses which define the boundaries of the memory address space occupied by a program or a series of programs. Memory maps can be produced by a high-level language such as FORTRAN.

Menu A common CAD/CAM input device consisting of a checkerboard pattern of squares printed on a sheet of paper or plastic placed over a data tablet. These squares have been preprogrammed to represent a part of a command, a command, or a series of commands. Each square, when touched by an electronic pen, initiates the particular function or command indicated on that square. See also Data tablet and Dynamic menuing.

Merge To combine two or more sets of related data into one, usually in a specified sequence. This can be done automatically on a CAD/CAM system to generate lists and reports. See also Data merge.

Microcomputer A smaller, lower-cost equivalent of a full-scale minicomputer. Includes a microprocessor (CPU), memory, and necessary interface circuits. Consists of one or more ICs (chips) comprising a chip set.

Microprocessor The central control element of a microcomputer, implemented in a single integrated circuit. It performs instruction sequencing and processing, as well as all required computations. It requires additional circuits to function as a microcomputer. See Microcomputer.

Minicomputer Traditionally a general purpose, single processor computer of limited flexibility and memory performance.

Mirroring A CAD design aid which automatically creates a mirror image of a graphic entity on the CRT by flipping the entity or drawing on its X or Y axis.

Mnemonic symbol An easily remembered symbol that assists the designer in communicating with the system (e.g., an abbreviation such as MPY for multiply).

Model, geometric A complete, geometrically accurate 3-D or 2-D representation of a shape, a part, a geographic area, a plant or any part of it, designed on a CAD system and stored in the data base. A mathematical or analytic model of a physical system used to determine the response of that system to a stimulus or load. See Modeling, geometric.

Modeling, geometric Constructing a mathematical or analytic model of a physical object or system for the purpose of determining the response of that object or system to a stimulus or load. First, the designer describes the shape under design using a geometric model constructed on the system. The computer then converts this pictorial representation on the CRT into a mathematical model later used for other CAD functions such as design optimization.

Modeling, solid A type of 3-D modeling in which the solid characteristics of an object under design are built into the data base, so that complex internal structures and external shapes can be realistically represented. This makes computer-aided design and analysis of solid objects easier, clearer, and more accurate than with wire-frame graphics.

Modem MOdulator—DEModulator. A device that converts digital signals to analog signals, and vice versa, for long-distance transmission over communications circuits such as telephone lines, dedicated wires, optical fiber, or microwave.

Module A separate and distinct unit of hardware or software which is part of the system.

Mouse A hand-held data entry device used to position a cursor on a data tablet. See Cursor.

Multiprocessor A computer whose architecture consists of more than one processing unit. See CGP, Microcomputer, and CPU.

NC See Numerical control (NC).

Nesting (1) Organizing design data into levels (i.e., a hierarchical structure) for greater efficiency in storing and processing repetitive design elements. In nesting, a design is first broken into major components or building blocks, which are then further subdivided into smaller components, and so on. With such a nested design, identical components need to be represented only once in the data base, saving memory storage and simplifying data retrieval and modification. (2) In computer-aided mechanical design, the arranging of multiple parts on a larger sheet or plate for optimum use of material. The parts are cut or burned out of the larger sheet. The objective of nesting is to minimize material costs and scrap.

Net A set of logically related connection points (pins) comprising a particular signal in an electrical or electronic design. Also called a logical net.

Net list A list, by name, of each signal, and each symbol component and pin logically connected to the signal (or net). No physical order is implied. A net list can be automatically generated by a computer-aided design system.

Network An arrangement of two or more interconnected computer systems to facilitate the exchange of information in order to perform a specific function. For example, a CAD/CAM system might be connected to a mainframe computer to off-load heavy analytic tasks. Also refers to a piping network in computer-aided plant design.

Node A reference point in a design displayed on the CRT to which a line (connection) or text can be attached via an interactive CAD input device.

Numerical control (NC) A technique of operating machine tools or similar equipment in which motion is developed in response to numerically coded commands. These commands may be generated by a CAD/CAM system on punched tapes or other communications media. Also, the processes involved in generating on the system the data or tapes necessary to guide a machine tool in the manufacture of a part.

Off-line Refers to peripheral devices not currently connected to and under the direct control of the system's computer.

On-line Refers to peripheral devices connected to and under the direct control of the system's computer, so that operator-system interaction, feedback, and output are all in real time.

Operating system A structured set of software programs that control the operation of the computer and associated peripheral devices in a CAD/CAM system, as well as the execution of computer programs and dataflow to and from peripheral devices. May provide support for activities and programs such as scheduling, debugging, input/output control, accounting, editing, assembly, compilation, storage assignment, data management, and diagnostics. An operating system may assign task priority levels, support a file system, provide drivers for I/O (input/output) devices, support standard system commands or utilities for on-line programming, process commands, and support both networking and diagnostics.

Optimization, design A process that uses a computer to determine the best graphic design to meet such criteria as fuel efficiency, cost of production, and ease of maintenance. In CAD, algorithms may be applied to rapidly evaluate many possible design alternatives in a comparatively short time, for example, to optimize PC board component placement in terms of minimal total length of all interconnections.

Orthographic A type of layout, drawing, or map in which the projecting lines are perpendicular to the plane of the drawing or map. In CAD, it is the commonly accepted way of showing mechanical objects. In computer-aided piping layouts, orthographic drawings are automatically generated on the system from projections of the 3-D, dimensioned piping data base. In computer-aided mapping, an orthographic map is an azimuthal projection in which the projecting lines are perpendicular to a tangent plane. Current CAD systems allow the fast conversion of surface models into maps of differing projections to serve specific needs.

Overlay A segment of code or data to be brought into the memory of a computer to replace existing code or data.

Oversizing See Undersizing, oversizing.

Output The end result of a particular CAD/CAM process or series of processes. The output of a CAD cycle can be artwork and hardcopy lists and reports. The output of a total design-to-manufacturing CAD/CAM system can also include numerical control tapes for manufacturing.

Pad An area of plated copper on a PC board which provides: (1) A contact for soldering component leads. (2) A means of copper-path transition from one side of the PC board to the other. (3) A contact for test probes.

Paint To fill in a bounded graphic figure on a raster display using a combination of repetitive patterns or line fonts to add meaning or clarity. See Font, line.

Paper-tape punch/reader A peripheral device that can read as well as punch a perforated paper tape generated by a CAD/CAM system. These tapes are the principal means of supplying data to an NC machine.

Parallel processing Executing more than one element of a single process concurrently on multiple processors in a computer system.

Part (1) The graphic and nongraphic representation of a physical part designed on a CAD system. (2) A product ready for sale, an assembly, subassembly or a component.

Password protection A security feature of certain CAD/CAM systems that prevents access to the system or to files within the system without first entering a password(i.e., a special sequence of characters).

Path In printed circuit board design, the copper interconnections between pins, or the route that an interconnection takes between nodes. Also a copper foil line.

Pattern generation Transforming CAD integrated circuit design information into a simpler format (rectangles only, or trapezoids only) suitable for use by a photo- or electron-beam machine in producing a reticle. (2) Using a pattern generator to physically produce an IC reticle.

PC board See Printed circuit (PC) board.

Pen plotter An electromechanical CAD output device that generates hardcopy of displayed graphic data by means of a ballpoint pen or liquid ink. Used when a very accurate final drawing is required. Provides exceptional uniformity and density of lines, precise positional accuracy, as well as various user-selectable colors.

Performance, CRT The degree to which the CRT achieves its specified result(s). Useful measurement criteria include: display screen resolution, picture element resolution, display writing speed, internal intelligence, working area, accuracy and precision. See also Addressability (CRT).

Performance, system The degree to which a system achieves its specified result(s). Performance can be expressed in quantitative terms such as speed, capacity, or accuracy. As indicated earlier (under benchmark), most prospective customers require benchmark tests to evaluate system performance. A performance time study might monitor and evaluate: throughput (by specific job and overall average); work unit costs; work unit volumes; and terminal utilization. System performance may also be measured in terms of the productivity ratio of CAD versus manual methods.

Peripheral (device) Any device, distinct from the basic system modules, that provides input to and/or output from the CPU. May include printers, keyboards, plotters, graphic display terminals, paper-tape reader/punches, analog-to-digital converters, disks, and tape drives.

Permanent storage A method or device for storing the results of a completed program outside the CPU, usually in the form of magnetic tape or punched cards.

Photo-pattern generation Production of an IC mask by exposing a pattern of overlapping or adjacent rectangular areas.

P & ID Piping and instrumentation diagram. A schematic, 2-D drawing which shows the major equipment, pipelines, and components to be used in a particular process plant design. Can be constructed on a CAD system.

Photoplotter A CAD output device that generates high-precision artwork masters photographically for printed circuit board design and IC masks.

Pin A connection point (node), on a component, PC board, or logic element, where electrical connections can be made. See also Node.

Piping and instrumentation diagram See P & ID.

Pixel The smallest portion of a CRT screen that can be individually referenced. An individual dot on a display image. Typically, pixels are evenly spaced, horizontally and vertically, on the display.

Placement The assignment of printed circuit components to permanent, fixed positions on the PC board layout. This can be done automatically on a CAD system.

Plasma panel A type of CRT utilizing an array of neon bulbs, each individually addressable. The image is created by turning on points in a matrix (energized grid of wires) comprising the display surface. The image is steady, long-lasting, bright, and flicker-free and selective erasing is possible.

Plotter A CAD peripheral device used to output for external use the image stored in the data base. Generally makes large, accurate drawings substantially better than what is displayed. Plotter types include: pen, drum, electrostatic, and flatbed.

Pocketing Mass removal of material within a predetermined boundary by means of NC machining. The NC tool path is automatically generated on the system. Machining begins at an inner point of the pocket and continues to the outer boundary in ever-widening machining passes.

Postprocessor A software program or procedure which formats graphic or other data processed on the system for some other purpose. For example, a postprocessor might format cutter centerline data into a form which a machine controller can interpret.

Precision The degree of accuracy. Generally refers to the number of significant digits of information to the right of the decimal point for data represented within a computer system. Thus, the term denotes the degree of discrimination with which a design or design element can be described in the data base. See also Accuracy.

Preplaced line (or bus) A run (or line) between a set of points on a PC board layout which has been predefined by the designer and must be avoided by a CAD automatic routing program.

Preprocessor A computer program that takes a specific set of instructions from an external source and translates it into the format required by the system.

Primitive A design element at the lowest stage of complexity. A fundamental graphic entity. It can be a vector, a point or a text string. The smallest definable object in a display processor's instruction set.

Printed circuit (PC) board A baseboard made of insulating materials and an etched copper-foil circuit pattern on which are mounted ICs and other components required to implement one or more electronic functions. PC boards plug into a rack or subassembly of electronic equipment to provide the brains or logic to control the operation of a computer, or a communications system, instrumentation, or other electronics systems. The name derives from the fact that the circuitry is connected not by wires but by copper-foil lines, paths, or traces actually etched onto the board surface. CAD/CAM is used extensively in PC board design, testing, and manufacture.

Process design In computer-aided plant design, the activity of stringing together a number of processing units (such as reactors and distillation columns) into a process flow sheet with the objective of schematically representing a means of converting raw material into desired product(s).

Process planning Specifying the sequence of production steps, from start to finish, and describing the state of the workpiece at each work station. Recently CAM capabilities have been applied to the task of preparing process plans for the fabrication or assembly of parts.

Process-simulation program A program utilizing a mathematical model created on the system to try out numerous process design iterations, with real-time visual and numerical feedback. Designers can see on the CRT what is taking place at every stage in the manufacturing process. They can therefore optimize a process and correct problems that could affect the actual manufacturing process downstream.

Processor In CAD/CAM system hardware, it is any device that performs a specific function. Most often used to refer to the CPU. In software, it refers to a complex set of instructions to perform a general function. See also CPU.

Product cycle The total of all steps leading from the design concept of a part to its final manufacture. How many of these steps can be aided or automated by a CAD/CAM system depends on the particular features or capabilities provided by the system.

Productivity As applied to labor productivity, it is the physical units of output per manhour, or the dollar output per manhour.

Productivity ratio A widely accepted means of measuring CAD/CAM productivity (throughput per hour) by comparing the productivity of a design/engineering group before and after installation of the system or relative to some standard norm, or potential maximum. The most common way of recording productivity is: Actual Manual Hours/Actual CAD Hours, expressed as 4:1, 6:1, etc.

Profiling Removing material around a predetermined boundary by means of numerically controlled (NC) machining. The NC tool path is automatically generated on the system.

Program A precise sequential set of instructions that direct a computer to perform a particular task or action, or solve a problem. A complete program includes plans for the transcription of data, coding for the computer, and plans for the absorption of the results into the system. As a verb, it means to develop a program. See also Computer program.

PROM (Programmable Read-Only Memory) A memory that, once programmed with permanent data or instructions, becomes an ROM (Read-Only Memory). See ROM.

Prompt A message or symbol generated automatically by the system, and appearing on the CRT, to inform the user of (1) a procedural error or incorrect input to the program being executed or (2) the next expected action, option(s), or input. See also Tutorial.

Properties Nongraphic data which may be associated, i.e., linked in a CAD/CAM data base, with their related entities such as parts or components. Properties in electrical design may include component name and identification, color, wire size, pin numbers, lug type, and signal values. See also Associativity.

Protocol The rules for controlling data communication between devices in computer systems or computer networks.

Puck A hand-held, manually controlled input device which allows coordinate data to be digitized into the system from a drawing placed on the data tablet or digitizer surface. A puck has a transparent window containing cross hairs.

Quality assurance (QA) Denotes both *quality control* and *quality engineering*, described here.

Quality control (QC) Establishing and maintaining specified quality standards for products.

Quality engineering The establishment and execution of tests to measure product quality and adherence to acceptance criteria.

Queue A priority-ranked collection of tasks waiting to be performed on the system.

RAM See Random-access memory (RAM).

Random-access memory (RAM) A main memory read/write storage unit which provides the CAD/CAM operator direct access to the stored information. The time required to access any word stored in the memory is the same as for any other word.

Raster display A CAD work-station display in which the entire CRT surface is scanned at a constant refresh rate. The bright, flicker-free image can be selectively written and erased. Also called a digital TV display.

Raster scan (video) Currently, the dominant technology in CAD graphic displays. Similar to conventional televison, it involves a line-by-line sweep across the entire CRT surface to generate the image. Raster scan features include: good brightness, accuracy, selective erase, dynamic motion capabilities, and the opportunity for unlimited color. The device can display a large amount of information without flicker, although resolution is not as good as with storage-tube displays.

Rat's nest A feature on PC design systems that allows users to view all the computer-determined interconnections between each component. This makes it easier to determine whether further component placement improvement is necessary to optimize signal routing.

Real time Refers to tasks or functions executed so rapidly by a CAD/CAM system that the feedback at various stages in the process can be used to guide the designer in completing the task. Immediate visual feedback through the CRT makes possible real time, interactive operation of a CAD/CAM system.

Rectangular array Insertion of the same entity at multiple locations on a CRT using the system's ability to copy design elements and place them at user-specified intervals to create a rectangular arrangement or matrix. A feature of PC and IC design systems.

Rectification A general-purpose, computer-aided mapping tool for adjusting the geometric information in a data base, based on updated values of a number of point after their position has been more accurately determined—typically, after a map has been digitized.

Redundancy The policy of building duplicate components into a system to minimize the possibility of a failure disabling the entire system. For example, redundancy of hardware performing steps critical to the performance of a CAD/CAM facility guarantees minimum interruption of service. An equally important function of redundancy is to maintain continuous throughput.

Reentrant A characteristic of software programs that allows interruption at any time before completion and subsequent restart. Thus, the designer can make modifications in the middle of a CAD/CAM automatic program without having to start it again later from the beginning.

Reference designator Text (e.g., a component name) used in CAD to identify a component and associate it with a particular schematic element.

Refresh (or vector refresh) A CAD display technology that involves frequent redrawing of an image displayed on the CRT to keep it bright, crisp, and clear. Refresh permits a high degree of movement in the displayed image as well as high resolution. Selective erase or editing is possible at any time without erasing and repainting the entire image. Although substantial amounts of high-speed memory are required, large, complex images may flicker.

Refresh rate The rate at which the graphic image on a CRT is redrawn in a refresh display, i.e., the time needed for one refresh of the displayed image.

Registration The degree of accuracy in the positioning of one layer or overlay in a CAD display or artwork, relative to another layer, as reflected by the clarity and sharpness of the resulting image.

Reliability The projected uptime of a system, expressed by the anticipated meantime between failures.

Repaint A CAD feature that automatically redraws a design displayed on the CRT.

Repeatability A feature of CAD/CAM systems to recalculate accurately for display a set of coordinates from computerized data.

Replicate To generate an exact copy of a design element and locate it on the CRT at any point(s), and in any size or scale desired.

Resolution The smallest spacing between two display elements which will allow the elements to be distinguished visually on the CRT. The ability to define every minute detail.

Response time The elapsed time from initiation of an operation at a work station to the receipt of the results at that work station. Includes transmission of data to the CPU, processing, file access, and transmission of results back to the initiating work station.

Restart To resume a computer program interrupted by operator intervention.

Restore To bring back to its original state a design currently being worked on in a CAD/CAM system after editing or modification which the designer now wants to cancel or rescind.

Resume A feature of some application programs that allows the designer to suspend the data processing operation at some logical break point, and restart it later from that point. See also Reentrant.

Reticle The photographic plate used to create an IC mask. See also photoplotter.

Robotics The use of computer-controlled manipulators or arms to automate a variety of manufacturing processes such as welding, material handling, painting, and assembly.

ROM (Read-Only Memory) A memory which cannot be modified or reprogrammed. Typically used for control and execute programs. See Execute files and PROM.

Rotate To turn a displayed 2-D or 3-D construction about an axis through a predefined angle relative to the original position.

Router A PC or IC design application program which automatically determines the optimal interconnection of signals based on design parameters established by the user. See also Autoroute.

Routine A computer program, or a subroutine in the main program. The smallest separately compilable source code unit. See Computer program and source.

Routing Positioning of the conductive interconnects between components on a printed circuit board or IC. A CAD program can automatically determine the optimal routing path for the interconnects on a PC board or IC layout. See also Autoroute.

Rubber banding A CAD capability which allows a component to be tracked (dragged) across the CRT screen, by means of an electronic pen, to a desired location, while simultaneously stretching all related interconnections to maintain signal continuity. During tracking the interconnections associated with the component stretch and bend, providing an excellent visual guide for optimizing the location of a component to best fit into the flow of the PC board, or other entity, minimizing total interconnect length and avoiding areas of congestion.

Satellite A remove system connected to another, usually larger, host system. A satellite differs from a remote intelligent work station in that it contains a full set of processors, memory and mass storage resources to operate independently of the host. See Host-satellite system.

Scale To enlarge or diminish the size of a displayed entity without changing its shape, i.e., to bring it into a user-specified ratio to its original dimensions. Scaling can be done automatically by a CAD system. Used as a noun, scale denotes the coordinate system for representing an object.

Schematic design See Logic design.

Schematic diagram See Electrical schematic.

Scissoring The automatic erasing of all portions of a design on the CRT which lie outside user-specified boundaries. See also Clipping.

Scroll To automatically roll up as on a spool a design or text message on a CRT to permit the sequential viewing of a message or drawing too large to be displayed all at once on the screen. New data appears on the CRT at one edge as other data disappears at the opposite edge. Graphics can be scrolled up, down, left or right.

Sectioning and paneling Computer-aided mapping functions that allow the cartographer to create new maps by joining a number of smaller scale maps. The two functions trim extraneous data, allow maps with common boundaries to be merged, and correct small inconsistencies.

Selective erase A CAD feature for deleting portions of a display without affecting the remainder or having to repaint the entire CRT display.

Shape fill The automatic painting in of an area on the IC or PC board layout, defined by user-specified boundaries; for example, the area to be filled by copper when the PC board is manufactured. Can be done on-line by CAD.

Signal The name associated with a net. See Net.

Signal highlighting A CAD editing aid to visually identify—by means of noticeably brighter lines—the pins (connection points) of a specific signal (net) on a PC design.

Silk screen A type of artwork which can be generated by a CAD/CAM system for printing component placement and/or identification information on a PC board.

Simulate To create on a CAD/CAM system the mathematical model or representation of a physical part under design. Thus, the behavior of the finished part under various structural and thermal loading conditions can be estimated, and design modifications made before final production.

Simulation A CAD/CAM computer program that simulates the effect of structural, thermal, or kinematic conditions on a part under design. Simulation programs can also be used to exercise the electrical properties of a circuit. Typically, the system model is exercised and refined through a series of simulation steps until a detailed, optimum configuration is arrived at. The model is displayed on a CRT and continually updated to simulate dynamic motion or distortion under load or stress conditions. A great variety of materials, design configurations, and alternatives can be tried out without committing any physical resources.

Smoothing Fitting together curves and surfaces so that a smooth, continuous geometry results.

Snap The action taken by a CAD/CAM graphics program when it interprets a user-specified location as the nearest of a set of reference locations. Thus, when a point is input by digitizing, the system may snap to the closest point on the grid.

Software The collection of executable computer programs including application programs, operating systems, and languages.

Source A text file written in a high-level language and containing a computer program. It is easily read and understood by people but must be compiled or assembled to generate machine-recognizable instructions. Also known as source code. See also High-level language.

Source code. See Source.

Source language A symbolic language comprised of statements and formulas used in computer processing. It is translated into object language (object code) by an assembler or compiler for execution by a computer.

Spline A subset of a B-spline wherein a sequence of curves is restricted to a plane. An interpolation routine executed on a CAD/CAM system automatically adjusts a curve by design iteration until the curvature is continuous over the length of the curve. See also B-spline.

Split equipment cross-reference report A hardcopy report which can be automatically generated by a CAD system, listing the exit and entry points of all common wiring appearing on two or more sheets of a wiring diagram.

Star network A computer network configuration in which work stations and/or processors are connected radially to a central host. See Network.

Stitch To interactively route a PC interconnect between layers and around obstructions with automatic insertion of vias when necessary through the use of powerful editing commands available on a CAD system.

Storage The physical repository of all information relating to products designed on a CAD/CAM system. It is typically in the form of a magnetic tape or disk. Also called memory.

Storage tube A common type of CRT which retains an image continuously for a considerable period of time without redrawing (refreshing). The image will not flicker regardless of the amount of information displayed. However, the display tends to be slow relative to raster scan, the image is rather dim, and no single element by itself can be modified or deleted without redrawing. See also Direct-view storage tube (DVST).

Stretch A CAD design/editing aid that enables the designer to automatically expand a displayed entity beyond its original dimensions.

String A linear sequence of entities, such as characters or physical elements, in a computer-aided design.

Stroke-writing (display) A CAD picture-generating technique. A beam is moved simultaneously in X and Y directions along a curve or straight path in much the same way as an Etch-A-Sketch children's toy.

Stylus A hand-held pen used in conjunction with a data tablet to enter commands and coordinate input into the system. Also called an electronic pen.

Subfigure A part or a design element which may be extracted from a CAD library and inserted intact into another part displayed on the CRT.

Surface machining Automatic generation of NC tool paths to cut 3-D shapes. Both the tool paths and the shapes may be constructed using the mechanical design capabilities of a CAD/CAM system.

Symbol Any recognizable sign, mark, shape or pattern used as a building block for designing meaningful structures. A set of primitive graphic entities (line, point, arc, circle, text, etc.) which form a construction that can be expressed as one unit and assigned a meaning. Symbols may be combined or nested to form larger symbols and/or drawings. They can be as complex as an entire PC board, or as simple as a single element such as a pad. Symbols are commonly used to represent physical things. For example, a particular graphic shape may be used to represent a complete device or a certain kind of electrical component in a schematic. To simplify the preparation of drawings of piping systems and flow diagrams, standard symbols are used to represent various types of fittings and components in common use. Symbols are also basic units in a language. The recognizable sequence of characters END may inform a compiler that the routine it is compiling is completed. In computer-aided mapping, a symbol can be a diagram, design, letter, character, or abbreviation placed on maps and charts which by convention or reference to a legend is understood to stand for or represent a specific characteristic or feature. In a CAD environment, symbol libraries contribute to the quick maintenance, placement, and interpretation of symbols.

Syntax (1) A set of rules describing the structure of statements allowed in a computer language. To make grammatical sense, commands and routines must be written in conformity to these rules. (2) The structure of a computer command language (i.e., the English-sentence structure of a CAD/CAM command language or, e.g., verb, noun, modifiers).

System An arrangement of CAD/CAM data processing, memory, display and plotting modules—coupled with appropriate software—to achieve specific objectives. The term CAD/CAM system implies both hardware and software. See also operating system (a purely software term).

Tablet An input device on which a designer can digitize coordinate data or enter commands into a CAD/CAM system by means of an electronic pen. See also Data tablet.

Tag To automatically attach an identifying mark (number or name) to a design element displayed on the CRT. Tags label geometric entities for easy identification.

Task (1) A specific project which can be executed by a CAD/CAM software program. (2) A specific portion of memory assigned to the user for executing that project.

Template The pattern of a standard, commonly used component or part which serves as a design aid. Once created, it can be subsequently traced instead of redrawn whenever needed. The CAD equivalent of a designer's template might be a standard part in the data base library which can be retrieved and inserted intact into an emerging drawing on the CRT.

Temporary storage Memory locations for storing immediate and partial results obtained during the execution of a program on the system.

Terminal See Work station.

Text editor An operating system program used to create and modify text files on the system.

Text file A file stored in the system in text format which can be printed and edited online as required.

Thematic map A map specifically designed to communicate geographic concepts such as the distribution of densities, relative magnitudes, gradients, spatial relationships, movements and all the required interrelationships and aspects among the distributional characteristics of the earth's phenomena. CAD systems allow the quick assignment and identification of both graphic and nongraphic properties, thus facilitating the use of thematic maps.

Thermal dot-matrix printer See Dot-matrix plotter.

Throughput The number of units of work performed by a CAD/CAM system or a work station during a given period of time. A quantitative measure of system productivity.

Time-sharing The use of a common CPU memory and processing capabilities by two or more CAD/CAM terminals to execute different tasks simultaneously.

Tolerance A term used in conjunction with the generation of a nonlinear tool path comprised of discrete points. The tolerance controls the number of these points. In general, the term denotes the allowed variance from a given standard (i.e., the acceptable range of data).

Tolerance stack-up A method of calculating the accumulation of tolerances on a group of selected linear dimensions.

Tool path Centerline on the tip of an NC cutting tool as it moves over a part produced on a CAD/CAM system. Tool paths can be created and displayed interactively or automatically by a CAD/CAM system, and reformatted into NC tapes, by means of a postprocessor, to guide or control machining equipment. See also Pocketing, Profiling, and Surface machining.

Track ball A CAD graphics input device consisting of a ball recessed into a surface. The designer can rotate it in any direction to control the position of the cursor used for entering coordinate data into the system.

Tracking Moving a predefined (tracking) symbol across the surface of the CRT with a light pen or an electronic pen.

Transform To change an image displayed on the CRT, for example, by scaling, rotating, translating, or mirroring.

Transformation The process of transforming a CAD display image. Also the matrix representation of a geometric space.

Translate (1) To convert CAD/CAM output from one language to another; for example, by means of a postprocessor such as Computervision's IPC-to-Numerics Translator program. (2) Also, by an editing command, to move a CAD display entity a specified distance in a specified direction.

Trap The area that is searched around each digitize to find a hit on a graphics entity to be edited. See also Digitize.

Traverse adjustment A computer-aided mapping feature which automatically distributes corrections through any surveying traverse to eliminate the error of closure, and to yield an adjusted position for each traverse station.

Turnaround time The elapsed time between the moment a task or project is input into the CAD/CAM system and the moment the required output is obtained.

Turnkey A CAD/CAM system for which the supplier/vendor assumes total responsibility for building, installing, and testing both hardware and software, and the training of user personnel. Also, loosely, a system which comes equipped with all the hardware and software required to do a specific application or applications. Usually implies a commitment by the vendor to make the system work, and to provide preventive and remedial maintenance of both hardware and software. Sometimes used interchangeably with standalone, although standalone applies more to system architecture than to terms of purchase.

Tutorial A characteristic of CAD/CAM systems. If the user is not sure how to execute a task, the system will show him how. A message is displayed to provide information and guidance.

Undersizing, oversizing CAD automatic editing tools for the systematic reduction or enlargement, respectively, of the areas in an IC design layout. This is typically performed to compensate for processing effects which may intrinsically tend to shift the edges of the layout areas either out or in.

Utilities Another term for system capabilities and/or features which enable the user to perform certain processes.

Vector A quantity that has magnitude and direction, and that in CAD is commonly represented by a directed line segment.

Verification (1) A system-generated message to a work station acknowledging that a valid instruction or input has been received (2) The process of checking the accuracy, viability and/or manufacturability of an emerging design on the system. See Design-rules checking (example).

Vertical integration A method of manufacturing a product, such as a CAD/CAM system, whereby all major modules and components are fabricated in-house under uniform company quality control and fully supported by the system vendor.

Very large-scale integrated circuit See VLSI (circuit).

Via A means of passing from one layer or side of a PC board to the other. A feedthrough. A CAD system can automatically optimize via placement by means of special application software.

View port A user-selected, rectangular view of a part, assembly, etc., which presents the contents of a window on the CRT. See Window.

VLSI (circuit) Very large scale integrated circuit. High-density ICs characterized by relatively large size (perhaps 1/4 inch on a side) and high complexity (10,000 to 100,000 gates). VLSI design, because of its complexity, makes CAD a virtual necessity.

Wafer A slice of silicon on which, typically, a large number of integrated circuit chips are simultaneously produced.

Window A temporary, usually rectangular, bounded area on the CRT which is user-specified to include particular entities for modification, editing, or deletion.

Wire chart The primary end-product of a CAD/CAM wiring diagram system, which generates it automatically. A wire chart lists all devices, connections, and properties in a wiring diagram indicating physical locations of devices and connections, as well as the optimum wiring order for each connection to be made.

Wire-frame graphics A computer-aided design technique for displaying a three-dimensional object on the CRT screen as a series of lines outlining its surface. See Finite-element analysis and Finite-element modeling.

Wire list A wire run list containing only two connections in each wire. A type of from-to list. See From-to.

Wire net A set of electrical connections in a logical net having equivalent characteristics and a common identifier. No physical order of connections is implied. A wire net can be generated automatically by a CAD system.

Wire net list This report, which can be generated automatically by a CAD system, lists the electrical connections of a wire net without reference to their physical order.

Wire tags Tags containing wire or net identification numbers and wrapped around both ends of each connection in an electrical system. Tags can be generated by a CAD/CAM system.

Wire wrap An interconnection technology which is an alternative to conventional etched printed circuit board technology. Wires are wrapped around the pins—a process normally done semiautomatically.

Wiring diagram (1) Graphic representation of all circuits and device elements of an electrical system and its associated apparatus or any clearly defined functional portion of that system. A wiring diagram may contain not only wiring system components and wires but also nongraphic information such as wire number, wire size, color, function, component label, pin number, etc. (2) Illustration of device elements and their interconnectivity as distinguished from their physical arrangement. (3) Drawing that shows how to hook things up. Wiring diagrams can be constructed, annotated, and documented on a CAD system.

Wiring elementary A wiring diagram of an electrical system in which all devices of that system are drawn between vertical lines which represent power sources. Can be generated by a CAD system. Also called a ladder diagram.

Word A set of bits (typically 16 or 32) that occupies a single storage location and is treated by the computer as a unit. See also Bit.

Work station The work area and equipment used for CAD/CAM operations. It is where the designer interacts (communicates) with the computer. Frequently consists of a CRT display and an input device as well as, possibly, a digitizer and a hardcopy device. In a distributed processing system, a work station would have local processing and mass storage capabilities. Also called a terminal or design terminal.

Work-around A software (sub-)routine, or programmed sequence of steps, used as a temporary expedient to bypass a bug until it can be permanently corrected. See also bug.

Working drawing In plant design, a detailed layout of a component with complete dimensions and notes, approved for production. It can be generated by a CAD/CAM system.

Working storage That part of the system's internal storage reserved for intermediate results (i.e., while a computer program is still in progress). Also called temporary storage.

Write To transfer information from CPU main memory to a peripheral device, such as a mass storage device.

Write-protect A security feature in a CAD/CAM data storage device that prevents new data from being written over existing data.

Yield In IC manufacture, the number of good chips obtainable per wafer. It is inversely proportional to the area of the chip—that is, as the area of a chip increases, the number of good chips on that wafer will decrease proportionately.

Z-position register A display controller device used to simulate the vector coordinates in the Z direction. The depth into and out of the display screen along the Z axis is simulated by varying the intensity of the displayed Z vector in proportion to the value of the Z coordinate.

Zero The origin of all coordinate dimensions defined in an absolute system as the intersection of the baselines of the X, Y, and Z axes.

Zero offset On an NC unit, this feature allows the zero point on an axis to be relocated anywhere within a specified range, thus temporarily redefining the coordinate frame of reference.

Zero shift Identical to *zero offset*, described above, except that the coordinate frame of reference is permanently redefined.

Zoom A CAD capability that proportionately enlarges or reduces a figure displayed on a CRT screen.

Index

Accounting, 42
Accuracy, 39
Alphanumeric terminal, 45
Analysis benefits, 34, 93, 94
Arithmetic base factor, 291
Assumptions used for analysis, 85

Benchmarking, 133
Boot-up, 209–210

CAD learning curve, 260
CAD/CAM
  applicatons, 23
  costs, 91
  savings, 91
  systems, 54
Career development, 171
Central processing unit (CPU), 43
  maintenance, 239
Centralized systems, 158
Change orders, 41
Closed shop, 155
Component arrangement, 151
Composite index, 292
Computer impact value, 295
Copy unit maintenance, 245
Cost justification, 81
Crash recovery, 211–212
Cursor control, 45

Daily operations, 221–223
Data base, 201
  creation, 36
  structure, 227–231
Data storage, 199

Decentralized systems, 158
Design, 34
  review, 36
  workstation, 55
Digitizers, 44, 56
Disk drives, 62
Disk maintenance, 238
Documentation, 206
Documentation preparation, 49
Drafting, 36
  procedures, 221–233
  standards, 205–220
Drawing release report, 300

Efficiency, 259
Evaluation, 249
Evaluation team, 4

Facility
  manager, 160
  organization, 155–161
  planning, 141–154
Financial analysis, 98
Finite-element analysis, 35
Framework components, 257
Framework for analysis, 256

Graphics terminal, 43
Gross domestic product, 256
Gross savings, 90

Hardcopy, 46
Help information, 212
Help list, 246
High speed line printer, 53
Human resources plan, 173–178

Implementation, 22
Inspection, 37

Job accounting packages, 300
Justification formulas, 82, 95

Kinematics, 66

Labor hours saved, 96
Layering, 202
  standards, 215–216
Learning curve milestones, 87, 88
Library organization, 201
Lighting, 149
Log-in, 210–211
Log-out, 211

MASS properties, 35
Manual vs. automated, 88
Manufacturing, 17
Mechanical design and drafting, 64
Memo tablet and pen, 48
Milestone chart, 141–144
Multiple shifts, 157
Multitask, 100

Naming parts, 213–215
New software, 219–220
Nominal group technique (NGT), 267
Numerical control programming, 37, 40

Open shop, 155
Operator selection, 165–169

Payback
  measurement, 22
  period, 12, 92
Performance ratios, 288
Personnel
  development, 171–188
  planning, 163–169
Plotter maintenance, 244–245
Plotters, 46, 61
Position description, 178–188
Power requirements, 144–145
Pray technique, 296
Presale consultation, 82
Preventive maintenance, 235–243
Product cycle, 85
Product, components, 87
Productivity
  basics, 262
  gains, 87
  measurement methods, 292
  report, 249
Project management, 42
Projected systems use, 99

Qualitative rationales, 11

Rebuilding a disk, 220–221
Request for proposal
  basic objectives, 100
  facilities design and management, 126
  family of parts, 108
  general description, 112
  mechanical design and drafting, 111
  multitask requirements, 100
  numerical control, 114
  plant design, 123
  printed circuit/electrical schematics, 117
[Request for proposal]
  processor, 101
  wiring diagrams, 120
Return on investment (ROI), 92

Secondary storage, 47
Select committee, 81
Service bureaus (pros and cons), 69
Single shifts, 158
Software
  control, 231–233
  maintenance, 231–233
  support, 203
Solid modeling, 65
Stack-ups, 35
Staffing, 31
Standard drawing formats, 212–213
System capacity calculations, 5
System efficiency report, 302
System
  environment, 145
  layout, 148
  planning, 199–204
  shut-down, 208
  start-up, 208
  taping, 223–226
  utilization, 303
Systems administration, 205–233

Tape drive maintenance, 241–242
Tape numbering, 216–217
Taping procedure, 216–219
Templates, 141
Terminal maintenance, 242–244
Three-dimensional design, 60
Tool design, 37, 40
Training, 41, 189–198

Value-added, 256
  per employee, 257
Vendor factor comparison, 5, 134
Vendor survey, 6
Windows, 149
Work analysis, 7
Workstation keyboard, 49